THE A - Z ENCYCLOPEDIA OF JOKES

Robinson Children's Books

Robinson Publishing Ltd
7 Kensington Church Court
London W8 4 SP

First published in the UK by Robinson Children's Books,
an imprint of Robinson Publishing Ltd, 1999

This collection © Robinson Publishing Ltd, 1999
Illustrations by Mike Phillips

A copy of the British Library Cataloguing-in-Publication Data
is available from the British Library

ISBN 1 85487 635 X

Printed and bound in the EC

10 9 8 7 6 5 4 3 2 1

Introduction

Instead of falling asleep in the classroom, on the train, or in front of the television, why not use this amazing joke encyclopedia to make life that little bit more fun. This book has no end of uses, and when you flick through the entries for each letter of the alphabet you'll soon realize why. For instance, next time an astronaut walks into your house, you can reach over for *The A–Z Encyclopedia of Jokes*, look under the letter A, and, hey presto, have a string of astronaut jokes at your fingertips! Your friendly astronaut will laugh his head off when you offer to cook him a *big launch* and say how much you like his *Apollo neck jumper* . . . Or when your school essay is grinding to a slow, sticky end, why not throw in a couple of howlers about broomsticks (look under B), chiropodists (look under C), and dinosaurs (look under D) – Just to lighten things up a little. Your teachers will be most amused. There's even a section at the end of the book for keeping a record of your favorite jokes. Or use the space for writing down your own jokes – yes, even *you* can become a creative joke-writer! If you need some inspiration, just take a look at the cartoons. And talking of cartoons, check out the cover of this book because it's covered with crazy pictures. There's one for every letter of the alphabet. All you have to do is find a joke to go with each picture. If you can't find one in the book, then make one up . . . Go on, dare you!

Abominable snowman

What kind of man doesn't like to sit in front of the fire?
An Abominable Snowman.

What did one Abominable Snowman say to the other?
I'm afraid I just don't believe in people.

What would you get if you crossed the Abominable Snowman and a vampire?
Frostbite.

Knock knock.
Who's there?
Chile.
Chile who?
Chile being an Abominable Snowman!

Doctor, doctor, I keep thinking I'm the Abominable Snowman.
Keep cool.

What is the Abominable Snowman's favorite book?
War and Frozen Peas.

Why did the Abominable Snowman send his father to Siberia?
Because he wanted frozen pop.

I Met An Abominable Snowman – by Anne Tarctic

Accident

"Now as I understand it, Sir," said the police officer to the motorist, "you were driving this vehicle when the accident occurred. Can you tell me what happened?"
"I'm afraid not, officer," replied the motorist. "I had my eyes shut!"

Did you hear about the millionaire who had a bad accident?
He fell off his wallet.

Actor

Why was the actor pleased to be on the gallows?
Because at last he was in the noose.

⁂

Fan: I've always admired you. Are your teeth your own?
Actor: Whose do you think they are?

⁂

Young Actor: Dad, guess what? I've just got my first part in a play. I play the part of a man who's been married for 30 years.
Father: Well, keep at it, son. Maybe one day you'll get a speaking part.

⁂

What's the definition of a good actor?
Somebody who tries hard to be everybody but himself.

⁂

"Jason," said the minister, "you've written here that Samson was an actor. What makes you think that?"
"Well, sir," said Jason, "I read that he brought the house down."

⁂

Neighbor: Haven't I seen you on TV?
Actor: Well, I do appear, on and off, you know. How do you like me?
Neighbor: Off.

Address

How do you address a monster?
Very politely.

⁂

How do you join the Dracula Fan Club?
Send your name, address and blood group.

⁂

Knock knock.
Who's there?
Insect.
Insect who?
Insect your name and address here.

⁂

Did you hear about the teacher who retired? His class gave him an illuminated address. They burned his house down.

Adult

What's the difference between an adult and a ghost?
One is all grown, the other is all groan.

Aftershave

What aftershave do monsters wear?
Brute.

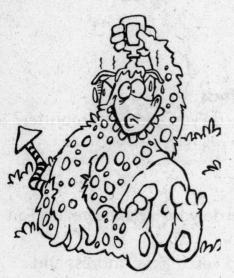

Age

"That's an excellent essay for someone your age," said the English teacher.
"How about for someone my Mom's age, Miss?"

Miss Simons agreed to be interviewed by John for the school magazine. "How old are you, ma'am?" asked John.
"I'm not going to tell you that," she replied.
"But Mr Hill the technical teacher and Mr Hill the geography teacher told me how old they were."
"Oh well," said Miss Simons. "I'm the same age as both of them."
The poor teacher was not happy when she saw what John wrote:
Miss Simons, our English teacher, confided in me that she was as old as the Hills.

※

"Now remember, boys and girls," said the science teacher, "you can tell a tree's age by counting the rings in a cross section. One ring for each year."
Susan went home for tea and found a chocolate roll on the table.
"I'm not eating that, Mom!" she said. "It's five years old."

※

Grandma: You've left all your crusts, Mary. When I was your age I ate every one.
Mary: Do you still like crusts, Grandma?
Grandma: Yes, I do.
Mary: Well, you can have mine.

※

Grandpa: You youngsters are soft and lazy today. When I was your age I got up at six o'clock every morning and walked five or six miles before breakfast. I used to think nothing of it.
Charlie: I don't blame you, Grandpa. I wouldn't think much of it myself.

＊

Doctor, doctor, my left leg is giving me a lot of pain.
I expect that's old age.
But my right leg is as old, and that doesn't hurt at all!

＊

George had reached the age of 46, and not only was he still unmarried but he had never had a girlfriend. "Come along now, George," said his father. "It's high time you got yourself a wife and settled down. Why, at your age I'd been married 20 years."
"But that was to Mom," said his son, "You can't expect me to marry a stranger!"

＊

An American tourist found himself in a sleepy country village, and asked one of the locals the age of the oldest inhabitant. "Well, sir," replied the villager, "we ain't got one now. He died last week."

＊

Agent

A monster decided to become a TV star, so he went to see an agent.
"What do you do?" asked the agent.
"Bird impressions," said the monster.
"What kind of bird impressions?"
"I eat worms."

Airplane

What is brown and yellow and buzzes at 36,000 feet in the air?
A bee in an airplane.

Two wrongs don't make a right.
But what did two rights make?
The first airplane.

＊

What do you get if you cross a witch with a werewolf?
A mad dog that chases airplanes.

Alarm Clock

Teacher: Why are you always late?
Roger: I threw away my alarm clock.
Teacher: But why did you throw away your alarm clock?
Roger: Because it always went off when I was asleep.

Algebra

A hillbilly dragged his protesting son to a new school which had just opened in a nearby village. When they arrived, he took his son to see the principal. "Howdy," said the hillbilly. "This here's my son, Arthur. Now what kind of learnin' are you teachin'?"

"Oh, all the usual subjects," said the principal, nodding at the boy. "Reading, writing, arithmetic."

"What's this?" interrupted the father. "Arith . . . arith . . . What did you say?"

"Arithmetic, sir," said the principal, "instruction in geometry, algebra and trigonometry."

"Trigonometry!" cried the hillbilly. "That's what my boy needs. He's the worst darn shot in the family."

❋

What do you mean, my spelling isn't much good – that's my algebra.

Alien

Two aliens from outer space landed in Las Vegas and were wandering around the casinos. One of them volunteered to go inside and see what was happening. He came out looking rather shocked. "What's the matter?" asked his friend.

"It's a very popular place," replied the first alien. "It's full of creatures that keep throwing up little metal discs."

❋

What did the alien say when his flying saucer landed in a stud farm? Take me to your breeder!

Why did the alien phone home on his mobile?
Because it was so ET.

※

What do you call an alien starship that drips water?
A crying saucer.

Ambush

Teacher: Why did the Romans build straight roads?
Alex: So the Britons couldn't lie in ambush round the corners.

American

Why is the silkworm not raised in America?
Because Americans get silk from the rayon which is larger and gives more silk.

※

Where do American ghosts go on holiday?
Lake Eerie.

※

What happened when two American stoats got married?
They became the United Stoats (States) of America

※

Where does an American cow come from?
Moo York.

※

Who rides a dog and was a Confederate general during the American Civil War?
Robert E. Flea.

※

"Where's your pencil, Bud?" the teacher asked an American boy who had just come to school in Britain.
"I ain't got one, Sir."
"You're in England now, Bud. Not ain't, haven't. I haven't got a pencil. You haven't got a pencil. They haven't got a pencil.
"Gee!" said Bud. "Pop said things were tough in this country, but I didn't know pencils were so hard to come by."

※

An American tourist was visiting a quaint country village, and got talking to an old man in the local pub. "And have you lived here all your life, Sir?" asked the American.
"Not yet, m'dear," said the villager wisely.

※

What's an American cat's favorite car?
A Catillac.

※

Why are American schoolchildren extremely healthy?
Because they have a good constitution.

※

Two neighbors were having a chat across the garden fence. "My son's learning to play football," said one. "Oh, really," said the other. "What position does he play?"
"The coach says he's a drawback."

※

A huge American car screeched to a halt in a sleepy English village, and the driver called out to a local inhabitant, "Say, am I on the right road for Shakespeare's birthplace?" "Ay, straight on, sir," said the rustic, "but no need to hurry. He's dead."

※

An Irishman joined the American Air Force and was making his first parachute jump. The instructor said, "When you jump out of the plane, shout Geronimo and pull the rip-cord." When the Irishman woke up in hospital a few days later the first thing he said was, "What was the name of that Indian again?"

※

What do you call an American with a lavatory on his head?
John.

Angel
On their first evening in their new home the bride went in to the kitchen to fix the drinks. Five minutes later she came back into the living-room in tears. "What's the matter, my angel?" asked her husband anxiously.
"Oh Michael!" she sobbed, "I put the ice-cubes in hot water to wash them and they've disappeared!"

Animal
What is the strongest animal in the world?
A snail, because it carries its home on its back.

※

What animal sleeps standing on its head?
Yoga Bear.

※

Teacher: Joe, name four animals of the Arctic.
Joe: Two walruses and two polar bears.

※

Which animal has the highest intelligence?
A giraffe.

※

It's obvious that animals are smarter than humans. Put eight horses in a race and 20,000 people will go along to see it. But put eight people in a race and not one horse will bother to go along and watch.

＊

Which animals were the last to leave the ark?
The elephants – they were packing their trunks.

＊

Which animal has a chip on its shoulder?
A chipmunk.

＊

One unfortunate teacher started off a lesson with the following instruction: I want you all to give me a list of the lower animals, starting with Georgina Clark . . .

Ant

What kind of ant is good at adding up?
An account-ant.

What do you call ant space travelers?
Cosmon-ants.

Boy: What's the biggest ant in the world?
Girl: My Aunt Fatima.
Boy: No, it's an elephant.
Girl: You obviously haven't met my Aunt Fatima.

＊

What do you call an ant with five pairs of eyes?
Ant-ten-eye

＊

What's worse than ants in your pants?
A bat in your bra.

＊

What do you get if you cross an ant with one leg of an overall?
Pant.

※

What do you call an ant that likes to be alone?
An independ-ant.

※

What do you call an ant with frog's legs?
An ant-phibian.

※

If ants are such busy insects, how come they find the time to turn up at all the picnics?

※

Ants – so, they can carry ten times their own body weight! Thousands of years on this planet and they still haven't worked out how to build a truck!

※

What do you call an eighty-year-old ant?
An antique.

※

Why don't anteaters get sick?
Because they're full of anty-bodies!

※

What's the biggest ant in the world?
An eleph-ant.
What is even bigger than that?
A gi-ant.

※

What do you call an ant who lives with your great-uncle?
Your great-ant.

※

What is smaller than an ant's dinner?
An ant's mouth.

※

How many ants are needed to fill an apartment?
Ten-ants.

※

Where do ants eat?
In a restaur-ant.

※

What do you call a smart ant?
Eleg-ant.

※

What kind of ants are very learned?
Ped-ants.

※

What do you call a foreign ant?
Import-ant.

※

Where do ants go for their holidays?
Fr-ants

What do you call a greedy ant?
An anteater.

What do you call a scruffy, lazy ant?
Decad-ant.

What do you get if you cross some ants with some tics?
All sorts of antics.

What do you call an ant who honestly hates school?
A tru-ant

Appearance

Two Irishmen bought two horses at a sale in County Cork. Both the horses were similar in appearance, so Pat said to Mike, "How shall we tell which horse is whose?"
"I tell you what," said Mike, "we'll bob the tail of one of them."
But by a mistake the tails of both horses were bobbed so they were still in the same predicament. "I know the answer," said Pat. "You take the white one, and I'll take the black one!"

Beautician: Did that mud pack I gave you for your wife improve her appearance?
Man: It did for a while – then it fell off.

Father: Jennifer, I've had a letter from your headmaster. It seems you've been neglecting your appearance.
Jennifer: Dad?
Father: He says you haven't appeared in school all week.

Appetite

Waiter, waiter! There's a mosquito in my soup.
Don't worry sir, mosquitoes have very small appetites.

Don't eat the cookies so fast – they'll keep.
I know, but I want to eat as many as I can before I lose my appetite.

Apple

What did one maggot say to the other who was stuck in an apple?
Worm your way out of that one, then!

Why didn't the two worms go into Noah's ark in an apple?
Because everyone had to go in pairs.

What's worse than finding a maggot in your apple?
Finding half a maggot in your apple.

✳

What lives in apples and is an avid reader?
A bookworm.

✳

First apple: You look down in the dumps. What's eating you?
Second apple: Worms, I think.

✳

What do you get if you cross an apple with a shellfish?
A crab apple.

✳

The first commandment was when Eve told Adam to eat the apple.

✳

Two girls were eating a snack lunch in the school yard. One had an apple and the other said, "Watch out for worms won't you!"
The first one replied, "Why should I? They can watch out for themselves."

✳

How do you get the most apples at Halloween?
Take a snorkel.

✳

Robert came rushing in to his Dad. "Dad!" he puffed, "Is it true that an apple a day keeps the doctor away?"
"That's what they say," said his Dad.
"Well, give me an apple quick – I've just broken the doctor's window!"

✳

School lunches are not generally popular with those that have to eat them, and sometimes with good reason. "What kind of pie do you call this?" asked one schoolboy indignantly.
"What's it taste of?" asked the cook.
"Glue!"
"Then it's apple pie – the plum pie tastes of soap."

✳

Doctor, doctor! I feel like an apple! We must get to the core of this.

Argument

Why do vampires hate arguments? Because they make themselves cross.

※

Two ghouls were in the middle of an argument. "I didn't come here to be insulted," yelled one.
"Really? Where do you usually go?"

Arithmetic

Teacher: Are you good at arithmetic?
Mary: Well, yes and no.
Teacher: What do you mean, yes and no?
Mary: Yes, I'm no good at arithmetic.

※

Mother: Samantha! You came bottom out of ten in arithmetic!
Samantha: Yes, Mum, but it could have been worse.
Mother: How?
Samantha: I could have been in Sarah's group and come bottom out of twenty.

※

Tom: Why are you scratching your head?
Harry: I've got those arithmetic bugs again.
Tom: Arithmetic bugs – what are they?
Harry: Well, some people call them head lice.
Tom: Then why do you call them arithmetic bugs?
Harry: Because they add to my misery, subtract from my pleasure, divide my attention and multiply like crazy!

※

Teacher: Now, Harrison, if your father borrows $10 from me and pays me back at $1 a month, at the end of 6 months how much will he owe me?
Harrison: $10, sir.
Teacher: I'm afraid you don't know much about arithmetic, Harrison.
Harrison: I'm afraid you don't know much about my father!

※

Mary arrived home from school covered in spots. "Whatever's the matter?" asked her mother.
"I don't know," replied Mary, "but the teacher thinks I may have caught decimals."

※

Teacher: I told you to write this poem out twenty times because your handwriting is so bad.
Girl: I'm sorry Miss – my arithmetic's not that good either.

What did the arithmetic book say to the geometry book?
Boy! Do we have our problems!

Arm
"Alec won't be at school today," said his mother on the telephone. "He's broken an arm."
"Well tell him we hope he gets better soon."
"Oh he's fine now," said the mother. "It was my arm he broke."

Mommy monster: Stop reaching across the table like that. Haven't you got a tongue?
Little monster: Yes, but my arm's longer.

Army
What's the maggot army called?
The apple corps.

Why did King Kong join the army?
He wanted to know about gorilla warfare.

Knock knock.
Who's there?
Army Ant.
Army Ant who?
Army Ants coming for tea then?

What do you get if you cross a centipede with a chicken?
Enough drumsticks for an army.

Mom: Jimmy, where are you off to now?
Jimmy: I'm going to join the army.
Mom: But legally you're only an infant.
Jimmy: That's all right. I'm going to join the infantry.

Art
"I told you to draw a picture of a cow eating grass," said the art teacher. "Why have you handed in a blank sheet of paper?"
"Because the cow ate all the grass – that's why there's no grass."
"But what about the cow?"
"There wasn't much point in it hanging around when there was nothing to eat, so it went back to the barn."

What's a ghost's favorite work of art?
A ghoulage.

A very posh lady was walking around an art gallery when she stopped by one particular exhibit. "I suppose this  picture of a hideous witch is what you would call modern art?" she asked very pompously.
"No, ma'am," replied the assistant, "it's what we call a mirror."

Why are art galleries like retirement homes for teachers?
Because they're both full of old masters.

Monica imagined herself a brilliant artist. But her teacher said she was so bad it was a wonder she could draw breath.

Why are vampires artistic?
They're good at drawing blood.

Did you hear about the two little boys who found themselves in a modern art gallery by mistake?
"Quick," said one, "run! Before they say we did it!"

Astronaut
Why don't astronauts get hungry after being blasted into space?
Because they've just had a big launch.

Teacher: What do you think astronauts wear to keep warm?
Girl: Apollo neck jumpers?

Athlete
What creepie crawlies do athletes break?
Tapeworms.

What is worse than a crocodile with toothache?
A centipede with athlete's foot.

Audience

What happened to the entertainer who did a show for an audience of cannibals?
He went down really well.

※

Soprano at concert: And what would you like me to sing next?
Member of audience: Do you know Old Man River?
Soprano: Er, yes.
Member of audience: Well, go jump in it.

※

At my piano teacher's last performance the audience cheered and cheered. The piano was locked!

Aunt

There was a young witch from Nantes
Who hated each one of her aunts
So she buried the lot
In her vegetable plot
And grew some remarkable plants.

※

Did you hear about the cannibal spider that ate his uncle's wife?
He was an aunt-eater.

※

Girl: We had Aunt Susan for lunch last Sunday.
Boy: Really? We had roast beef.

A rather stern aunt had been staying with Sharon's parents, and one day she said to the little girl, "Well, Sharon, I'm going tomorrow. Are you sorry?"
"Oh yes, Auntie," replied Sharon, "I thought you were going today."

※

Mother: John, why did you put a slug in your aunt's bed?
John: Because I couldn't find a snake.

※

My Aunt Helen has got so many double chins it looks like she is peering over a pile of pancakes.

※

My Aunt Edna is so fat, Uncle Tom has to stand up in bed each morning to see if it's daylight.

※

My aunt has a sore throat. What should she do?
Take aunti-septic.

✳

Auntie Gladys bought herself a new rear-engine European car. She took an old friend for a drive, but after only half a mile the car broke down. Both women got out and opened up the front of the car.
"Oh, Gladys," said her friend, "you've lost your engine!"
"Never mind, dear," said auntie. "I've got a spare one in the trunk."

✳

Crazy Aunt Muriel received a letter one morning, and upon reading it burst into floods of tears.
"What's the matter?" asked her companion.
"Oh dear," sobbed Auntie, "It's my favorite nephew. He's got three feet."
"Three feet?" exclaimed her friend. "Surely that's not possible?"
"Well," said Auntie, "his mother's just written to tell me he's grown another foot!"

✳

Australia
Teacher: Who was that on the phone, Samantha?
Samantha: No one important, Miss. Just some man who said it was long distance from Australia, so I told him I knew that already.

Ax
Father monster came home from the Monster Repair Company to find his son Brad in disgrace.
"He's been fighting again. It's those terrible Slime children down the road. They're such a bad influence on him. He learned all about punching and kicking from them."
"Yes," interrupted Brad, "but hitting them on the head with an ax was my own idea."

✳

MUNCH!
MUNCH!

Baby

Knock knock.
Who's there?
Baby Owl.
Baby Owl who?
Baby Owl see you later, baby not.

✳

How can you tell if a snake is a baby snake?
It has a rattle.

✳

What did the mommy snake say to the crying baby snake?
Stop crying and viper your nose.

✳

What do baby pythons play with?
Rattle-snakes.

✳

What would you get if you crossed a new-born snake with a basket-ball?
A bouncing baby boa.

✳

What is a baby bee?
A little humbug.

✳

Which is the only day you are safe in a cannibal village?
Sitter days (when they eat the baby-sitter instead).

✳

How did the witch almost lose her baby?
She didn't take it far enough into the woods.

✳

What are baby witches called?
Halloweenies.

✳

Why did the vampire baby stop having baby food?
He wanted something to get his teeth into.

✳

Baby snake to its mother: Are we poisonous?
Mother: Why?
Baby: Because I've just bitten my tongue!

✳

Knock knock.
Who's there?
Underwear.
Underwear who?
Underwear my baby is tonight?

✳

Witch: My new baby is the image of his father.
Doctor: Never mind. Just so long as he's healthy.

✳

Witch: Doctor, doctor, my baby's swallowed a bullet.
Doctor: Well don't point him at anyone until I get there.

George: My mom's having a new baby.
Drew: What's wrong with the old one?

✹

Cry Baby – by Liza Weeping

✹

Definition of a baby: A soft pink thing that makes a lot of noise at one end and has no sense of responsibility at the other.

✹

Why did you drop the baby?
Well, Mrs Smith said he was a bonny bouncing baby, so I wanted to see if he did.

✹

It can't go on! It can't go on!
What can't go on?
This baby's vest – it's too small for me.

✹

Did you hear about Mrs Dimwit's new baby? She thought babies should be pink, so she took this one to the doctor because it was a horrible yeller.

✹

Mom, are the Higginbottoms very poor people?
I don't think so, Jimmy. Why do you ask?
Because they made such a fuss when their baby swallowed half a dollar.

✹

Daddy, daddy, can I have another glass of water, please?
But that's the tenth one I've given you tonight!
Yes, but the baby's bedroom is still on fire.

✹

Doctor, doctor, my baby's swallowed a watch!
Give it some Epsom Salts: that should help it pass the time.

✹

A scoutmaster asked one of his troop what good deed he had done for the day. "Well, Skip," said the scout, "Mom had only one dose of castor oil left, so I let my baby brother have it."

✹

Why are babies always gurgling with joy?
Because it's a nappy time.

※

Mrs Brown: Who was that at the door?
Veronica: A lady with a baby in a buggy.
Mrs Brown: Tell her to push off.

※

"I see the baby's nose is running again," said a worried father.
"For goodness sake!" snapped his wife. "Can't you think of anything other than horse racing?"

※

A distraught mom rushed into the back yard, where eight-year-old Tommy was banging on the bottom of an old upturned tin bath with a poker. "What do you think you're doing?" she demanded.
"I'm just entertaining the baby," explained Tommy.
"Where is the baby?" asked his Mom.
"Under the bath."

※

How do you get a baby astronaut to sleep?
You rock-et.

Bachelor
Cannibal to his daughter: Now you are nearly old enough to be married, we must start looking around for an edible bachelor.

※

Was Dracula ever married?
No, he was a bat-chelor.

Bacon
What is small, furry and smells like bacon?
A hamster.

※

What's the best day to eat bacon?
Fry-day.

Bag
What do you get if you cross a bag of snakes with a cupboard of food?
Snakes and Larders.

※

Where does a witch keep her purse?
In a hag bag.

※

Why are glow-worms good to carry in your bag?
They can lighten your load.

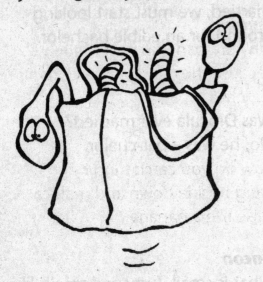

At the school concert, Wee Willie had volunteered to play his bagpipes. The noise was dreadful, like a choir of cats singing off-key. After he'd blown his way through *The Flowers of the Forest* he asked, "Is there anything else you'd like me to play?"
"Yes!" cried a voice from the back of the hall. "Dominoes!"

Bald
A wizard who's as bald as a bat
Spilt hair tonic over the mat
It's grown so much higher
He can't see the fire
And he thinks that it's smothered his cat.

First boy: My dad saw a horrible witch and didn't turn a hair!
Second boy: I'm not surprised – your dad's bald!

What do you call an English teacher, five feet tall, covered from head to toe in boils and totally bald?
Sir!

Look at that bald man over there. It's the first time I've seen a parting with ears.

America's oldest lady was 115 years old today, and she hasn't got a grey hair on her head.
How come?
She's completely bald.

What's your dad getting for Christmas?
Bald and fat.

Doctor, doctor, can you give me something for my baldness?
How about a few pounds of pig manure?
Will that cure my baldness?
No, but with that on your head no one will come near enough to notice you're bald.

Ball

Captain: Why didn't you stop the ball?
Player: I thought that was what the net was for.

As two boys were passing the church, the minister leaned over the wall and showed them a ball.
"Is this yours?" he asked.
"Did it do any damage?" asked one of the boys.
"No," replied the minister.
"Then it's mine," came the reply.

Ballet

"Ann," said the dance teacher. "There are two things stopping you becoming the world's greatest ballerina."
"What are they, ma'am?" asked Ann.
"Your feet."

What is a toad's favorite ballet? Swamp lake.

Banana

Why are bananas never lonely? Because they hang around in bunches.

How do you catch King Kong? Hang upside down and make a noise like a banana.

Time flies like an arrow, but fruit flies like a banana.

Tom: What did the banana say to the elephant?
Nick: I don't know.
Tom: Nothing. Bananas can't talk.

Mandy: Our teacher went on a special banana diet.
Andy: Did she lose weight?
Mandy: No, but she sure could climb trees well!

How can you tell the difference between a monster and a banana? Try picking it up. If you can't, it's either a monster or a giant banana.

What's the easiest way to make a
banana split?
Cut it in half.

　※

Why did the banana go out with
the prune?
Because he couldn't find a date.

　※

What's yellow and sniffs?
A banana with a bad cold.

　※

The last time I saw a face like yours
I threw it a banana.

　※

They're not going to grow bananas
any longer.
Really? Why not?
Because they're long enough
already.

Band

What's the grasshoppers' favorite
band?
Buddy Holly and the Crickets.

　※

What is the worms' favorite band?
Mud.

　※

Waiter, waiter! What's this creepy
crawly thing doing waltzing round
my table?
It's the band, sir, it's playing his
tune.

Bang

What goes "eek, eek, bang?"
A mouse in a minefield.

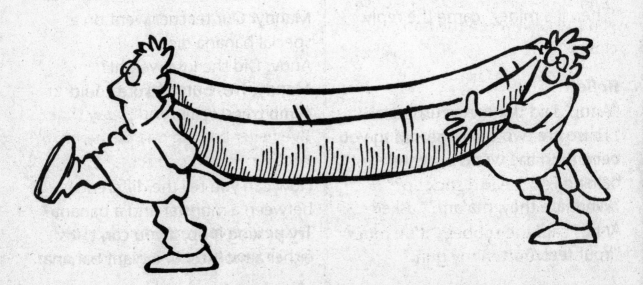

Bank

Where do vampires keep their savings?
In blood banks.

※

Why was the robber bionic?
He was holding up a bank.

※

A gang of witches broke into a blood bank last night and stole a thousand pints of blood. Police are still hunting for the clots.

※

Teacher: Why do you want to work in a bank, Alan?
Alan: 'Cuz there's money in it, sir.

※

"Dad," said Billy to his father, who was a bank robber. "I need $50 for the school trip tomorrow."
"OK, son," said his dad, "I'll get you the cash when the bank closes."

※

A stupid bank robber rushed into a bank, pointed two fingers at the clerk and said, "This is a muck up!"
"Don't you mean a stick up?" asked the girl.
"No," said the robber, "it's a muck-up. I've forgotten my gun."

※

At the scene of a bank raid the police officer came running up to his inspector and said, "He got away, sir!"
The inspector was furious. "But I told you to put a man on all the exits!" he roared. "How could he have got away?"
"He left by one of the entrances, sir!"

※

When Dave Doyle was applying for a credit card, the manager of the credit card company asked him if he had much money in the bank. "I have," said Dave.
"How much?" asked the manager.
"I don't know exactly," said Dave, "I haven't shaken it lately."

Bar

What did the cowboy maggot say when he went into the saloon bar?
Gimme a slug of whiskey.

※

Father: There are fifty-four bars in Buffalo and I'm proud to say that I've never been in one of them.
Mother: Which one is that?

※

Do you serve women in this bar?
No sir, you have to bring your own.

※

25

A man with a newt on his shoulder walked into a bar. "What do you call him?" asked the barmaid.
"Tiny," said the man.
"Why do you call him Tiny?"
"Because he's my newt!"

A man walked into a bar holding a cow pat in his hand. "Look everyone!" he cried. "See what I almost stood on!"

Barbecue
What did one termite say to the other termite when he saw a house burning?
Barbecue tonight!

Two cannibals were walking along the road when they passed a line of people waiting for a bus. "Oh look," said one of them, "A barbecue."

Barber
Why do barbers make good drivers?
Because they know all the short cuts.

A man sitting in a barber's chair noticed that the barber's hands were very dirty. When he commented on this, the barber explained, "Yes, sir, no one's been in for a shampoo yet."

A punk walked into a barber's shop and sat in an empty chair. "Haircut, sir?" asked the barber.
"No, just change the oil, please!"

Mean man: How much for a haircut?
Barber: Fifteen dollars.
Mean man: How much for a shave?
Barber: Ten dollars.
Mean man: Right – shave my head.

Bargain
Why do witches get good bargains?
Because they like to haggle.

Trader: Roll up, roll up! Come to our mammoth sale. Mammoth bargains to be had in our mammoth sale.
Customer: Forget it! No one round here's got room in their houses for a mammoth.

Bark

What happened to the werewolf who ate garlic?
His bark was worse than his bite.

Baseball

Why do vampires like playing baseball?
Because they've got plenty of bats.

※

What's the very lowest game you can play?
Baseball.

Basketball

What game can you play with a shopping bag?
Basketball.

Bat

What animal is best at cricket?
A bat.

※

What did the bat pop group call themselves?
The Boom Town Bats.

※

What did one bat say to another?
Let's hang around together.

※

What do bats sing when it's raining?
Raindrops keep falling on my feet.

※

What did a mommy bat say to her naughty son?
You bat boy.

※

What is the best way to hold a bat?
By its handle.

※

What do bats do at night?
Aerobatics.

※

What is the first thing that bats learn at school?
The alphabat.

※

What do you call a little bat?
A battle.

※

What do you call a bat in a belfry?
A dingbat.

※

What do little witches like to play at school?
Bat's cradle.

※

First bat: Fancy going out for a bite tonight?
Second bat: No. I think I'll just hang around.

Knock knock.
Who's there?
Bat.
Bat who?
Bat you'll never guess!

A wizard went to the doctor one day complaining of headaches. "It's because I live in the same room as two of my brothers," he said. "One of them has six goats and the other has four pigs and they all live in the room with us. The smell is terrible."
"Well, couldn't you just open the windows?" asked the doctor.
"Certainly not," he replied, "my bats would fly out."

Keith: Our teacher's an old bat.
Kevin: You mean he's bad-tempered?
Keith: Not only that, he hangs around us all the time.

How does a vampire enter his house?
Through the bat flap.

Boris the monster knocked on a witch's door and asked for something to eat. "You look familiar," said the witch. "Didn't I give you some bat's blood soup last week?"
"Yes," said the monster, "but I'm better now."

Bath

How do vampire football players get the mud off?
They all get in the bat-tub.

Which villains steal soap from the bath?
Robber ducks.

Boy: Dad, dad, there's a spider in the bath.
Dad: What's wrong with that? You've seen spiders before.
Boy: Yes, but this one is three feet wide and using all the hot water!

Doctor: And did you drink your medicine after your bath, Mrs Soap?
Mrs Soap: No, doctor. By the time I'd drunk the bath there wasn't room for medicine.

The plumber was working in a house when the lady of the house said to him, "Will it be alright if I have a bath while you're having your lunch?"

"It's okay with me lady," said the plumber, "as long as you don't splash my sandwiches."

※

Robot: I have to dry my feet carefully after a bath.
Monster: Why?
Robot: Otherwise I get rusty nails.

※

Dr Frankenstein: I've just invented something that everyone in the world will want! You know how you get a nasty ring around the bathtub every time you use it, and you have to clean the ring off?
Igor: Yes, I hate it.
Dr Frankenstein: Well, you need never have a bathtub ring again! I've invented the square tub . . .

Did you hear about the idiot who had a new bath put in? The plumber said, "Would you like a plug for it?"
The idiot replied, "Oh, I didn't know it was electric."

※

Hotel guest: Can you give me a room and a bath, please?
Porter: I can give you a room, but you'll have to wash yourself.

※

Mom: Joe, time for your medicine.
Joe: I'll run the bath then.
Mom: Why?
Joe: Because on the bottle it says "to be taken in water."

※

Does your brother keep himself clean?
Oh, yes. He takes a bath every month whether he needs one or not.

Bathroom
Witch: I'd like some tiles for my bathroom.
Salesman: But this is a pet shop.
Witch: That's all right – I want reptiles.

※

"But she's so young to get married," sobbed Diana's mother. "Only seventeen!"
"Try not to cry about it," said her husband soothingly. "Think of it as not losing a daughter but as gaining a bathroom."

❋

You have to be a good singer in our house, you know.
Why's that ?
There's no lock on the bathroom door.

Batman

What did The Terminator say to Batman?
I'll be bat!

❋

Who is the bat's favorite hero?
Batman, of course!

❋

What do you get if a huge hairy monster steps on Batman and Robin?
Flatman and Ribbon.

Battery

What did one lightning bug say to another when his light went out?
Give me a push, my battery is dead.

Bean

Waiter, waiter! There's a fly in my bean soup.
Don't worry sir, I'll take it back and exchange it for a bean.

❋

"Why is your son crying?" the doctor asked a young woman in his surgery.
"He has four baked beans stuck up his nose."
"And why is his little sister screaming?"
"She wants the rest of her lunch back."

❋

There was a young man called Art,
Who thought he'd be terribly smart,
He ate ten cans of beans,
And busted his jeans,
With a loud and earth-shattering ****!

Bear

What do baby witches play with?
Deady bears.

❋

"It's cruel," said the papa bear to his family on seeing a car load of humans, "to keep them caged up like that."

❋

What do Paddington Bear and Winnie the Pooh pack for their holidays?
The bear essentials.

✳

"Who's been eating my porridge?" squeaked Baby Bear.
"Who's been eating my porridge?" cried Mother Bear.
"Burp!" said Father Bear.

✳

Why do bears wear fur coats?
They'd look silly in yellow raincoats.

Beard

Bob: Our teacher is very musical you know.
Ben: Musical? Mr Jenkinson?
Bob: Yes. He's always fiddling with his beard.

✳

I can't get over that new beard of yours. It makes your face look just like a busted sofa.

Beauty

First witch: I spend hours in front of the mirror admiring my beauty. Do you think that's vanity?
Second witch: No, it's imagination.

✳

Who won the Monster Beauty Contest?
No one.

First Witch: I went to the beauty parlor yesterday. I was there for three hours.
Second Witch: Oh, what did you have done?
First witch: Nothing, I was just going in for an estimate.

✳

Mrs Saggy: Mrs Wrinkly tried to have a facelift last week.
Mrs Baggy: Tried to?
Mrs Saggy: Yes, they couldn't find a crane strong enough to lift her face!

✳

They say Margaret is a raving beauty.
You mean she's escaped from the funny farm?

✳

First witch: My beauty is timeless.
Second witch: Yes, it could stop a clock.

※

A witch went into a beauty parlor and asked the assistant how much it would cost to make her look like a film star. "Nothing," replied the assistant.
"Nothing?" she asked, "but how can I look like a film star?"
"Haven't you seen a film called *The Creature from the Black Lagoon*?" replied the assistant.

※

A monster went to the doctor with a branch growing out of his head. "Hmm," said the doctor. "I've no idea what it is." The next week the branch was covered in leaves and blossom. "I'm stumped," said the doctor, "but you can try taking these pills." When the monster came back a month later the branch had grown into a tree, and just a few weeks later he developed a small pond, surrounded by trees and bushes, all of them on top of his head. "Ah!" said the doctor, "I know what it is. You've got a beauty spot."

※

Peggy: I've just come back from the beauty parlour.
Piggy: Pity it was closed!

※

Bed

Who stole the sheets from the bed?
Bed buglars.

※

What should you do if you find a snake in your bed?
Sleep in the wardrobe.

※

What do you call a python with a great bedside manner?
A snake charmer.

※

What should you do if you find a witch in your bed?
Run!

※

A cannibal known as Ned
Ate potato chips in his bed.
His mother said, Sonny
It's not very funny
Why don't you eat people instead?

※

Father: Why did you put a toad in your sister's bed?
Son: I couldn't find a spider.

※

Wizard: Doctor, doctor, I'm having difficulty sleeping.
Doctor: Well maybe it's your bed.
Wizard: Oh, I'm all right at night, it's in the day I have problems.

※

Doctor, doctor, I keep dreaming there are great, gooey, bug-eyed monsters playing tiddley winks under my bed. What shall I do?
Hide the tiddley winks.

✳

Witch: Doctor, doctor, I don't feel well.
Doctor: Don't worry, you'll just have to go to bed for a spell.

✳

The hotel we stayed in for our holiday offered bed and board, but it was impossible to say which was the bed and which was the board.

✳

A little boy came downstairs crying late one night. "What's wrong?" asked his mother.
"Do people really come from dust, like they said in church?" he sobbed.
"In a way they do," said his mother.
"And when they die so they turn back to dust?"
"Yes, they do."
The little boy began to cry again. "Well, under my bed there's someone either coming or going."

✳

Doctor, doctor, every night I dream there are a thousand witches under my bed. What can I do?
Saw the legs off your bed.

✳

Two friends who lived in the town were chatting. "I've just bought a pig," said the first.
"But where will you keep it?" said the second. "Your yard's much too small for a pig!"
"I'm going to keep it under my bed," replied his friend.
"But what about the smell?"
"He'll soon get used to that."

✳

When Mr Maxwell's wife left him, he couldn't sleep.
Why was that?
She had taken the bed.

✳

Why did the composer spend all his time in bed?
He wrote sheet music.

✳

I don't think my Mom knows much about children.
Why do you say that?
Because she always puts me to bed when I'm wide awake, and gets me up when I'm sleepy!

✳

I was once in a play called *Breakfast In Bed*.
Did you have a big role?
No, just toast and marmalade.

❋

Did you hear about the granny who plugged her electric blanket into the toaster by mistake?
She spent the night popping out of bed.

Bee
What did the mommy bee say to the naughty little bee?
Bee-hive yourself!

❋

What goes "hum-choo, hum-choo?"
A bee with a cold.

❋

What kind of bee hums and drops things?
A fumble bee.

❋

What did the confused bee say?
To bee or not to bee.

❋

What goes zzub, zzub?
A bee flying backwards.

❋

Which is the bees' favorite pop group?
The Bee Gees.

❋

Why do bees hum?
Because they don't know the words.

❋

What do you get if you cross a bee with a door-bell?
A hum-dinger.

❋

How many bees do you need in a proper bee choir?
A humdred.

❋

What does a bee say before it stings you?
This is going to hurt me much more than it hurts you.

❋

What do you call a bee that can shelter a plane?
An air-drone.

❋

Knock knock.
Who's there?
Bee.
Bee who?
Bee careful out there!

❋

Waiter, waiter! There's a bee in my alphabet soup.
Yes, sir, and I hope there's an A, a C and all the other letters, too.

Beef

Waiter, couldn't you make this corned beef lean?
Which way?

✳

Teacher: Eat up your roast beef, it's full of iron.
Sarah: No wonder it's so tough.

✳

What do you get if you cross a chicken with a cow?
Roost beef.

Beer

What do you get if you cross a glow-worm with a pint of beer?
Light ale.

✳

My sister thinks that a juggernaut is an empty beer mug.

Beetle

What happened to the man who turned into an insect?
He beetled off.

✳

Waiter, waiter! There's a fly in my soup.
What do you expect for two dollars, sir? A beetle?

✳

Waiter, waiter! There's a beetle in my soup.
Sorry, sir, we're out of flies today.

✳

Waiter, waiter! There's a teeny beetle in my broccoli.
I'll see if I can find a bigger one, ma'am.

✳

Waiter, waiter, there's a dead beetle in my gravy.
Yes, sir. Beetles are terrible swimmers.

✳

What did the spider say to the beetle?
Stop bugging me.

Bell

Mouse I: I've trained that crazy science teacher at last.
Mouse II: How have you done that?
Mouse I: I don't know how, but every time I run through that maze and ring the bell, he gives me a piece of cheese.

✳

The school teacher was furious when Brad knocked him down with his new bicycle in the school yard. "Don't you know how to ride that yet?" he roared.

"Oh yes!" shouted Brad over his shoulder. "It's the bell I can't work yet."

Teacher: Didn't you know the bell had gone?
Silly Sue: I didn't take it, Miss.

Knock, knock.
Who's there?
Bella.
Bella who?
Bella not working, that'sa why I knocka.

Bicycle
What is a ghost-proof bicycle?
One with no spooks in it.

"Lie flat on your backs, class, and circle your feet in the air as if you were riding your bikes," said the gym teacher. "Alec! What are you doing? Move your feet, boy."
"I'm freewheeling, sir."

Did you hear about the vampire bicycle that went round biting people's arms off?
It was a vicious cycle.

My dog is a nuisance. He chases everyone on a bicycle. What can I do?
Take his bike away.

Romeo: Your cheeks are like petals.
Juliet: Really?
Romeo: Yes, bicycle pedals.

Bikini
Sandra's mother said no young man in his right mind would take her to the school dance in her bikini, so she decided to go with her friend's stupid brother.

Biology
Thinking he would play a trick on the biology teacher, Jim glued a beetle's head to a caterpillar's body and very carefully attached some

butterfly wings, ant's legs and a fly's tail. The teacher was very impressed. "I've never seen anything like this, Jim," he said. "Tell me. Did it hum when you caught it?"

"Why yes, sir. Quite loudly."

"I thought so. It's a humbug."

Bird

What's the difference between a fly and a bird?
A bird can fly but a fly can't bird.

☀

What do you get if you cross an owl with a witch?
A bird that's ugly but doesn't give a hoot.

☀

Why did the boy carry a clock and a bird on Halloween?
It was for "tick or tweet."

☀

Waiter, waiter, there's a bird in my soup.
That's all right, sir. It's bird-nest soup.

☀

Teacher: Why do birds fly south in winter?
Jim: Because it's too far to walk.

☀

Dave: The trouble with our teachers is that they all do bird impressions.
Maeve: Really? What do they do?
Dave: They watch us like hawks.

Birthday

Young vampire: Dad, dad, I know what you're getting for your birthday.
Vampire: Really? How?
Young vampire: I felt your presence.

☀

First boy: Are you having a party for your birthday?
Second boy: No, I'm having a witch do.
First boy: What's a witch do?
Second boy: She flies around on a broomstick casting spells.

☀

Come here, you greedy wretch. I'll teach you to eat all your sister's birthday chocolates!
It's all right, Dad, I know how.

☀

Flash Harry gave his girlfriend a mink stole for her birthday. Well, it may not have been mink, but it's fairly certain it was stole.

☀

Good news! I've been given a goldfish for my birthday. . .the bad news is that I don't get the bowl until my next birthday!

The housewife answered a knock on the door and found a total stranger standing on the doorstep. "Excuse me for disturbing you, ma'am," he said politely, "but I pass your house every morning on my way to work, and I've noticed that every day you appear to be hitting your son on the head with a loaf of bread."

"That's right."

"Every day you hit him on the head with a loaf of bread, and yet this morning you were beating him with a chocolate cake."

"Well, today is his birthday."

Jane: Have you noticed that your mother smells a bit funny these days?
Wayne: No. Why?
Jane: Well, your sister told me she was giving her a bottle of toilet water for her birthday.

Simon: I was going to buy you a handkerchief for your birthday.
Sarah: That was a kind thought. But why didn't you?
Simon: I couldn't find one big enough for your nose.

Emma: I'd like to say something nice about you as it's your birthday.
Gemma: Why don't you?
Emma: Because I can't think of a single thing to say!

Black cat
Why are black cats such good singers?
They're very mewsical.

First Witch: My boyfriend's gone and stolen my black cat.
Second witch: You mean your familiar.
First witch: Well, we were, but I'm not speaking to him now.

When it is unlucky to see a black cat?
When you're a mouse.

What did the black cat say to the fish-head?
I've got a bone to pick with you.

＊

"I'm sorry to call you out at this time of night," said the witch, "but it's my poor black cat. He's just lying there telling me he wants to die."
The monster vet licked his lips. "Well, you've done the right thing by sending for me . . . "

＊

What is a black cat's favorite TV program?
Miami Mice.

＊

What did one black cat say to the other?
Nothing. Cats can't speak.

＊

What did the black cat do when its tail was cut off?
It went to a re-tail store.

Black eye

Brian: How did you manage to get a black eye?
Ben: You see that tree in the playground?
Brian: Yes.
Ben: Well, I didn't.

＊

Darren came home with two black eyes and a face covered in blood. His mother was horrified. "You've been fighting," she said. "Who did this to you?"
"I don't know his name," replied Darren. "But I'd know him if I met him again. I've got half his left ear in my pocket."

＊

Father: Alan! You mustn't fight! You must learn to give and take!
Alan: But I did! I gave him a black eye and took his football!

＊

Blackboard

"Teacher is a bore!" was scrawled on the blackboard one day. "I do not want to see that on my blackboard," he thundered when he saw it.
"Sorry, sir! I didn't realize you wanted it kept secret."

米

The ghost teacher was giving her pupils instructions on how to haunt a house properly. "Has everyone got the hang of walking through walls?" she asked. One little ghoul at the front of the class looked uncertain. "Just watch the blackboard everyone," instructed the teacher, "and I'll go through it one more time."

Blind

Why are bats blind?
Well, your eyesight wouldn't be too good if you hung upside down all day would it?

Blood

What's a vampire's favorite drink?
A Bloody Mary.

米

What is small and grey, sucks blood and eats cheese?
A mouse-quito.

米

Why did the vampire take up acting?
It was in his blood.

米

Knock knock.
Who's there?
Buster.
Buster who?
Buster blood vessel?

米

What do vampires think of blood transfusions?
New-fang-led nonsense.

米

Why are vampire families so close?
Because blood is thicker than water.

米

What's Dracula's car called?
A mobile blood unit.

米

What do you get if you cross a midget with Dracula?
A vampire that sucks blood from your kneecaps.

米

What happened when the vampire went to the blood bank?
He asked to make a withdrawal.

米

Barber: Oops! Sorry, I've just cut your chin.
Vampire: Don't worry, it's not my blood.

※

Knock knock.
Who's there?
Blood.
Blood who?
Blood brothers.

※

Where do vampires go fishing?
In the blood stream.

※

Why are vampires artistic?
They're good at drawing blood.

※

What sort of group do vampires join?
A blood group.

※

Did you hear about the two blood cells?
They loved in vein.

Blue

When is a blue school book not a blue school book?
When it is read.

※

And what goes into the water pink and comes out blue?
A swimmer on a cold day!

※

What do you do with a blue witch?
Try to cheer her up.

※

What do you call a man who's black and blue all over?
Bruce.

※

What is ugly, scary and very blue?
A vampire holding his breath.

※

What has blue blood, lives in a palace and goes "woof"?
The Queen's corgi.

Bluebottle

Bluebottle: I must fly.
Bee: OK, I'll give you a buzz later.

※

I went fly-fishing yesterday.
Catch anything?
Yes, a three-pound bluebottle.

Boar

We had roast boar for dinner last night.
Was it a wild boar?
Well, it wasn't very pleased.

※

Boat

What happened to the boat that sank in the sea full of piranha fish?
It came back with a skeleton crew.

※

How can you save school dumplings from drowning?
Put them in gravy boats.

※

When is a boat like a fall of snow?
When it is a drift.

Body

Classified advertisement: For sale. 1926 hearse. Excellent condition; original body.

※

Why didn't the skeleton go to the party?
He had no body to go with.

※

Frankenstein: Doctor, I'd like to leave my body to science.
Doctor: Don't bother. We couldn't find a cure for it.

※

What has a purple-spotted body, ten hairy legs and eyes on stalks?
I don't know.
Neither do I, but there's one creeping up your back!

※

Max: I've bought a book on body building and I've been doing the exercises every day for a month.
Alexis: Is it having any effect?
Max: You bet. I can now lift the book above my head.

※

What did the skeleton say to his girlfriend?
I love every bone in your body.

※

Teacher: I was going to read you a story called *The Invasion of the Body Snatchers*, but I've changed my mind.
Class: Oh why, sir?
Teacher: Because we might get carried away.

※

What did the zombie say when he knocked on Eddie's door?
Eddie body home?

※

Madge: Your body's quite well organized.
Martin: What do you mean?
Madge: The weakest part – your brain – is protected by the strongest – your thick skull!

※

What sort of soup do skeletons like?
One with plenty of body in it.

※

What do you call a foreign body in a chip pan?
An Unidentified Frying Object.

※

Did you hear about the film star who had so many facelifts that when she went for the next one they had to lower her body instead?

Bone
Did you hear about the wizard who can sculpt lots of things out of skull bones?
Apparently he has a high degree of witchcraftsmanship.

※

Knock knock.
Who's there?
Bones.
Bones who?
Bones upon a time . . .

※

How to Feed Werewolves – by Nora Bone

※

Darren: I've just swallowed a bone.
Alexis: Are you choking?
Darren: No, I'm serious.

Bonfire
A little demon came running into the house saying, "Mom, Dad's fallen on the bonfire!"
Mom said, "Great, we'll have a barbecue."

Book
What's a witch's favorite book?
Broom at the Top.

※

What do young ghosts write their homework in?
Exorcise books.

What's a flea's favorite science fiction book?
The Itch-hiker's Guide to the Galaxy.

What's a man-eating monster's favorite book?
Ghouliver's Travels.

What's the difference between a schoolboy and an angler?
One hates his books. The other baits his hooks.

What's the difference between a boring teacher and a boring book?
You can shut the book up.

The class went to a concert. Afterwards Jacqui asked the music teacher why members of the orchestra kept looking at a book while they played. "Those books are the score," replied the teacher. "Really?" replied Jacqui, "who was winning?"

Creepy Book Title: Never Make a Witch Angry – by Sheila Tack

It says in this book that Eskimos eat raw fish and blubber.
I'm not surprised. You'd blubber, too, if you had to eat raw fish.

Bookworm

What would you do if you found a bookworm chewing your favorite book?
Take the words right out of its mouth.

What is a bookworm's idea of a big feast?
War and Peace.

What did the bookworm say to the school librarian?
Can I burrow this book please?

Boomerang

Did you hear about the stupid Australian who received a new boomerang for his birthday?
He spent two days trying to throw the old one away.

Boot

Why did the cowboy die with his boots on?
'Cos he didn't want to stub his toes when he kicked the bucket.

Bore

What's the difference between a flea-bitten dog and a bored visitor?
One's going to itch. The other's itching to go.

Vegetarian: I've lived on nothing but vegetables for years.
Bored listener: That's nothing. I've lived on Earth all my life.

You might find my sister a bit dull until you get to know her. When you do you'll discover she's a real bore!

Holly: Do you ever find life boring?
Dolly: I didn't until I met you.

The seaside resort we went to last year was so boring that one day the tide went out and never came back.

Box

Why did the monster paint himself in rainbow colors?
Because he wanted to hide in the crayon box.

Wizard: Doctor, doctor, I need something to keep my falling hair in.
Doctor: How about a matchbox.

Boxer

If a boxer was knocked out by Dracula, what would he be?
Out for the Count.

Maeve: You remind me of my favorite boxer.
Dave: Mike Tyson?
Maeve: No, he's called Fido.

Jonathan ought to be a boxer. Someone might knock him conscious.

My brother's a professional boxer.
Heavyweight?
No, featherweight. He tickles his opponents to death.

Boxing
Which weight do ghosts box at?
Phantom weight.

Did you hear about the boxing referee who used to work at a space rocket launching site?
If a fighter was knocked down he'd count Ten, nine, eight, seven . . .

Boyfriend
What did a cannibal's parents say when she brought her boyfriend home?
Lovely, dear, he looks good enough to eat!

First Witch: What's your new boyfriend like?
Second Witch: He's mean, nasty, ugly, smelly, and totally evil – but he has some bad points, too.

"My boyfriend says I look like a dishy Italian!" said Miss Conceited.
"He's right," said her brother.
"Sophia Loren?"
"No – spaghetti!"

Your sister's boyfriend certainly has staying power. In fact, he never leaves.

My boyfriend only has two faults – everything he says and everything he does!

Brain
Did you hear about the dentist who became a brain surgeon?
His drill slipped.

Why do we know that insects have amazing brains?
Because they always know when you're having a picnic.

What happened when the idiot had a brain transplant?
The brain rejected him.

"You can have that brain there for $3,000," said the brain surgeon to the man who was going to have a brain transplant. "It used to belong to a bank manager. This one's $4,000: it was a dancer's. And this one's $50,000: it belonged to a school teacher."
"Why's it ten times more than the others?" gasped the man.
"It's been used ten times less than theirs!"

※

"The girl beside me in math is very clever," said Alec to his mother. "She's got enough brains for two."
"Perhaps you'd better think of marriage," said Mom.

※

Doctor, doctor, I'm nervous, this is the first brain operation I've had.
Don't worry, it's the first I've performed.

※

Brian: How long can someone live without a brain?
Ryan: How old are you?

※

They call him Baby-face.
Does that mean he's got a brain to match?

※

Bread
Cannibal: Doctor, doctor, I keep thinking I'm a slice of bread.
Doctor: You've got to stop loafing around.

※

Waiter, waiter! There's a fly in my soup!
Don't worry sir, the spider in your bread will get it.

※

Did you hear about the teacher who was trying to instil good table manners in her girls?
She told them that a well-brought-up girl never crumbles her bread or rolls in her soup.

※

The effect of TV advertising on young viewers can be gauged from this version of part of the Lord's Prayer, as rendered by a small boy: Give us this day our oven-fresh, slow-baked, vitamin-enriched, protein-packed, nour-ishing, delicious, wholemeal daily bread!

※

They say she has a sharp tongue.
Yes, she can slice bread with it.

※

Breakfast

What is a termite's favorite breakfast?
Oak-meal.

What do nasty monsters give each other for breakfast?
Smacks in the mouth.

What do witches' cats eat for breakfast?
Mice Krispies.

What do demons have for breakfast?
Deviled eggs.

What do ghouls eat for breakfast?
Dreaded Wheet.

What noise does a witch's breakfast cereal make?
Snap, cackle, pop!

What do cannibals eat for breakfast?
Buttered host.

Brick

The Broken Window – by Eva Brick

A jeweler standing behind the counter of his shop was astounded to see a man come hurtling head-first through the window. "What on earth are you up to?" he demanded. "I'm terribly sorry," said the man, "I forgot to let go of the brick!"

Bricklayer

Dr Frankenstein decided to build an extension to his laboratory, so he crossed a cement mixer, a ghoul and a chicken. Now he's got a demon bricklayer.

Bridge

Monster: Doctor, doctor, I think I'm a bridge.
Doctor: What on earth's come over you?
Monster: Six cars, two trucks and a bus.

Two fish were swimming in a stream when it began to rain. "Quick," said one fish to the other, "let's swim under that bridge, otherwise we'll get wet!"

British

What airline do vampires travel on?
British Scareways.

Broomstick

What does a witch get if she's a poor traveler?
Broom sick.

✳

What do you call a motor bike belonging to a witch?
A brrooooom stick.

✳

Why do witches ride on broomsticks?
It's easier than walking.

✳

Why do witches fly on broomsticks?
Because vacuum cleaners are too heavy.

✳

What happens to a witch when she loses her temper riding her broomstick?
She flies off the handle.

What do you call two witches who share a broomstick?
Broom-mates.

✳

What do you call it when a witch's cat falls off her broomstick?
A catastrophe.

✳

Witch: I want you to come round the world with me on a broomstick.
Wizard: Are you taking me for a ride?

✳

Did you hear about the boy who saw a witch riding on a broomstick? He said, "What are you doing on that?"
She replied, "My sister's got the vacuum cleaner."

✳

Why do witches only ride their broomsticks after dark?
That's the time to go to sweep.

✳

What's the difference between a broomstick and a pumpkin?
You can't make broomstick pie.

※

If a flying saucer is an aircraft, does that make a flying broomstick a witchcraft?

Brother

Mommy monster: What are you doing with that saw and where's your little brother?
Young monster: Hee, hee, he's my half-brother now.

※

A ghost was sitting in a haunted house all alone when another ghost came in. It said, "Hello, I'm your long lost brother."
The first ghost said "Oooo?"

※

"What's your father's occupation?" asked the school secretary on the first day of the new term.
"He's a conjurer, Ma'am," said the new boy.
"How interesting. What's his favorite trick?"
"He saws people in half."
"Golly! Now next question. Any brothers and sisters?"
"One half brother and two half sisters."

※

"Ann!" the teacher shouted one day at the girl who had been daydreaming. "If India has the world's second largest population, oranges are 50 cents for six, and it costs $3 for a day return to Austin, how old am I?"
"Thirty-two," replied Ann.
"What makes you say that?"
"Well, my brother's sixteen and he's half mad!"

※

My big brother is such an idiot. The other day I saw him hitting himself on the head with a hammer. He was trying to make his head swell so his hat wouldn't fall over his eyes.

※

Did the bionic monster have a brother?
No, but he had lots of trans-sisters.

※

My brother's just opened a store.
Really? How's he doing?
Six months. He opened it with a crowbar.

※

My brother's one of the biggest stick-up men in town.
Gosh, is he really?
Yes, he's a six foot six bill-poster.

※

Little brother: Look, Sis, I've got a pack of cards.
Big sister: Big deal!

※

Alexis: Why is your brother so small?
Max: He's my half-brother.

※

My brother said he'd tell me everything he knows.
He must have been speechless.

※

Peter: My brother wants to work badly.
Anita: As I remember, he usually does.

※

My dad once stopped a man ill-treating a donkey. It was a case of brotherly love.

※

My brother's looking for a wife.
Trouble is, he can't find a woman who loves him as much as he loves himself.

※

Jan: My little brother is a real pain.
Nan: Things could be worse.
Jan: How?
Nan: He could be twins.

※

Brown

What is white one minute and brown the next?
A rat in a microwave oven.

※

What is brown one minute and white the next?
A rat in a freezer.

※

What's yellow and brown and covered in blackberries?
A bramble bee.

※

What's yellow, brown and hairy?
Cheese on toast dropped on the carpet.

※

What's brown and furry on the inside and clear on the outside?
King Kong in clingfilm.

※

When a girl falls over, why can't her brother help her up?
Because he can't be a brother and assist her (a sister) too.

※

Why did King Kong paint the bottoms of his feet brown?
So that he could hide upside down in a jar of peanut butter.

Bubble
What do you get if you cross a mouse with a packet of soap powder?
Bubble and Squeak.

Bucket
What happened when the monster fell down a well?
He kicked the bucket.

What's the difference between school lunches and a bucket of fresh manure?
School lunches are usually cold.

Police officer: Why are you driving with a bucket of water on the passenger seat?
Driver: So I can dip my headlights.

Buffalo
What did the buffalo say to his son when he went on vacation?
Bison!

Bug
What do you call an amorous insect?
The Love Bug.

Which fly makes films?
Stephen Spielbug.

What do you call a nervous insect?
Jitterbug.

What do you call an insect from outer space?
Bug Rogers.

What do you get if you cross a praying mantis with a termite?
A bug that says grace before eating your house.

How do insects travel when they go on holiday?
They go for a buggy ride.

Why was the insect kicked out of the park?
It was a litterbug.

What do you call singing insects?
Humbugs.

Knock knock.
Who's there?
Bug.
Bug who?
Bugsy Malone.

Doctor, doctor, I keep seeing an insect spinning round.
Don't worry, it's just a bug that's going round.

What do you get if you cross a flea with a rabbit?
A bug's bunny.

Bull

Another country boy was being interviewed for a job on a farm.
"You must be healthy," said the farmer. "Have you had any illnesses?"
"No, sir," said the boy.
"Any accidents?"
"No, sir."
"But you walked in here on crutches," said the farmer. "Surely you must have had an accident?"
"Oh that! I was tossed by a bull – but it weren't no accident, sir. He did it on purpose!"

What kind of bull doesn't have horns?
A bullfrog.

Where does Sitting Bull's ghost live?
In a creepy tepee.

What did the bull say when he came out of the china shop?
I've had a smashing time.

Bulldog

The agitated woman had rung 911. "Police, fire or ambulance?" asked the operator.
"I want a vet!" demanded the panic-stricken woman.
"A vet?" said the emergency service operator in surprise. "What for?"
"To open my bulldog's jaws."
"But why did you ring 911?"
"There's a burglar in them."

Sign in the window of a pet store: FOR SALE Pedigree bulldog. House trained. Eats anything. Very fond of children.

Bully

"I'm not going to school today," Alexander said to his mother. "The teachers bully me and the boys in my class don't like me."
"You're going. And that's final. I'll give you two good reasons why."
"Why?"
"Firstly, you're 35 years old. Secondly, you're the principal."

What's the difference between an iced lolly and the school bully?
You lick one, the other licks you.

Maureen: I hear Mattie likes hockey.
Doreen: That's because she's such a bully!

Bun

How did the baker get an electric shock?
He stood on a bun and a current ran up his leg.

Burglar

First cannibal: We had burglars last night.
Second cannibal: Did they taste good?

A woman woke her husband in the middle of the night. "There's a burglar downstairs eating the cake that I made this morning."
"Who shall I call," her husband asked, "police or ambulance?"

Pattie: We had a burglary last night, and they took everything except the soap and towels.
Peter: The dirty crooks.

Why did the burglar take a shower?
He wanted to make a clean getaway.

Bus

Cross-eyed monster: When I grow up I want to be a bus driver.
Witch: Well, I won't stand in your way.

How do eels get around the seabed?
They go by octobus.

What did the bus conductor say to the frog?
Hop on.

✳

Why did the bat miss the bus?
Because he hung around for too long.

✳

What do monsters play when they are in the bus?
Squash.

✳

What would you get if you crossed King Kong with a skunk?
I don't know but it could always get a seat on a bus!

✳

What kinds of wizards can jump higher than a bus?
All kinds – buses can't jump.

✳

What's big and red and lies upside down in a gutter?
A dead bus.

✳

Why couldn't the skeleton pay his bus fare?
Because he was skint.

✳

Roger was sitting in a very full bus when a fat woman opposite said, "If you were a gentleman, young man, you'd stand up and let someone else sit down."
"And if you were a lady," replied Roger, "you'd stand up and let four people sit down."

✳

What's the difference between a bus driver and a cold?
A bus driver knows the stops, and a cold stops the nose.

✳

A man standing at a bus-stop was eating a hamburger. Next to him stood a lady with her little dog, which became very excited at the smell of the man's supper and began whining and jumping up at him. "Do you mind if I throw him a bit?" said the man to the lady.
"Not at all," she replied, whereupon the man picked the dog up and threw it over a wall.

✳

Teacher: Tommy Russell, you're late again.
Tommy: Sorry, sir. It's my bus – it's always coming late.
Teacher: Well, if it's late again tomorrow, catch an earlier one.

✳

How can you kill an idiot with half a dollar?
Throw it under a bus.

✳

Passenger: Will this bus take me to New York?
Driver: Which part?
Passenger: All of me, of course!

Bush
Where do greedy monsters find their babies?
Under the guzzle-berry bush.

Business
What business is King Kong in?
Monkey business.

✳

Did you hear about the businessman who is so rich he has two swimming pools, one of which is always empty?
It's for people who can't swim!

✳

Monster: Stick 'em down.
Ghost: Don't you mean, stick 'em up.
Monster: No wonder I'm not making much money in this business.

✳

What happens when business is slow at a medicine factory?
You can hear a cough drop.

✳

What did the ruthless businessman say to his employees?
If at first you don't succeed – you're fired!

✳

How's your business coming along?
I'm looking for a new cashier.
But you had a new one only last week!
That's the one I'm looking for.

Butcher
Why was the werewolf arrested in the butcher's shop?
He was chop-lifting.

✳

The butcher's boy had been dismissed for insolence, and vowed vengeance on his ex-employer. The following Saturday morning, when the shop was packed with customers, he marched in, elbowed his way to the counter and slapped down one very, very dead cat. "There you are, boss!" he called out cheerily, "that makes up the dozen you ordered."

✳

An angry woman went into the butcher's shop and snapped, "That meat you sold me was awful!"
"Why, ma'am, was it tough?" asked the butcher.
"Tough!" said the woman. "I should say it was. Why, I couldn't even get my fork into the gravy!"

꙳

Mr Butcher, have you got a sheep's head?
No, ma'am, it's just the way I part my hair.

Butter

What do ghosts eat?
Dread and butter pudding.

꙳

How do you know that a werewolf's been in the fridge?
There are paw prints in the butter.

꙳

"And what's your name?" the secretary asked the next new boy.
"Butter."
"I hope your first name's not Roland," smirked the secretary.
"No, ma'am. It's Brendan."

꙳

Why was the cannibal expelled from school?
Because he kept buttering up the teacher.

꙳

Dim Dinah wrote in her homework book: Margarine is butter made from imitation cows.

꙳

Millicent! What did I say I'd do if I found you with your fingers in the butter again?
That's funny, Mom. I can't remember either.

Butterfly

How do you make a butterfly?
Flick it out of the dish with a butter knife.

꙳

Why did the butterfly?
Because it saw the ice-cream float.

꙳

Doctor, doctor, I keep thinking I'm a butterfly.
Will you say what you mean and stop flitting about?

꙳

Cabbage

Mommy! Mommy! Have you seen my Cabbage Patch Doll?
Be quiet and finish your coleslaw!

Cake

My Aunt Maud had so many candles on her last birthday cake that all her party guests got sunburnt.

＊

Flo: Try some of my sponge cake.
Joe: It's a bit tough.
Flo: That's strange. I only bought the sponge from the chemist this morning.

＊

Knock knock.
Who's there?
Chrysalis.
Chrysalis who?
Chrysalis the cake for you.

＊

Knock knock.
Who's there?
Woodworm.
Woodworm who?
Woodworm cake be enough or would you like two?

＊

What do witches eat at Halloween?
Spook-etti, Halloweenies, Devil's food cake and Boo-berry pie.

＊

Girl: Did you like that cake, Mrs Jones?
Mrs Jones: Yes, very much.
Girl: That's funny. My mom said you didn't have any taste.

＊

What cake wanted to rule the world?
Attila the Bun.

＊

A little boy went into a baker's.
"How much are those cakes?" he asked.
"Two for 25 cents," said the baker.
"How much does one cost?" asked the boy.
"13 cents," said the baker.
"Then I'll take the other one for 12 cents!" said the boy.

Camel

He's so stupid he thinks Camelot is where Arabs park their camels.

PARK HERE

A man buying a camel was advised that to make it walk he should say Few!, to make it run he should say Many!, and to make it stop he should say Amen! At his first ride all went well. Few! he called, and off the camel went. Many! he shouted, and the camel began to run – straight for the edge of a cliff. But the new owner had forgotten the word to make the animal stop! As the cliff edge came closer he cried out in terror. Lord save me! Lord save me! Amen! And of course the camel stopped – right on the edge the fearsome precipice.
Whereupon the rider mopped his brow in relief and said, Phew, that was clo- AAAAGH!

Camera

Doctor, doctor, I've just swallowed the film from my camera.
Well, let's hope nothing develops.

Why did Mr and Mrs Werewolf call their son Camera?
Because he was always snapping.

Canary

What is large, yellow, lives in Scotland and has never been seen?
The Loch Ness Canary.

Donald: My canary died of flu.
Dora: I didn't know canaries got flu.
Donald: Mine flew into a car.

"May I have another slice of lemon?" a man asked the barmaid. We don't have any lemons in this bar!
"Oh no!" said the man. "If that's true, I've just squeezed your canary into my gin and tonic!"

Candle

First witch: Shall I buy black or blue candles?
Second witch: Which one burns longer?
First witch: Neither, they both burn shorter.

Why did the mouse eat a candle?
For light refreshment.

What's a cold, evil candle called?
The wicked wick of the north.

Witch: How much are your black candles?
Salesman: Five dollars each.
Witch: That's candleous!

Cannibal

When do cannibals cook you?
On Fried-days.

※

What does a cannibal eat with cheese?
Pickled organs.

※

How can you help a starving cannibal?
Give him a helping hand.

※

What happened when the cannibals ate a comedian?
They had a feast of fun.

※

What happens if you upset a cannibal?
You get into hot water.

※

What did the cannibal say when he came home and found his wife chopping up a python and a pygmy?
Oh no, not snake and pygmy pie again!

※

What did the cannibal say when he was full?
I couldn't eat another mortal.

※

Why was the cannibal fined by the judge?
He was caught poaching.

※

What happened when the cannibal ate the speaking clock?
It repeated on him.

※

How did the cannibal turn over a new leaf?
He became a vegetarian.

※

What is a cannibal's favorite food?
Baked Beings.

※

Why did the cannibal live on his own?
He was fed up with other people.

※

Why did the Scottish cannibal live on a sugar plantation?
He said, "So that I can feed my lads with m'lasses."

※

Why do cannibals make suitcases out of people's heads?
Because they're headcases.

※

What happened when a cannibal went on a self-catering holiday?
He ate himself.

※

There was a young cannibal from Kew,
Whose girlfriend said "I'll be true,
But please understand
That as well as my hand
The rest of me comes along, too."

※

First cannibal: I can't find anything to eat!
Second cannibal: But the jungle's full of people.
First cannibal: Yes, but they're all very unsavory.

※

Did you hear about the cannibals who captured a scrawny old hunter?
It sure gave them something to chew over.

※

Did you hear about the cannibal family who were caught spying by the witch-doctor?
They were given a right roasting.

※

Two cannibals were having their dinner. One said to the other "I don't like your friend."
The other one said, "Well, put him to one side and just eat the vegetables."

※

The cannibal priest told his flock to close their eyes and say grace. "For whosoever we are about to eat, may the Lord make us truly thankful."

※

"Well, children," said the cannibal cooking teacher. "What did you make of the new English teacher?"
"Burgers, ma'am."

※

Two cannibals were having lunch.
"Your wife makes a great soup," said one to the other.
"Yes!" agreed the first. "But I'm going to miss her terribly."

※

First Cannibal: Who was that girl I saw you with last night?
Second Cannibal: That was no girl, that was my supper.

※

Canoe
Knock, knock.
Who's there?
Canoe.
Canoe who?
Canoe help me with my homework, please, Dad. I'm stuck.

Captain

"Who was Captain Kidd?" asked the history teacher.
"He was a contortionist."
"What makes you think that, Alec?"
"Well, it says in the history book that he spent a lot of time sitting on his chest."

✳

Did you hear about the monster who was known as Captain Kirk? He had a left ear, a right ear and a final front ear.

Car

How do you stop a werewolf howling in the back of a car?
Put him in the front.

✳

What car do insects drive?
A Volkswagen automobile.

✳

My dad is stupid. He thinks a fjord is a Norwegian motor car.

✳

Two wizards in a car were driving along and the police were chasing them for speeding. One said, "What are we going to do?"
The other replied, "Quick, turn the car into a side street."

✳

What happens when a frog's car breaks down?
It gets toad away.

Why did the car judder to a stop when it saw a ghost?
It had a nervous breakdown.

✳

If you watch the way that many motorists drive you will soon reach the conclusion that the most dangerous part of a car is the nut behind the wheel.

✳

What should a teacher take if he's run down?
The number of the car that hit him.

✳

What sort of a car has your dad got?
I can't remember the name. I think it starts with T.
Really? Ours only starts with gas.

✳

A man was in court charged with parking his car in a restricted area. The judge asked if he had anything to say in his defense. "They shouldn't put up such misleading notices," said the man. "It said FINE FOR PARKING HERE."

On Fred's 17th birthday, his Dad said he'd take him out for his first driving lesson. As they got in the car, the father said, "Just one thing, Fred. If you're going to hit anything, make sure it's cheap."

Cards
Witch: Why have you stopped playing cards with my sister?
Wizard: Well, would you play with someone who cheats all the time, is a poor loser and keeps tearing up the cards?
Witch: No, I wouldn't.
Wizard: No, she won't either.

Career
Teacher: Who can tell me what an archeologist is?
Tracey: It's someone whose career is in ruins.

Cartoon
My sister is so dim she thinks that a cartoon is a song you sing in a car.

Cat
What has four legs, a tail, whiskers and goes round and round for hours?
A cat in a tumble-drier.

A man out for a walk came across a little boy pulling his cat's tail. "Hey, you!" he called. "Don't pull the cat's tail!"
"I'm not pulling!" replied the little boy. "I'm only holding on – the cat's doing the pulling!"

Why is a frog luckier than a cat?
Because a frog croaks all the time – a cat only croaks nine times.

What has six legs and flies?
A witch giving her cat a lift.

Why did the girl feed her cat with pennies?
She wanted to put them in the kitty.

64

What do you call a cat who never comes when she's called?
Im-puss-able.

What do you call a cat with no legs?
Anything you like – she won't be able to come anyway.

What do you call a cat who can spring from the ground to her mistress's hat in one leap?
A good jum-purr.

What do you call a witch's cat who can do spells as well as her mistress?
An ex-purr-t.

There once was a very strong cat
Who had a big fight with a bat;
The bat flew away
At the end of the day,
And the cat had a scrap with a rat.

What does a cat go to sleep on?
A caterpillar.

"Won't you let me live one of my own lives?" said the put-upon young cat to its parents.

How does a cat go down the highway?
Mee-oww-oww!

A guy went into a police station and put a dead cat on the counter. "Somebody threw this into my front yard," he complained.
"Okay, sir," said the officer. "You come back in six months and if no one's claimed it, you get to keep it."

First cat: Where do fleas go in winter?
Second cat: Search me!

What kind of cats love water?
Octopusses.

Catapult
Father: How did the greenhouse get smashed?
Arthur: I was cleaning my catapult and it went off.

Caterpillar
What's green and dangerous?
A caterpillar with a hand-grenade.

Two caterpillars were crawling along a twig when a butterfly flew by. "You know," said one caterpillar to the other, "when I grow up, you'll never get me in one of those things."

What's the definition of a caterpillar?
A worm in a fur coat.

Cave
After years of travelling around the world in his search, the wicked Abanazar finally discovered the enchanted cave in which he believed lay the magic lamp which would make him millions. He stood before the boulders which sealed the cave, and uttered the magic words, "Open sesame!"
There was a silence, and then a ghastly voice from within moaned, "Open says-a-who?"

Cell
News report: Two prisoners escaped from their cells today. One is seven feet tall and the other is four feet six inches. The authorities are looking high and low for them.

A man is in a prison cell with no windows and no doors; there are no holes in the ceiling or trapdoors in the floor, yet in the morning the jailers find him gone. How did he get out?
Through the doorway – there were no doors remember!

Cent
Did you hear about the very well behaved little wizard? When he was good his father would give him a cent and a pat on the head. By the time he was sixteen he had $25 and a totally flat head.

Centipede
Why did the insects drop the centipede from their football team?
It took him too long to put his boots on.

Why was the centipede late?
Because she was playing "This Little Piggy" with her baby.

What is worse than a crocodile with toothache?
A centipede with athlete's foot.

What did one centipede say to another? "You've got a lovely pair of legs, pair of legs, pair of legs. . ."

What has 100 legs and goes in one ear and out the other?
A centipede in a corn field.
(geddit?)

Chair
Did you hear about the man in the electric chair who asked the executioner to reverse the charges?

Champion
Why did the champion monster give up boxing?
He didn't want to spoil his looks.

Chandelier
A pretentious woman was showing a friend round her new home. "It's very lovely," her friend admitted, "but what you need in this big room is a chandelier."
"I know, my dear," said her gracious hostess, "but nobody in the family plays one."

Why did the teacher fix her bed to the chandelier?
Because she was a light sleeper.

Cheese
What did the snake say when he was offered a piece of cheese for dinner?
Thank you, I'll just have a slither.

What musical instrument goes with cheese?
Pickle-o.

Billy: I thought there was a choice for lunch today.
School Cook: There is.
Billy: No, there isn't. There's only cheese pie.
School Cook: You can choose to eat it or leave it.

What cheese is made backwards?
Edam.

Chemistry
Baby Skunk: But, Mom, why can't I have a chemistry set for my birthday?
Mother: Because it would stink the house out, that's why.

"Philip," asked the chemistry teacher, "what is HNO 3?"
"Oh, er. . .just a minute, sir, er. . .it's on the tip of my tongue. . ."
"Well in that case – spit it out. It's nitric acid!"

Chicken

On which side does a chicken have the most feathers?
On the outside.

※

An idiot decided to start a chicken farm so he bought a hundred chickens to begin with. A month later he returned to the dealer for another hundred chickens because all of the first lot had died. A month later he was back at the dealer for another hundred chickens for the second lot had also died. "But I think I know where I'm going wrong," said the idiot, "I think I'm planting them too deep."

Billy's mother was called into the school one day by the principal.
"We're very worried about Billy," he said. "He goes round all day cluck, cluck, clucking."
"That's right," said Billy's mother. "He thinks he's a chicken."
"Haven't you taken him to a psychiatrist?"
"Well, we would, but we need the eggs."

※

What do you call a witch who likes the beach but is scared of the water?
A chicken sand-witch.

※

What happened to the baby chicken that misbehaved at school?
It was eggspelled.

※

Why should a school not be near a chicken farm?
So the pupils don't overhear fowl language.

※

Did you hear about Dr Frankenstein's invention for cooking breakfast?
He crossed a chicken with an electric organ and now he's got Hammond eggs.

※

The young teacher was complaining to her friends about how badly she was being paid. "We get a really poultry amount each month," she said.
"You mean 'paltry'," corrected one of her friends.
"No, I don't, I mean 'poultry'," replied the teacher. "What I earn is chicken feed."

What do you call a team of chickens playing football?
Fowl play.

Children
Mrs Turbot, the biology teacher, was very fond of fish. She was also rather deaf, which was great for the children in her class. "What Mrs Turbot needs," said one of her colleagues, "is a herring-aid."

Why was the lightning bug unhappy?
Because her children were not very bright.

Why was the mother flea feeling down in the dumps?
Because she thought her children were all going to the dogs.

"What were you before you came to school, boys and girls?" asked the teacher, hoping that someone would say "babies."
She was disappointed when all the children cried out, "Happy!"

Sign in shop window: FOR SALE Pedigree bulldog. House trained. Eats anything. Very fond of children.

A woman telephoned her local newspaper to let them know that she had just given birth to eighteen children. The reporter didn't quite hear the message and said, "Would you repeat that?"

"Not if I can help it," replied the woman.

Chinese

What is a cloak?
The mating call of a Chinese toad.

Why didn't King Kong go to Hong Kong?
He didn't like Chinese food.

Why was the cannibal looking peeky?
Because he'd just eaten a Chinese dog.

Where do Chinese vampires come from?
Fanghai.

A group of Chinamen who were on safari in Africa came across a pride of lions. "Oh look," said one of the lions. "A Chinese takeaway."

Chiropodist

What kind of jokes does a chiropodist like?
Corny jokes.

Chocolate

There once was a schoolboy named Rhett,
Who ate ten Hershey Bars for a bet.
When asked "Are you faint?"
He said, "No, I ain't.
But I don't feel like flying a jet."

Countess Dracula: Say something soft and sweet to me.
Dracula: Marshmallows, chocolate fudge cake. . .

Mom: Sue, there were two chocolate cakes in the larder yesterday, and now there's only one. Why?
Sue: I don't know. It must have been so dark I didn't see the other one.

I went to see my doctor to see if he could help me give up smoking.
What did he say?
He suggested that every time I felt like a smoke I should reach for a bar of chocolate.
Did that do any good?
No – I can't get the chocolate to light.

Choir

The dentist looked into his patient's mouth and said, "The only way I can cure your bad breath is to take out all your teeth."

"Will I be able to sing in the church choir afterwards?" asked the patient.

"I don't see why not," replied the dentist .

"Well, I wasn't good enough to sing in it last time I auditioned."

Christmas

What did the witch write in her Christmas card?
Best vicious of the season.

✳

For our next Christmas dinner I'm going to cross a turkey with an octopus.
What on earth for?
So we can all have a leg each.

At Christmas the school went to a special service in church. The teacher asked if they had enjoyed it, and if they had behaved themselves. "Oh yes, ma'am," said Brenda. "A lady came round and offered us a plate full of money, but we all said no thank you."

✳

Two teachers were reminiscing about their deprived childhood. "I lived in a tough neighborhood," said the first. "People were afraid to walk the streets after dark."
"That's nothing," said the other, "Whenever I hung my Christmas stocking up by the fireplace, Santa Claus stole it."

✳

A child one Christmas time asked for some paper and crayons in order to draw a crib. Eventually the artistic masterpiece was displayed for parental approval. The manger, the shepherds, Jesus, and the Holy Family were duly admired. "But what's that in the corner?" asked mother.
"Oh, that's their TV," replied the child.

✳

Alfie had been listening to his sister practice her singing. "Sis," he said, "I wish you'd sing Christmas carols."

"That's nice of you Alfie," she said, "why?"

"Then I'd only have to hear you once a year!"

Church

Mrs Jones and her little daughter Karen were outside the church watching all the comings and goings of a wedding. After it was over, Karen said to her mother, "Why did the bride change her mind, Mommy?"

"What do you mean, change her mind?" asked Mrs Jones.

"Well," said Karen, "she went into the church with one man and came out with another."

Circus

After a visit to the circus, Geoff and Don were discussing the thrills and marvels they had seen. "I didn't think much of the knife-thrower, did you?" said Geoff.

"I thought he was great!" enthused Don.

"Well, I didn't," said Geoff. "He kept throwing those knives at that soppy girl but he didn't hit her once."

Why did the vampire attack the clown?
He wanted the circus to be in his blood.

City

Which capital city cheats at exams?
Peking.

City boy (visiting country for the first time) : That farmer's a magician.
Country boy: What – old Farmer Giles? How do you know?
City boy: He told me he was going to turn his cow into a field.

Did you hear about the farmer's boy who hated the country?
He went to the big city and got a job as a shoe-shine boy, and so the farmer made hay while the son shone!

What's the smelliest city in America?
Phew York.

Mick: Tim's gone to live in the city.
Nick: Why's that?
Mick: He'd read in the papers that the country was at war.

Class

Why was the big, hairy, two-headed monster top of the class at school?
Because two heads are better than one.

※

Anna: I was top of the class last week.
Mom: How did you manage that?
Anna: I managed to answer a question about elephants.
Mom: What question?
Anna: Well, the teacher asked us how many legs an elephant had, and I said five.
Mom: But that wasn't right.
Anna: I know, but it was the nearest anyone got.

※

"Don't worry Miss Jones," said the principal to the new teacher.
"You'll cope with your new class, but they'll keep you on your toes."
"How's that, sir?" asked the teacher.
"They always put thumbtacks on the chairs."

※

Alexis: I'm the most advanced boy in my class.
Max: How do you know?
Alexis: I sit at the front!

※

"Ann," said the teacher, "point out Australia for me on the map.
Ann went to the front of the class, picked up the pointer and showed the rest of the class where Australia was.
"Well done! Now, Alec! Can you tell us who discovered Australia?"
"Er . . . Ann, sir?"

※

Joan's teacher got so fed up with her fooling around in class that he wrote a letter of complaint to her father. "What's all this about?" roared Dad, "Your teacher says he finds it impossible to teach you anything."
"I told you he was no good," said Joan.

※

"I did not come into the classroom to listen to you lot being impertinent," complained the teacher.
"Oh! Where do you usually go, sir?"

※

Father: I want to take my girl out of this terrible math class.
Teacher: But she's top of the class.
Father: That's why I think it must be a terrible class.

73

Cleopatra

Why was Cleopatra so cantankerous?
She was Queen of Denial.

Cliff

The Monster Hanging off the Cliff –
by Alf Hall

Knock knock.
Who's there?
Cliff.
Cliff who?
Cliffhanger.

Clock

The teacher glanced up at the clock and then checked the time with his watch. "That clock's fast," he told the class.
"I hope so, sir. If it isn't, it'll fall down and break."

You're late for work again, Lamport!
Yes, I'm sorry, sir. I overslept.
I thought I told you to get an alarm clock.
I did, sir, but there are nine of us in our family.
What's that got to do with it?
The alarm was only set for eight!

Hickory dickory dock
The mice ran up the clock.
The clock struck one,
And the rest got away with minor injuries.

You are so ugly your face would stop a clock.
And yours would make one run.

The proud owner of an impressive new clock was showing it off to a friend. "This clock," he said, "will go for 14 days without winding."
"Really," replied his friend. "And how long will it go if you do wind it?"

Clothes

Nicky and Vicky were talking about a famous, very glamorous film star.
"What do you think of her clothes?" asked Nicky.
"I'd say they were chosen to bring out the bust in her," replied Vicky.

Why did the girl keep her clothes in the fridge?
She liked to have something cool to slip into in the evening.

※

What do you call a hairy beast with clothes on?
A wear-wolf.

※

At a very exclusive boarding school, one of the teachers who was going out for a grand dinner appeared wearing a tuxedo, evening shirt and black tie. "Oh, sir," said one of the boys. "You're not wearing those clothes are you? You know they always give you a headache in the morning."

※

Sign in a launderette: Those using automatic washers should remove their clothes when the lights go out.

Coat

What coat has the most sleeves?
A coat of arms.

※

What likes to spend the summer in a fur coat and the winter in a swim-suit?
A moth.

※

First Monster: That orange and red checked coat of yours is a bit loud.
Second Monster: It's okay when I put my muffler on.

Cockroach

Waiter, waiter! There's a cockroach on my steak.
They don't seem to care what they eat, do they, sir?

※

Waiter, waiter, what's this cockroach doing on my ice-cream sundae?
I think it's skiing downhill.

※

Waiter, waiter! What's this cockroach doing in my soup?
We ran out of flies.

Coconut

What is brown, hairy, wears dark glasses and carries a pile of term papers?
A coconut disguised as a teacher.

※

What is hairy and coughs?
A coconut with a cold.

Coffee

Waiter, waiter, this coffee tastes like mud.

I'm not surprised, sir, it was ground only a few minutes ago.

Coffin

Why does Dracula always travel with his coffin?

Because his life is at stake.

＊

Did you hear someone has invented a coffin that just covers the head?

It's for people like you who're dead from the neck up!

＊

What do vampires have at eleven o'clock every day?

A coffin break.

＊

What kind of medicine does Dracula take for a cold?

Coffin medicine.

＊

Knock knock.
Who's there?
Coffin.
Coffin who?
Coffin and spluttering.

＊

Doctor: Is your cough any better now?

Zombie: Yes, I've been coffin nicely for weeks, thank you.

＊

A monster and a zombie went into the undertaker's. "I'd like to order a coffin for a friend of mine who has just died," said the monster. "Certainly, sir," said the undertaker, "but there was really no need to bring him with you."

Coke

How do you make a vampire float?

Take two scoops of ice-cream, a glass of Coke and add one vampire.

＊

What do frogs drink?
Croaka Cola.

Cold

What do you get if you cross a witch with an iceberg?
A cold spell.

What happened when the ice monster had a furious row with the zombie?
He gave him the cold shoulder.

Color

What kind of ant can you color with?
A cray-ant.

＊

Art Teacher: What color would you paint the sun and the wind?
Brian: The sun rose, and the wind blue.

＊

Eat up all your spinach, Jemima. It'll put color in your cheeks.
But who wants to have green cheeks?

Comb

Mommy, mommy, teacher keeps saying I look like a werewolf.
Be quiet dear and go and comb your face.

＊

What do you part with, but never give away?
A comb.

＊

Comedian

Did you hear about the comedian who entertained at a werewolves' party?
He had them howling in the aisles.

Cook

Why are school cooks cruel?
Because they batter fish and beat eggs.

＊

A cannibal caught a missionary in the jungle. "Now how shall I cook you?" said the cannibal, "Are you best roasted or grilled?"
"To tell you the truth," replied the missionary, "I'm a friar."

＊

Boy to Mother: Our school cook really knows her new technology as well as her history. For school lunch today we had micro-chips with ancient grease.

＊

Jane: I'll cook dinner. What would you like?
Shane: Good life insurance.

＊

Cookies

How do you get six monsters in a cookie tin?
Take the cookies out first.

꙳

Boy: What's black, slimy, with hairy legs and eyes on stalks?
Mom: Eat the cookies and don't worry about what's in the tin.

꙳

Why do stupid people eat cookies?
Because they're crackers.

꙳

An irate woman burst into the baker's shop and said, "I sent my son in for two pounds of cookies this morning but when I weighed them there was only one pound. I suggest you check your scales."
The baker looked at her calmly for a moment or two and then replied, "Ma'am, I suggest you weigh your son."

꙳

Jimmy, how many more times must I tell you to come away from that cookie tin?
No more, mom. It's empty.

꙳

What's the difference between a vampire and a cookie?
You can't dip a vampire in your tea.

꙳

Why did the cookie cry?
Because its mother had been a wafer too long.

꙳

Three cookies were crossing the road when the first one was knocked down. What did the third cookie say as he reached the pavement in safety?
Crumbs!

꙳

What did the cookies say to the almonds?
You're nuts and we're crackers!

Cop

"I'll have to report you, sir," said the traffic cop to the speeding driver. "You were doing 85 miles an hour."
"Nonsense, officer," declared the driver. "I've only been in the car for ten minutes."

Cornflakes

Two flies were on a cornflakes packet. "Why are we running so fast?" asked one.
"Because," said the second, "it says 'tear along the dotted line'!"

Cousin

Tim once took his small cousin with him while he went fishing. When he returned, he was looking very fed up. "I'll never do that again," he complained to his Dad.
"Did she frighten off the fish?" enquired Dad.
"No," replied Tim. "She sat on the bank and ate all my maggots."

Cow

Dad, is an ox a sort of male cow?
Sort of, yes.
And equine means something to do with horses, doesn't it?
That's right.
So what's an equinox?

⁂

Joe: Did you ever see a horse fly?
Pete: No, but I once saw a cow jump off a cliff.

⁂

What do you get if you cross a cow and a camel?
Lumpy milkshakes!

⁂

What do you call a man with cow droppings all over his shoes?
An incowpoop.

⁂

When the cow fell over the cliff, little Sarah couldn't stop laughing. After all, there was no point in crying over spilt milk.

⁂

What do you get if you cross a cow with a mule?
Milk with a kick in it.

Cowboy

Who do zombie cowboys fight?
Deadskins.

⁂

What did the cowboy maggot say when he went into the saloon bar?
Gimme a slug of whiskey.

⁂

Who is in cowboy films and is always broke?
Skint Eastwood.

⁂

What do you call a frog who wants to be a cowboy?
Hoppalong Cassidy.

⁂

A police officer saw a man dressed as a cowboy in the street, complete with huge stetson hat, spurs, and six shooters. "Excuse me, sir," said the police officer, "who are you?"
"My name's Tex, officer," said the cowboy.
"Tex, eh?" said the police officer, "Are you from Texas?"
"Nope, Louisiana."
"Louisiana? So why are you called Tex?"
"Don't want to be called Louise, do I?"

Visitor: Wow, you have a lot of flies buzzing round your horses and cows. Do you ever shoo them?
Cowboy: No we just let them go barefoot.

The swing doors of the Wild West saloon crashed open and in came Little Pete, black with fury. "All right!" he raged, "all right! Who did it? What goldarned varmint painted my horse blue?"
The huge figure of Black Jake, notorious gunfighter and town baddie rose from a chair by the door. "It was me, shrimp," he drawled, bunching his gigantic fists, "what about it?"
"Oh, well, er," stammered little Pete wretchedly, "all I wanted to say was. . .when are you going to give it another coat?"

Coyote
What's the difference between a coyote and a flea?
One howls on the prairie, and the other prowls on the hairy.

Cream
Why did the girl have to stop eating strawberry shortcake?
She was thick to her stomach.

What did the middle-aged lady say as she tucked into her dessert?
I'm afraid all this food is going to waist.

Doctor, doctor, I've just been sprayed by a skunk. Should I put some cream on it?
Well, you could. But I doubt if you'll be able to catch it.

Cricket

What happened when the frog joined the cricket team?
He bowled long hops.

✳

First witch: (Before a cricket match) How do you hold a bat?
Second witch: By the wings of course!

✳

Knock knock.
Who's there?
Cricket.
Cricket who?
Cricket neck means I can't bend over.

✳

Why is it better to be a grasshopper than a cricket?
Because grasshoppers can play cricket but there's no such game as "grasshopper."

Criminal

Newsflash: Two criminals have escaped from prison today. One is orange and 9ft tall, and the other is green and yellow and 2ft 6in tall. The police are searching high and low for them.

✳

Did you hear about the burglar who fell in the cement mixer?
Now he's a hardened criminal.

✳

When the school was broken into, the thieves took absolutely everything – desks, books, blackboards, everything apart from the soap in the lavatories and all the towels. The police are looking for a pair of dirty criminals.

Crocodile

A woman went into a shoe shop.
"I'd like some crocodile shoes, please," she said.
"Certainly, ma'am," said the salesgirl. "How big is your crocodile?"

✳

What do you get if you cross a crocodile with a flower?
I don't know, but I'm not going to smell it.

✳

What's a crocodile's favorite game?
Snap!

First crocodile: My dad's so tough
he can kill another crocodile by
blinking his eyes.
Second crocodile: My dad's so
tough it took me six hours in the
microwave to cook him.

Crossword
What's the difference between a
crossword expert, a greedy boy
and a pot of glue?
A crossword expert is a good
puzzler and the greedy boy's a pud
guzzler. The pot of glue? Ah, that's
where you get stuck.

Cucumber
He's so dumb he
thinks a cucumber
is something you
play snooker
with.

Cup
Knock knock.
Who's there?
Larva.
Larva who?
Larva cup of coffee.

Cyclops
Why were the two cyclops always
fighting?
They could never see eye to eye
over anything.

Why did the cyclops
give up teaching?
Because he only
had one pupil.

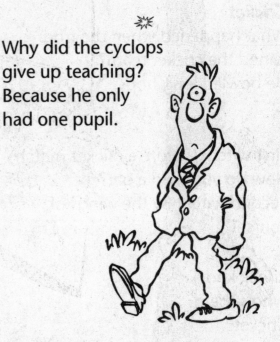

Why did the cyclops buy a very
small TV?
Because he only had one eye.

What do you call a one-eyed
monster who rides a motorbike?
Cycle-ops.

Dance

How do hens dance?
Chick to chick.

※

Why did the vampire enjoy ballroom dancing?
He could really get into the vaultz.

※

Why shouldn't you dance with a Yeti?
Because if it trod on you you might get flat feet.

※

How does a witch-doctor ask a girl to dance?
Voodoo like to dance with me?

※

What do ghosts dance to?
Soul music.

※

Where can you dance in California?
San Fran-disco.

※

Ghost: I've been invited to an avoidance.
Monster: An avoidance? What's that?
Ghost: It's a dance for people who hate each other.

Daughter

Freddie had persuaded Amanda to marry him, and was formally asking her father for his permission. "Sir," he said, "I would like to have your daughter for my wife."
"Why can't she get one of her own?" said Amanda's father, disconcertingly.

※

School Doctor to Parent: I'm afraid your daughter needs glasses.
Parent: How can you tell?
School Doctor: By the way she came in through the window.

Dead

What's the difference between a very old, shaggy Yeti and a dead bee?
One's a seedy beast and the other's a deceased bee.

※

What lies on the ground 100 feet up in the air and smells?
A dead centipede.

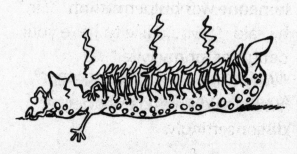

What is the difference between a musician and a dead body?
One composes and the other decomposes.

✹

What has four legs, a tail, whiskers and flies?
A dead cat.

✹

What do you call a man who has been dead and buried for thousands of years?
Pete.

✹

What's a zombie's favorite pop song?
Dead sails in the sunset.

✹

What do you find in a zombie's veins?
Dead blood corpuscles.

✹

Where do ghosts go for their holidays?
The Dead Sea.

✹

There was an old man called Jake
Who had a poisonous snake
It bit his head
And now he's dead
So that was the end of Jake.

✹

First ghoul: You don't look too well today.
Second ghoul: No, I'm dead on my feet.

✹

Did you hear about the man who left his job at the mortuary?
It was a dead end job.

✹

Did you hear about the two men who were cremated at the same time?
It was a dead heat.

✹

If a man was born in England, raised in America and died in Spain, what does that make him?
Dead.

✹

Doctor, doctor, I feel dead from the waist down.
I'll arrange for you to be half-buried.

＊

Waiter, waiter! There's a dead fly in my soup.
Oh no! Who's going to look after his family?

＊

Why did the monster take a dead man for a drive in his car?
Because he was a car-case.

＊

Teacher: If I had ten flies on my desk, and I swatted one, how many flies would be left?
Girl: One – the dead one!

Deaf
Boy: Did you know the most intelligent kid in our class is deaf?
Girl: That's unfortunate.
Boy: What did you say?

＊

A man sat on a train chewing gum and staring vacantly into space, when suddenly an old woman sitting opposite said, "It's no good you talking to me, young man, I'm stone deaf!"

＊

Why can't the deaf teacher be sent to prison?
Because you can't condemn someone without a hearing.

＊

What do you call a deaf teacher?
Anything you like, he can't hear you.

＊

Death
The man who was about to die said to the Sheriff, "Say, do I really have to die swinging from a tree?"
"Course not," replied the Sheriff. "We just put the rope round your neck and kick the horse away. After that it's up to you."

＊

A chemist, a shopkeeper and a teacher were sentenced to death by firing squad. The chemist was taken from his cell and as the soldiers took aim he shouted "Avalanche!" The soldiers panicked and in the confusion the chemist escaped. The shopkeeper was led out next. As the soldiers took aim he shouted "Flood!" and escaped. The teacher was then lead out. The squad took aim and the teacher, remenbering how the other two had escaped, shouted "Fire!"

＊

Knock knock.
Who's there?
Barry.
Barry who?
Barry the dead.

⁂

At the inquest into her husband's death by food poisoning Mrs Wally was asked by the coroner if she could remember her husband's last words. "Yes," she replied. "He said 'I don't know how that shop can make a profit from selling this salmon at only 20 cents a tin . . .'."

Deer
What's the difference between a deer running away and a small witch?
One's a hunted stag and the other's a stunted hag.

⁂

What do you call a deer with no eyes?
No idea.
What do you call a deer with no eyes and no legs?
Still no idea.

Demon
What happened to the demon who fell in the marmalade jar?
Nothing, he was a jammy devil.

⁂

What do you call a demon who slurps his food?
A goblin.

Why was the demon so good at cooking?
He was a kitchen devil.

Dentist
Monster: Doctor, doctor, I'm a blood-sucking monster and I keep needing to eat doctors.
Doctor: Oh what a shame. I'm a dentist.

⁂

Little Jackie's mother was on the telephone to the boy's dentist. "I don't understand it," she complained, "I thought his treatment would only cost me $20, but you've charged me $80."
"It is usually $20, ma'am," agreed the dentist, "but Jackie yelled so loudly that three of my other patients ran away!"

⁂

Nigel: You said the school dentist would be painless, but he wasn't.
Teacher: Did he hurt you?
Nigel: No, but he screamed when I bit his finger.

※

Why are you laughing?
My silly dentist just pulled one of my teeth out.
I don't see much to laugh about in that.
Ah, but it was the wrong one!

※

What did the werewolf eat after he'd had his teeth taken out?
The dentist.

Desert
Did you hear about the vampire that was seen crawling through the desert crying "Blood, blood."

Diamond
A little thing, a pretty thing, without a top or bottom. What am I?
A diamond ring.

※

What's the best place to find diamonds?
In a pack of cards.

Dinner
What does a monster mom say to her kids at dinnertime?
Don't talk with someone in your mouth.

※

I smother my dinner with honey.
I've done it all my life.
It makes the food taste funny.
But the peas stay on my knife.

"How do you spell 'blancmange'?" the cook asked her assistant when she was chalking up the lunch menu.
"Er . . . b.l.a.m . . . no . . . er b.l.a.a . . . no . . ."
"Never mind," said the cook.
"Tony," she shouted to the other assistant. "Open a tin of rice pudding will you?"

※

What did the school cook say when the teacher told her off for putting her finger in his soup?
It's all right, it isn't hot.

※

Ben, sniffing: Smells like UFO for dinner tonight, chaps.
Ken: What's UFO?
Ben: Unidentified Frying Objects.

＊

What did the baby ghost eat for dinner?
A boo-loney sandwich.

＊

Pupil to a school cook: Excuse me, but I have a complaint.
School cook: This is the cafeteria, not the doctor's office.

＊

The food at the club dinner was awful. The soup tasted like dishwater, the fish was spoiled, the meat was overcooked, the vegetables were obviously old. The last straw for one member was the custard which was lumpy. "This meal is disgusting!" he roared. "And what's more, I'm going to bring it up at the annual meeting next week!"

＊

"Is my dinner hot?" asked the excessively late husband.
"It should be," said his furious wife, "It's been on the fire since seven o'clock!"

Dinosaur

What do you get if you cross a dinosaur with a wizard?
A Tyrannosaurus hex.

＊

How did dinosaurs pass exams?
With extinction.

＊

What do you call a dinosaur that steps on everything in its way?
Tyrannosaurus wrecks.

Doctor

Doctor: It's bad news, I'm afraid. You've only got five minutes to live.
Patient: But doctor, isn't there anything you can do for me?
Doctor, after some thought: Well, I could boil you an egg.

＊

Did you hear about the vain monster who was going bald? The doctor couldn't do a hair transplant for him so he shrunk his head to fit his hair.

A man rushed into the doctor's office, jumped on the doctor's back, and started screaming, "One! Two! Three! Four!"
"Wait a minute!" yelled the doctor, struggling to free himself. "What do you think you're doing?"
"Well, doctor," said the eccentric man, "they did say I could count on you!"

❄

Doctor, doctor, there's an invisible ghost in the waiting room.
Tell him I can't see him without an appointment.

❄

Doctor: Good morning, Mrs Feather. Haven't seen you for a long time.
Mrs Feather: I know, doctor. It's because I've been ill.

❄

What did the vampire sing to the doctor who cured him of amnesia?
Fangs for the Memory.

❄

Doctor, doctor, I think I'm turning into a frog.
Oh, you're just playing too much croquet.

❄

Boy: Mom, mom I've just swallowed a spider.
Mom: Shall I get the doctor to give you something for it?
Boy: No, let it starve to death.

❄

Ghost: Doctor I want to go on a diet.
Doctor: Why do you want to do that?
Ghost: Because I want to keep my ghoulish figure.

❄

What happened when a doctor crossed a parrot with a vampire?
It bit his neck, sucked his blood and said, "Who's a pretty boy then?"

❄

Doctor, doctor, I keep thinking I'm a frog.
What's wrong with that?
I think I'm going to croak.

❄

"What did the doctor say to you yesterday?" asked the teacher.
"He said I was allergic to horses."
"I've never heard of anyone suffering from that. What's the condition called?"
"Bronco-itis."

✳

"Ugh! You smell terrible," said a doctor to a patient.
"That's odd," said the patient, "That's what the other doctor said."
"If you were told that by another doctor, why have you come to me?"
"Because I wanted a second opinion."

✳

A doctor had been attending a rich old man for some time, but it became apparent that the old chap had not long to live. Accordingly, the doctor advised his wealthy patient to put his affairs in order.
"Oh yes, I've done that," said the old gentleman. "I've only got to make a will. And do you know what I'm going to do with all my money? I'm going to leave it to the doctor who saves my life."

Dog
What fish do dogs chase?
Catfish.

✳

My dog plays chess.
Your dog plays chess? He must be really clever!
Oh, I don't know. I usually beat him three times out of four.

Teacher: Who can tell me what "dogma" means?
Cheeky Charlie: It's a lady dog that's had puppies, sir.

✳

What do you call a dog owned by Dracula?
A blood hound.

✳

Would you like to play with our new dog?
He looks very fierce. Does he bite?
That's what I want to find out.

✳

Mother: Keep that dog out of the house, it's full of fleas.
Son: Keep out of the house, Fido, it's full of fleas.

✳

Why did the skeleton run up a tree?
Because a dog was after its bones.

Jim: Our dog is just like one of the family.
Fred: Which one?

My dog saw a sign that said: "Wet Paint" – so he did!

"Keep that dog out of my garden. It smells disgusting!" a neighbor said to a small boy one day. The boy went home to tell everyone to stay away from the neighbor's garden because of the smell!

A blind man went into a shop, picked up his dog by the tail and swung it around his head. "Can I help you?" asked the assistant. "No thanks," said the blind man, "I'm just looking around."

What dog smells of onions?
A hot dog.

So you are distantly related to the family next door, are you ?
Yes – their dog is our dog's brother.

A man who bought a dog took it back, complaining that it made a mess all over the house. "I thought you said it was house-trained," he moaned.
"It is," said the previous owner. "It won't go anywhere else."

"Why are you crying, little boy?"
"'Cos we've just had to have our dog put to sleep!" sobbed the lad.
"Was he mad?" asked the old lady.
"Well, he wasn't too happy about it."

Doll
"Why are you crying, Amanda?" asked her teacher.
"'Cos Jenny's broken my new doll," she cried.
"How did she do that?"
"I hit her on the head with it."

Dollar

Have you heard about the new aftershave that drives women crazy?
No! Tell me about it.
It smells of 50 dollar bills.

※

She once had a million-dollar figure. Trouble is, inflation set in.

Door

Knock knock.
Who's there?
Czech.
Czech who?
Czech before you open the door!

※

Mr Jones met a neighbor carrying a front door. "Why are you carrying that, Tom?" asked Mr Jones.
"I've lost my key," replied Tom.
"Oh," said Mr Jones, "so how will you get in?"
"It's all right – I've left the window open."

※

Witch: I got up really early this morning and opened the door in my pajamas!
Wizard: That's a funny place to keep a door.

※

When a Wizard Knocks on Your Door – by Wade Aminit

※

Knock knock.
Who's there?
Adair.
Adair who?
Adair you to open this door and see my fangs.

A man who was very upset walked in to see his doctor. "Doctor, you've got to help me!" he wailed.
"What seems to be the trouble?" asked the doctor.
"I keep having the same dream, night after night. There's this door with a sign on it, and I push and push the door but I can't get it open."
"What does the sign say?" asked the Doctor.
"Pull," said the patient.

※

As he was walking along the street the minister saw a little girl trying to reach a high door knocker. Anxious to help, the minister went over to her. "Let me do it, dear," he said, rapping the knocker vigorously.

"Great!" said the girl. "Now run like hell."

Did you hear about the absent-minded professor who went round and round in a revolving door for three hours?
He didn't know whether he was coming or going!

Double Glazing

He's so stupid he thinks double glazing means a man wearing glasses who's had too much to drink.

Doughnut

Why did the doughnut maker retire?
He was fed up with the hole business.

I say waiter, there's a fly in my soup!
Well, throw him a doughnut – they make fantastic life belts!

Dracula

Why did Dracula go to the dentist?
He had fang decay.
Why did he have fang decay?
He was always eating fangcy cakes.

Why does Dracula have no friends?
Because he's a pain in the neck.

How does Dracula like to have his food served?
In bite-sized pieces.

What do you get if you cross Dracula with Al Capone?
A fangster.

What does Mrs Dracula say to Mr Dracula when he leaves for work in the evening?
Have a nice bite!

How does Dracula keep fit?
He plays batminton.

What does Dracula say when you tell him a new fact?
Well, fangcy that!

Did you know that Dracula wants to become a comedian?
He's looking for a crypt writer.

Why did Dracula go to the orthodontist?
He wanted to improve his bite.

What is Dracula's favorite pudding?
Leeches and scream.

What do you get if you cross Dracula with a snail?
The world's slowest vampire.

Don't Go Near Dracula – by Al Scream

The Witch meets Dracula – by Pearce Nex

Why did Dracula miss lunch?
Because he didn't fancy the stake.

When he's out driving, where does Dracula like to stop and eat?
The Happy Biter.

What do you think of Dracula films?
Fangtastic!

Dream
Witch: Doctor, doctor, I keep dreaming of bats, creepy-crawlies, demons, ghosts, monsters, vampires, werewolves and yetis.
Doctor: How interesting. Do you always dream in alphabetical order?

I had a funny dream last night, Mom.
Did you?
I dreamed I was awake, but when I woke up I found I was asleep.

Dress

What do you get if you cross a fashion designer with a sea monster?
The Loch Dress Monster.

✳

Mommy monster: Did you catch everyone's eyes in that dress, dear?
Girl monster: Yes, mom, and I've brought them all home for Cedric to play marbles with.

✳

Knock knock.
Who's there?
Maggot.
Maggot who?
Maggot me this new dress today.

✳

What should you do if you find yourself surrounded by Dracula, Frankenstein, a zombie and a werewolf?
Hope you're at a fancy dress party.

✳

How do people dress in mid-January?
Quickly.

✳

Did you hear about the lady ghoul who went to buy a dress in the Phantom Fashion boutique? "I'd like to try on that shroud in the window," she told the ghoul in charge.
"Yes, ma'am," said the ghoul, "but wouldn't you prefer to use the changing-room instead?"

✳

Yes, I do like your dress – but isn't it a little early for Halloween?

Drink

A man went into a diner and ordered a drink. He tasted it, pulled a face and called the waiter over.
"Is this tea or coffee?" he asked.
"It's disgusting – it tastes like disinfectant."
"In that case it's tea," said the waiter. "Our coffee tastes like soap."

✳

Why do wizards drink tea?
Because sorcerers need cuppas.

✳

Uncle Hubert noticed that his nephew Johnny was watching him the whole time. "Why are you always looking at me?" he asked.
"I was just wondering when you were going to do your trick," replied Johnny.
"What trick?" enquired Uncle Hubert.
"Well, Mom and Dad say you drink like a fish."

Why did the monster drink ten liters of anti-freeze?
So that he didn't have to buy a winter coat.

Driver
Learner driver: What happens when everything's coming your way?
Instructor: You're in the wrong lane.

Why did the stupid racing driver make ten pit stops during the Indy 500?
He was asking for directions.

"Take the wheel, Harry!" said the nervous lady driver. "There's a tree coming straight for us!"

A man whose son had just passed his driving test went home one evening and found that the boy had driven slap into the living room. "How did you manage to do that?" he fumed.
"Quite simple, Dad. I came in through the kitchen and turned left!"

Drunk
First witch: See my cat? He's just drunk 83 saucers of milk.
Second witch: That must be a lap record.

Teacher: Martin, put some more water in the fish tank.
Martin: But, Sir, they haven't drunk the water I gave them yesterday.

"What makes you think the prisoner was drunk?" asked the judge.
"Well, Your Honor," replied the arresting officer, "I saw him lift up a manhole cover and walk away with it, and when I asked him what it was for he said, 'I want to listen to it on my record-player!'"

A ghost came home one night and his wife said, "Are you drunk again?"

He said, "No, of course, not. How dare you!"

She replied, "Well, you look legless."

Duck

Two monsters went duck-hunting with their dogs but without success. "I know what we're doing wrong," said the first one.

"What's that then?" asked the second.

"We're not throwing the dogs high enough!"

Would you like a duck egg for supper?

Only if you quack it for me.

How do you make a tame duck wild?

Annoy it.

Doctor, doctor, my wife thinks she's a duck.

You better bring her in to see me straight away.

I can't do that – she's already flown south for the winter.

Dynamite

Did you hear about the mad scientist who put dynamite in his fridge?

They say he blew his cool.

Eagle

What do you get if you cross an eagle with a skunk?
A bird that stinks to high heaven.

Ear

What kind of monster has the best hearing?
The eeriest.

Little monster: Daddy, daddy, you've got carrots sprouting out of your ears.
Big monster: That's funny, I planted radishes.

Witch: I'm on a diet and it's making me irritable. Yesterday I bit someone's ear off!
Doctor: Oh dear, that's a lot of calories.

What did the earwig say when it fell down the stairs?
Ear we go!

Claire's singing is improving. People are putting cotton wool in only one ear now.

A monster walked into the city rent office with a $5 bill stuck in one ear and a $10 bill in the other. You see, he was $15 in arrears.

Earl

The eighth Earl of Jerry was showing Americans round his ancestral home, Jerry Hall, when one of them pointed to a moth-eaten, stuffed polar bear. "Gee! That beast sure smells," said the American. "Why d'ya keep it?"
"For sentimental reasons. It was shot by my mother when she and my father were on a trip to the Arctic."
"What's it stuffed with?" asked the American.
"The seventh Earl of Jerry!"

Earth

What did one worm say to another when he was late home?
Why in earth are you late?

"Why have you written that Shakespeare was a corset manufacturer before he became a playwright?" asked the English teacher.
"Because he wrote that he could put a girdle round the earth in 40 minutes."

※

What did ET's mother say to him when he got home?
Where on Earth have you been?

Eel
What is wet and slippery and likes Latin American music?
A conga eel.

※

Why did the slippery eel blush?
Because the sea weed.

※

What do you get if you cross an electric eel and a sponge?
Shock absorbers.

※

What do you get if you cross an eel with a shopper?
A slippery customer.

Knock, knock.
Who's there?
Eel.
Eel who?
Eel meet again.

Egg
What do you get if you cross a Scottish legend and a bad egg?
The Loch Ness pongster.

※

How does a witch make scrambled eggs?
She holds the pan and gets two friends to make the stove shake with fright.

※

At a party, a conjurer was producing egg after egg from a little boy's ear. "There!" he said proudly. "I bet your Mom can't produce eggs without hens, can she?"
"Oh yes, she can," said the boy. "She keeps ducks."

※

How can you drop an egg six feet without breaking it?
By dropping it seven feet – it won't break for the first six.

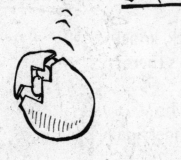

Mick: I see you've got your Easter shirt on.
Nick: Why do you call it that?
Mick: Because you've spilt egg all down the front.

What happens if you play table-tennis with a bad egg?
First it goes ping, then it goes pong.

Did you hear about the wizard who turned his friend into an egg?
He kept trying to poach his ideas.

Egypt

What do you get if you cross an Egyptian mummy with a car mechanic?
Toot and Car Man.

What did the Pharaohs use to keep their babies quiet?
Egyptian dummies.

Why were ancient Egyptian children confused?
Because their daddies were mummies.

Elastic

Wizard: Doctor, doctor, I keep thinking I'm an elastic band.
Doctor: Stretch yourself out on the couch.

With whom does an elastic trumpet player play?
With a rubber band.

A man stood up in a crowded restaurant and shouted, "Anybody lost a roll of ten dollar bills with an elastic band round them?" There was a rush of people claiming to be the loser. The first to arrive was an old tramp.
"Here you are," said the man, "I've found your elastic band."

Electric

Why did the teacher decide to become an electrician?
To get a bit of light relief.

❋

What do you get if you cross a bottle of water with an electric eel?
A bit of a shock really!

❋

A man was sitting in the electric chair. The executioner said, "Look, I'm sorry but I'm going to have to throw the switch in a minute."
The man said, "Do me a favor and throw it out the window!"

❋

Science teacher: Can you tell me one substance that conducts electricity, Jane?
Jane: Why, er. . .
Science teacher: Wire is correct.

❋

Science teacher: What happened when electricity was first discovered?
Alex: Someone got a nasty shock.

The apprentice electrician was on his first job. "Take hold of those two wires, Jim," said his boss, "and rub them together." Jim did as he was told, and his boss said, "Do you feel anything?"
"No," said Jim.
"That's good – so don't touch those other two wires, they must be the live ones!"

❋

Frankenstein: Help, I've got a short circuit!
Igor: Don't worry, I'll lengthen it.

❋

Ivan: What are you reading?
Andrea: It's a book about electricity.
Ivan: Oh, current events?
Andrea: No, light reading.

Elephant

Why did the elephant paint her head yellow?
To see if blondes really do have more fun.

How can you prevent an elephant from charging?
Take away his credit card.

Why did the elephant put his trunk across the trail?
To trip up the ants.

What do you get if you cross an elephant with a spider?
I don't know but if it crawled over your ceiling the house would collapse.

How do you make an elephant sandwich?
First of all, you get a very large loaf. . .

What do you get if you cross an elephant and peanut butter?
Either peanut butter that never forgets, or an elephant that sticks to the roof of your mouth.

Reports are coming in of an elephant doing a ton in the highway. Police ask motorists to drive carefully and to yield right of way.

An elephant ran away from a circus and ended up in a little old lady's back garden. Now she had never seen an elephant before, so she rang the police. "Please come quickly," she said to the police officer who answered the phone. "There's a strange-looking animal in my garden picking up cabbages with its tail."
"What's it doing with them?" asked the police officer.
"If I told you," said the old lady, "You'd never believe me!"

How does an elephant go up a tree?
It stands on an acorn and waits for it to grow.

What do you get if you cross an elephant with the abominable snowman?
A jumbo yeti.

✳

"Why are you tearing up your homework notebook and scattering the pieces around the playground?" a furious teacher asked one of the kids in his class.
"To keep the elephants away, sir."
"There are no elephants!"
"Shows how effective it is then, doesn't it?"

Escalator
A man went into the local department store where he saw a sign on the escalator – Dogs must be carried on this escalator. The man then spent the next two hours looking for a dog.

Eskimo
Did you hear about the Eskimo teacher who was reciting Little Jack Horner to her class of five-year-olds?
She'd got as far as "Little Jack Horner sat in a corner" when one little girl put up her hand and said, "Please, ma'am, what's a corner?"

✳

What did the Eskimo children sing when their principal was leaving?
Freeze a Jolly Good Fellow.

✳

What did the Eskimo schoolboy say to the Eskimo schoolgirl?
What's an ice girl like you doing in a place like this?

Essay
An English teacher asked her class to write an essay on what they'd do if they had $1,000,000. Alec handed in a blank sheet of paper.
"Alec!" yelled the teacher. "You've done nothing. Why?"
"'Cos if I had $1,000,000 that's exactly what I would do."

✳

When Dad came home he was astonished to see Alec sitting on a horse, writing something. "What on earth are you doing there?" he asked.

"Well, teacher told us to write an essay on our favorite animal. That's why I'm here and that's why Susie's sitting in the goldfish bowl!"

✳

The class was set an essay on Shakespeare. Jacqui wrote in her book: Shakespeare wrote tragedy, comedy, and errors.

✳

Teacher: Colin, one of your essays is very good but the other one I can't read.
Colin: Yes, sir. My mother is a much better writer than my father.

Evil

What is evil and ugly on the inside and green on the outside?
A witch dressed as a cucumber.

✳

What is evil and ugly and goes at 125mph?
A witch in a high-speed train.

✳

What is evil and ugly, puts spells on people and is made of leaves?
A witch (the leaves were just a plant).

✳

What is evil and ugly and bounces?
A witch on a trampoline.

What's evil and ugly and goes up and down all day?
A witch in an elevator.

✳

What is evil and bearded and lives under the sea?
A wizard with an aqualung.

✳

Why is a turkey like an evil little creature?
'Cos it's always a-gobblin'. . .

Exam

Which animals do you have to beware of when you take exams?
Cheetahs.

✳

A teacher was correcting exam papers when he came across Simon's effort: a sheet of paper, blank apart from his name and Act II Macbeth. Scene V. Line 28. The teacher reached for his Shakespeare and turned to Macbeth where he found that the 28th line of the fifth scene of the second act read, "I cannot do this bloody thing."

❋

Student: Excuse me, sir, but I don't think I deserve a mark of 0 for this exam paper.
Teacher: Neither do I, but it's the lowest mark I can give.

Teacher: In this exam you will be allowed ten minutes for each question.
Boy: How long is the answer?

❋

Why did the flea fail his exams?
He wasn't up to scratch.

❋

Why did the skeleton schoolgirl stay late at school?
She was boning up for her exams.

Excuse

A teacher in a county school received the following letter from one his student's mothers: Dear Teacher, Please excuse Phil from school last week. His father was ill and the pig had to be fed. Yours sincerely,

❋

Coach: Why did you miss that shot?
Player: I sprained my ankle.
Coach: That's a lame excuse.

Eyes

The police are looking for a thief with one eye?
Why don't they use two?

❋

What did one of the monster's eyes say to the other?
Between us is something that smells.

What's big, red and prickly, has three eyes and eats rocks.
A big, red, prickly, three-eyed, rock-eating monster.

What kinds of wizards have their eyes closest together?
The smallest ones.

There was a big monster called Ned
Who had eyes at the back of his head.
When asked where he's going
"I've no way of knowing.
But I know where I've been to," he said.

First monster: That pretty girl over there just rolled her eyes at me.
Second monster: Well you'd better roll them back to her, she might need them.

Knock knock.
Who's there?
Reuben.
Reuben who?
Reuben my eyes 'cos I can't believe what a big monster you are.

I have two noses, three eyes and only one ear. What am I?
Very ugly.

A man who tests people's eyes is called an optimist.

Did you hear about the vampire who had an eye for the ladies?
He used to keep it in his back pocket.

Did you hear about the monster with one eye at the back of his head, and one at the front?
He was terribly moody because he couldn't see eye to eye with himself.

What did the little eye say to the big eye?
Aye, aye, Captain!

His left eye must be fascinating.
Why do you say that?
Because his right eye looks at it all the time.

Face

What is grey and hairy and lives on a man's face?
A mousetache.

Susannah was watching her big sister covering her face with cream. "What's that for?" she asked. "To make me beautiful," came the reply. Susannah then watched in silence as she wiped her face clean. "Doesn't work, does it?" was her comment.

What happened when the witch went for a job as a TV presenter? The producer said she had the perfect face for radio.

Johnny: You have the face of a saint.
Jilly: Really? Which one?
Johnny: A Saint Bernard.

Ben: You've got a Roman nose.
Jen: Like Julius Caesar?
Ben: No, it's roamin' all over your face.

Witch: Doctor, I can't help pulling ugly faces.
Doctor: Well there's nothing terrible about that.
Witch: It is when the people with ugly faces don't like them being pulled.

A little boy came running into the kitchen. "Dad, dad," he said, "there's a monster at the door with a really ugly face."
"Tell him you've already got one," said his father.

Boy Monster: You've got a face like a million dollars.
Girl Monster: Have I really?
Boy Monster: Yes – it's green and wrinkly.

Ben's new girlfriend uses such greasy lipstick that he has to sprinkle his face with sand to get a better grip.

Father monster: Johnny, don't make faces at that man. I've told you before not to play with your food.

A woman just back from Arizona was telling her friends about the trip. "When my husband first saw the Grand Canyon, his face dropped a mile," she said. "Why, was he disappointed with the view?" "No, he fell over the edge."

✳

Two boys were watching TV when the fabulous face and figure of Pamela Anderson appeared on the screen. "If I ever stop hating girls," said one to the other, "I think I'll stop hating her first."

✳

I never forget a face, but in your case I'll make an exception.

✳

Did you hear about the witch who was so ugly that when a tear rolls down her cheek it takes one look at her face and rolls straight up again?

✳

Gill: Your sister uses too much make-up.
Jen: Do you think so?
Gill: Yes. It's so thick that if you tell her a joke, five minutes after she's stopped laughing her face is still smiling!

✳

Wife to Husband: I'll have you know I've got the face of a teenager!
Husband to Wife: Then you should give it back, you're wearing it out.

✳

Patient: The trouble is, doctor, I keep pulling ugly faces.
Doctor: Don't worry, I don't expect anyone will notice.

✳

Knock, knock.
Who's there?
Alec.
Alec who?
Alec most people but I don't like your face.

✳

Chris: Do you like my new hairstyle?
Fliss: In as much as it covers most of your face, yes.

✳

You can read his mind in his face.
Yes, it's usually a complete blank.

✳

First Witch: I like your toad. He always has such a nice expression on his face.
Second Witch: It's because he's a hoptimist.

Fairy

A ghost was out haunting one night and met a fairy fluttering through the forest. "Hello," said the ghost. "I've never met a fairy before. What's your name?"

"Nuff," said the fairy.

"That's a very odd name," said the ghost.

"No, it's not," said the fairy, offended, "haven't you heard of Fairy Nuff?"

False Teeth

What did the vampire call his false teeth?

A new fangled device.

❈

What happened to the man who put his false teeth in backwards?
He ate himself!

Why did the old lady cover her mouth with her hands when she sneezed?
To catch her false teeth.

❈

A man coughed violently, and his false teeth shot across the room and smashed against the wall. "Oh, dear," he said, "whatever shall I do? I can't afford a new set."

"Don't worry," said his friend. "I'll get a pair from my brother for you."

The next day the friend came back with the teeth, which fitted perfectly. "This is wonderful," said the man. "Your brother must be a very good dentist."

"Oh, he's not a dentist,"replied the friend, "he's an undertaker."

❈

Knock, knock.
Who's there?
Dishes.
Dishes who?
Dishes the way I talk now I've got false teeth.

Family

Girl: Do you know what family the octopus belongs to?
Boy: No one in our street.

❈

Lee: Our family's descended from royalty.
Dee: King Kong?

❈

At a very Ivy-league school the girls were discussing their family pets. "We've got a beautiful spaniel at our place," said one girl. "Does it have a pedigree?" asked another. "It does on its mother's side. And its father comes from a very good neighborhood."

✳

On the first day at school the children were sizing each other up and boasting, trying to make good impressions on each other. "I come from a one-parent family," said one little girl proudly. "That's nothing. Both my parents remarried after they got divorced. I came from a four-parent family."

✳

Ronnie: I can trace my family tree way back.
Bonnie: Yes, back to the time you lived in it!

Famous

What do you get if you cross a skeleton with a famous detective?
Sherlock Bones.

✳

Who was the most famous scientist ant?
Albert Antstein.

✳

What do you call the famous eighteenth-century skeleton who was cremated?
Bone-ash (Beau Nash. . . geddit?)

✳

What did the cannibal say when he met the famous explorer?
Dr Livingstone, I consume?

✳

First Monster: Every time we meet, you remind me of a famous film star.
Second Monster: Meryl Streep? Madonna? Racquel Welch?
First Monster: No, ET.

Fan

What kind of letters did the snake get from his admirers?
Fang mail.

✳

If you want to know more about Dracula what do you have to do?
Join his fang club.

Fangs

Where did vampires go to first in America?
New-fang-land.

What do you get if you cross a snake with a hotdog?
A fangfurther.

What's a vampire's favorite soup?
Sharks' fang soup.

What is the American national day for vampires?
Fangsgiving Day.

How do vampires keep their breath smelling nice?
They use extractor fangs.

Why was Dracula thought of as being polite?
He always said fangs.

What's a vampire's favorite dance?
The Fang Tango.

Knock knock.
Who's there?
Fang.
Fang who?
Fangs for the memory.

Knock knock.
Who's there?
Adair.
Adair who?
Adair you to open this door and see my fangs.

How does a vampire get through life with only one fang?
He has to grin and bare it.

What has webbed feet and fangs?
Count Quackula.

What do you think of Dracula films?
Fangtastic!

Farm

We had a wonderful act at the club last week – a man who did farmyard impressions.
What was wonderful about it?
He didn't do the sounds – he did the smells. . .

Farmer

How did the aliens hurt the farmer?
They trod on his corn.

✳

What did the neurotic pig say to the farmer?
You take me for grunted.

✳

"Why did you come back early from your holidays?" one of Alec's friends asked him.
"Well, on the first day we were there one of the chickens died and that night we had chicken soup. The next day one of the pigs died and we had pork chops. . .
"But why did you come back?"
"Well, on the third day the farmer's father-in-law died. What would you have done?"

Fat

What was proved when the fat man was run over by a steam-roller?
That he had a lot of guts.

✳

What's the difference between a square peg in a round hole and a pound of lard?
One's a fat lot of good and the other's a good lot of fat!

✳

A fat witch who lived on the Rhine
Was asked at what hour she would dine.
She said, "At seven,
And half past eleven,
With a snack at a quarter to nine."

✳

Did you hear about the two fat men who ran in the New York Marathon?
One ran in short bursts, the other in burst shorts!

✳

What did the speak-your-weight machine say when the fat lady stepped on?
One at a time, please.

There was an old man from Brazil
Who always ate more than his fill
He thought it no matter
That his waist line grew fatter
But he burst.
Doesn't that make you ill?

Father

Rob: I must rush home and cut the lawn for my father.
Teacher: Did he promise you something if you cut it?
Rob: No, he promised me something if didn't!

✳

Mom: Jackie, go outside and play quietly. Your father can't read his paper.
Jackie: Wow, I'm only eight, and I can read it!

✳

Mother: What did your father say about your report?
Girl: Well, if you want me to cut out the swear words, he didn't really say anything.

Fear

What is the witches' favorite musical?
My Fear Lady.

✳

First Explorer: There's one thing about Jenkinson.
Second Explorer: What's that?
First Explorer: He could go to headhunters' country without any fear – they'd have no interest in him.

✳

Max: Did you hear about the man who didn't know the meaning of the word "fear"?
Alexis: How come?
Max: He was too afraid to ask.

Feet

What lies down a hundred feet in the air?
A centipede.

✳

Centipede: Doctor, doctor, when my feet hurt, I hurt all over.
Can you stand on your head?
I've tried, but I can't get my feet up high enough.

Chuck: Do have holes in your underpants?
Teacher: No, of course not.
Chuck: Then how do you get your feet through?

❋

Two monsters were in hospital and they were discussing their operations and ailments. "Have you had your feet checked?" one asked the other.
"No," came the reply. "They've always been purple with green spots."

❋

Joan, pick up your feet when you walk.
What for, Mom? I've only got to put them down again.

❋

How do ghosts keep their feet dry?
By wearing boo-ts.

❋

Why are feet like ancient tales?
Because they are leg-ends.

❋

"If you're going to work here, young man," said the boss, "one thing you must learn is that we are very keen on cleanliness in this firm. Did you wipe your feet on the mat as you came in?"

"Oh, yes, sir."
"And another thing, we are very keen on truthfulness. There is no mat."

Female
What is a myth?
A female moth.

❋

My sister is so dumb, she thinks that a buttress is a female goat.

Fence
Did you hear that in the recent gales the fence blew down around the Pink and Pimply Nudist Camp? A group of construction workers is looking into it.

❋

Paddy was telling Mick of his plans to make a lot of money. "I intend to buy a dozen swarms of bees and every morning at dawn I'm going to let them into the park opposite my house to spend all the day making honey, while I relax."
"But the park doesn't open until nine o'clock," protested Mick.
"I realize that," said Paddy, "but I know where there's a hole in the fence."

❋

A young lad was helping his dad put up a yard fence. "You know, son," said the father, "you're just like lightning with that hammer."

"Fast, eh?" said the boy.

"Oh, no – you never strike in the same place twice."

Fiend

What is the demons' favorite TV sit-com?

Fiends.

＊

Why was Baron Frankenstein never lonely?

Because he was good at making fiends.

＊

Rumors that Count Dracula is about to marry Glenda the Ghoul are not true.

They're just good fiends.

＊

First Ghoulish Fiend: I had a nice man to dinner last night.

Second Ghoulish Fiend: So you enjoyed having him?

First Ghoulish Fiend: Oh, yes, he was delicious.

Fight

What do you do when two snails have a fight?

Leave them to slug it out.

＊

There once was a snake named Drake
Who started a fight with a rake.
It cut off his tail
Drake went very pale
And that's the short end of my tale.

＊

Boy: Dad, dad, come out. My sister's fighting this ten-foot gargoyle with three heads.

Dad: No, I'm not coming out. He's going to have to learn to look after himself.

＊

Mom: Alexis, you've been fighting again. You've lost your front teeth!

Alexis: No I haven't, Mom. They're in my pocket.

＊

There was a fight in the restauarant last night – a whole lot of fish got battered!

❄

Steve, you've been fighting again, haven't you?
Yes, Mom.
You must try to control your temper. Didn't I tell you to count to ten?
Yes, but Vic's Mom only told him to count up to five, so he hit me first!

❄

I hear she was a war baby.
I'm not surprised – I expect her parents took one look at her and started fighting.

File
What do cannibal secretaries do with left-over fingernails?
They file them.

❄

It's a pity you've gone on hunger strike, said the convict's wife on visiting day.
Why?
I've put a file in your cake.

Film
What is the bees' favorite film?
The Sting.

❄

Insect Films: The Fly; Batman; Beetlejuice; The Sting; The Good, the Bug and the Ugly; Spawn; The Frog Prince; Four Webbings and a Funeral; Seven Bats for Seven Brothers.

❄

What happened when the old witch went to see a funny film?
The manager told her to cut the cackle.

❄

What do you do if a witch in a pointy hat sits in front of you in the cinema?
Miss most of the film.

❄

Why did the vampire actress turn down so many film offers?
She was waiting for a part she could get her teeth into.

❄

Romeo: You remind me of a film star.
Juliet: Which one?
Romeo: Lassie.

Finger
Why are witches' finger nails never more than eleven inches long?
Because if they were twelve inches they'd be a foot.

❄

What did the monster want to eat in the restaurant?
The finger bowl.

Dad, what are all the holes in the new garden shed?
They're knot-holes.
What do you mean they're not holes? I can put my finger into them.

💥

My husband really embarrassed me yesterday. We were drinking tea at a friend's house and he drank his with his little finger sticking out.
But that's considered polite in some circles.
Not with the teabag hanging from it, it's not.

💥

Mommy monster: Agatha, how often must I tell you not to eat with your fingers.
Agatha monster: Sorry, Mom.
Mommy monster: I should think so! Use a shovel like I do.

Fire
What happened to the skeleton who stayed by the fire all night?
He was bone dry.

💥

Mommy, mommy, why do you keep poking Daddy in the ribs?
If I don't, the fire will go out.

Firefly
Why did the firefly keep stealing things?
He was light-fingered.

💥

What goes 'snap, crackle, pop'?
A firefly with a short circuit.

💥

How do fireflies start a race?
Ready, steady, glow!

💥

What did one firefly say to another?
Got to glow now.

💥

A little firefly was in school one day and he put up his hand. "Please, ma'am, may I be excused?"
"Yes," replied the teacher, "when you've got to glow, you've got to glow."

💥

What do you get if you cross a moth with a firefly?
An insect that can find its way around a dark closet.

First

What does a polite monster say when he meets you for the first time?
Pleased to eat you!

＊

When a witch falls into a pond what is the first thing that she does?
Gets wet.

＊

What is the first thing a wizard does in the morning?
He wakes up.

＊

What happened when the young wizard met the young witch?
It was love at first fright.

＊

The games teacher had broken off her engagement. The science teacher asked her what had happened. "I thought it was love at first sight," said the science teacher.
"It was, but it was the second and third sights that changed my mind."

＊

Hil: Who was the fastest runner in history?
Bill: Adam. He was first in the human race.

＊

What's the first thing a ghost does when it gets into the front seat of a car?
Fasten the sheet belt.

＊

Two men were arranging to meet. "If I get there first I'll put a chalk cross on the wall, Paddy."
"Right you are Mick," said Paddy. "And if I get there first, I'll rub it off."

＊

"I just want you to remember one thing, Boyce," said the managing director to the new sales manager. "If at first you don't succeed – you're fired!"

＊

My sister fell in love at second sight. When she first met him she didn't know how rich he was.

＊

Fish

Doctor, doctor, my husband smells like a fish.
Poor sole!

What is a sea monster's favorite dish?
Fish and ships.

What sort of fish performs surgical operations?
A sturgeon.

Did you hear about the stupid angler who poured whiskey into the river?
He thought the fish would come up ready canned.

An irate customer in a restaurant complained that his fish was bad, so the waiter picked it up, smacked it and said, "Naughty, naughty, naughty!"

Doctor, doctor! I think need glasses!
You certainly do, madam. This is a fish and chip shop.

Fisherman

Two shark fishermen were sitting on the side of their boat just off the coast of Florida, cooling their feet in the sea. Suddenly an enormous shark swam up and bit off one fisherman's leg. "A shark's just bitten off my leg," yelled the fisherman.
"Which one?"

Two fishermen were out in their boat one day when a hand appeared in the ocean. "What's that?" asked the first fisherman. "It looks as if someone's drowning!"
"Nonsense," said the second. "It was just a little wave."

Passer-by (to fisherman): Is this river any good for fish?
Fisherman: It must be. I can't get any of them to leave it.

Fishing

Where do vampires go fishing?
In the blood stream.

A man was fishing in the jungle. After a while another angler came to join him. "Have you had any bites?" asked the second man. "Yes, lots," replied the first one, "but they were all mosquitoes."

※

Retired colonel, talking of the good old days: Have you ever hunted bear?

His grandson's teacher: No, but I've been fishing in shorts.

※

An old lady saw a little boy with a fishing-rod over his shoulder and a jar of tadpoles in his hand walking through the park one Sunday. "Little boy," she called, "don't you know you shouldn't go fishing on a Sunday?"

"I'm not going fishing, ma'am," he called back, "I'm going home."

※

The little kid sat on the side of the road with a fishing line down the drain. Feeling sorry for him, and wanting to humor him, a lady gave him 50 cents, and kindly asked "How many have you caught?"

"You're the tenth this morning," was the reply.

※

What kind of musical instrument can you use for fishing?
The cast-a-net.

Flagpole
Wally Woollynut was given the job of painting a flagpole but he didn't know how much paint he would need. "Lay it down and measure it," suggested a mate.

"That's no good," said Wally. "I need to know the height, not the length."

Flat
What do you get if King Kong sits on your best friend?
A flat mate.

※

What do you get if King Kong sits on your piano?
A flat note.

※

Why shouldn't you dance with a Yeti?
Because if it trod on you, you might get flat feet.

※

How do you know if a monster is musical?
He's got a flat head.

※

Why won't a witch wear a flat cap?
Because there's no point in it.

✳

Why do elephants have flat feet?
From jumping out of tall trees.

Flea

What's the name of the opera
about a mouse and a flea?
Der Fleadermouse.

✳

What did one amorous flea say to
the other?
I love you aw-flea.

✳

A fly and a flea in a flue
Were wondering what they should
do.
Said the fly, "Let us flee!"
Said the flea, "Let us fly"
So they flew, through a flaw in the
flue.

✳

Did you hear about the angry flea?
He was hopping mad.

✳

Knock knock.
Who's there?
Flea.
Flea who?
Flea's a jolly good feller.

✳

Knock knock.
Who's there?
Flea.
Flea who?
Flea thirty!

✳

Waiter, waiter! There's a flea in my
soup.
Tell him to hop it.

✳

How do you find out where a flea
has bitten you?
Start from scratch.

✳

What's the difference between fleas
and dogs?
Dogs can have fleas but fleas can't
have dogs.

✳

What did the idiot do to the flea in
his ear?
Shot it!

✳

What did one flea say to another
after a night out?
Shall we walk
home or take
a dog?

What is the most faithful insect on the planet?
Fleas. Once they find someone they like they stick to them.

❋

If a flea and a fly pass each other what time is it?
Fly past flea.

❋

What do you call a cheerful flea?
A hop-timist.

❋

A flea jumped over the swinging doors of a saloon, drank three whiskeys and jumped out again. He picked himself up from the dirt, dusted himself down and said, "OK, who moved my dog?"

Flies
What has four wheels and flies?
A trash can.

❋

If there are five flies in the kitchen, which one is the American football player?
The one in the sugar bowl.

❋

Why were the flies playing football in a saucer?
They were playing for the cup.

❋

Waiter, I must say that I don't like all the flies in this dining room!
Tell me which ones you don't like and I'll chase them out for you.

❋

What did one frog say to the other?
Time's sure fun when you're having flies!

❋

Boy: My sister's the school swot.
Girl: Does she do well in exams.
Boy: No, but she kills a lot of flies.

❋

Waiter, waiter! There are two flies in my soup.
That's all right sir. Have the extra one on me.

❋

Doctor, doctor, I don't like all these flies buzzing around my head.
Pick out the ones you like and I'll swat the rest.

Flood
A charming young singer named Hannah,
Got caught in a flood in Savannah;
As she floated away,
Her sister – they say;
Accompanied her on the piannah!

❋

Floodlight

Why did the idiot have his sundial floodlit?
So he could tell the time at night.

✳

How did Noah see to the animals in the Ark?
By floodlighting.

Floor

Why did the moth nibble a hole in the carpet?
He wanted to see the floor show.

✳

What do you call a wizard who lies on the floor?
Matt.

✳

Girl: Mom, mom a monster's just bitten my foot off.
Mom: Well keep out of the kitchen, I've just washed the floor.

✳

Waiter, waiter, you have your thumb on my steak!
I know sir, I don't want it to fall on the floor again!

✳

Why did the ghost go trick or treating on the top floor?
He was in high spirits.

✳

Did you hear about the very stupid monster who sat on the floor?
He fell off.

✳

Doctor! Doctor! My sister thinks she's an elevator.
Tell her to come in.
I can't. She doesn't stop at this floor.

✳

Doctor, how can I cure myself of sleepwalking?
Sprinkle thumb-tacks on your bedroom floor.

Florist

Did you hear about the florist who had two children?
One's a budding genius and the other's a blooming idiot.

✳

Stupid florist: I used to wear a flower in my lapel.
Customer: Why did you stop?
Florist: Because the pot kept hitting me in the stomach.

Flower

What do you get if you cross a vampire with a rose?
A flower that goes for your throat when you sniff it.

What's a python's favorite flower?
Coily-flowers.

What is a frog's favorite flower?
The croakus.

What did the bee say to the flower?
Hello, honey.

Why did the bees go on strike?
Because they wanted more honey and shorter working flowers.

What kind of flower is a witch's favorite?
A triffid.

What are the bees' favorite flowers?
Bee-gonias

Flu

What do you call an insect that has just flown by?
A flu bug.

How did the yeti feel when he had flu?
Abominable.

How does a flu germ know when it has won?
When it brings its victim to his sneeze.

Fly

Why did the fly fly?
Because the spider spied her.

Why did the robin fly into the library?
It was looking for bookworms.

Waiter, waiter! There's a fly in my custard.
I'll fetch him a spoon sir.

How do you make a moth bawl?
Hit him with a fly swatter.

Can bees fly in the rain?
Not without their little yellow jackets.

What is big, hairy and can fly faster than sound.
King Koncord.

Knock knock.
Who's there?
Fly.
Fly who?
Fly away soon.

Waiter, waiter! There's a fly in my soup!
Yes, sir, he's committed insecticide.

Waiter, waiter! There's a fly in my soup.
Not fussy what they eat are they sir?

Waiter, waiter, there's a fly in my soup.
Just a minute sir, I'll get the fly spray.

Waiter, waiter! There's a fly in my starter. Get rid of it would you?
I can't do that, sir, he hasn't had his main course yet.

Waiter, waiter! There's a fly in my soup.
Go ahead and eat him. There are plenty more where he came from.

Sir, you haven't touched your custard.
No, I'm waiting for the fly to stop using it as a trampolene.

Waiter, waiter! There's a fly in my soup!
Just wait until you see the main course.

Waiter, waiter! Did you know there is a fly in my soup?
That's not a fly sir, it's just dirt in the shape of a fly.

※

Waiter, waiter! What's this fly doing in my soup?
I think it's drowning sir.

※

The wizard who had invented a flying carpet was interviewed for a local radio station. "What's it like, Merlin, to fly on a magic carpet?" asked the radio presenter. "Rugged," replied Merlin.

※

Waiter, waiter! What is this fly doing in the alphabet soup?
Learning to spell.

Flying
What does a witch do if her broom is stolen?
She calls the Flying Squad.

※

What's the best way to see flying saucers?
Pinch the waitress.

※

What do you call a starship full of wizards?
Flying sorcery.

※

What do you get if you cross a vampire with a mummy?
A flying bandage.

※

If a flying saucer is an aircraft, does that make a flying broomstick a witchcraft?

Fog
What do you get if you cross a toad with a mist?
Kermit the Fog.

※

Did you hear about the boy who was known as Fog?
He was thick and wet.

Foghorn
What goes "croak, croak" when it's foggy?
A frog-horn.

※

First Witch: Every time it's misty, I hear a strange croaking noise coming from your house.
Second Witch: That would be my frog horn.

Food

Waiter, this food isn't fit for a pig!
All right, I'll get you some that is.

Alex and Alan took their lunches to the local cafe to eat. "Hey!" shouted the proprietor. "You can't eat your own food in here!"
"Okay," said Alex. So he and Alan swapped their sandwiches.

Brian: Our school must have very clean kitchens.
Bill: How can you tell?
Brian: All the food tastes of soap.

My brother's on a seafood diet.
Really?
Yes, the more he sees food the more he eats.

Fool

Alexis: Do you think I'm a fool?
Bruce: No. But what's my opinion against thousands of others?

Did you hear about the fool who keeps going round saying "no"?
No.
Oh, so it's you!

A man went into a pet shop to buy a parrot. He was shown an especially fine one which he liked the look of, but he was puzzled by the two strings which were tied to its feet. "What are they for?" he asked the pet shop manager.
"Ah well, sir," came the reply, "that's a very unusual feature of this particular parrot. You see, he's a trained parrot, sir, he used to be in the circus. If you pull the string on his left foot he says 'Hello' and if you pull the string on his left foot he says 'Goodbye'."
"And what happens if you pull both strings at once?"
"I fall off my perch, you fool!" screeched the parrot.

Foot

Monster: Doctor, doctor, how do I stop my nose from running?
Doctor: Stick out your foot and trip it up.

Doctor, doctor, I've got bad teeth, foul breath and smelly feet.
Sounds like you've got foot and mouth disease.

Football

What do ghosts say when a girl football player is sent off?
Ban-she, ban-she!

Why is the ghouls' football pitch wet?
Because players keep dribbling on it.

✻

George knocked on the door of his friend's house. When his friend's mother answered he said, "Can Albert come out to play?"
"No," said the mother, "it's too cold."
"Well, then," said George, "can his football come out to play?"

I thought, Jessop, that you wanted yesterday afternoon off because you were seeing your dentist?
That's right, sir.
So how come I saw you coming out of the football stadium with a friend at the end of the game?
That was my dentist.

✻

Why do centipedes make such poor football players?
By the time they put their boots on, the match is nearly over.

✻

Some more vampires went to see Dracula. They said, "Drac, we're going to start a football team."
"Great," he said, "I'll be ghoulie."
They said, "When we've had a bit of practice we'll challenge the human beings to a game."
Dracula said, "Be careful, the stakes will be high."
They said," No, we've got this brilliant idea. We'll have these very long games which'll tire them out. The first half will run from dusk to midnight and the second half from midnight till dawn."
Dracula said, "And what happens if it goes to extra time?"

Fork
I wonder where I got that puncture?
Maybe it was at that last fork in the road. . .

Forked Tongue
Why can't you trust snakes?
They speak with forked tongue.

Fork Lift Truck

How do you raise a baby monster that has been abandoned by its parents?
With a fork-lift truck.

Fortune

My uncle spent a fortune on deodorants before he found out that people didn't like him anyway.

Fortune Telling

In My Crystal Ball – by Thea Lot

Why did the witch give up fortune telling?
There was no future in it.

"Five dollars for one question!" said the woman to the fortune teller.
"That's very expensive, isn't it?"
"Next!"

Fountain Pen

What do you get if you cross a tall green monster with a fountain pen?
The Ink-credible Hulk.

France

Which ghost was president of France?
Charles de Ghoul.

First witch: I'm going to France tomorrow.
Second witch: Are you going by broom?
First witch: No, by hoovercraft.

Tommy was saying his prayers as his father passed by his bedroom door. "God bless Mommy, and God bless Daddy, and please make Calais the capital of France."
"Tommy," said his father, "why do you want Calais to be the capital of France?"
"Because that's what I wrote in my geography test!"

Frankenstein

How does Frankenstein sit in his chair?
Bolt upright.

What did one of Frankenstein's ears say to the other?
I didn't know we lived on the same block.

How did Frankenstein's monster
eat his lunch?
He bolted it down.

✳

Why did Frankenstein squeeze his
girl-friend to death?
He had a crush on her.

✳

How did Dr Frankenstein pay the
men who built his monster?
On a piece rate.

✳

Frankenstein was sitting in his cell
when suddenly through the wall
came the ghost of his monster,
with a rope round his neck.
Frankenstein said, "Monster,
monster, what are you doing
here?"
The monster said, "Well, boss, they
hanged me this morning so now
I've come to meet my maker."

✳

What happened to Frankenstein's
monster on the road?
He was stopped for speeding, fined
$50 and dismantled for six months.

✳

What does Frankenstein's monster
call a screwdriver?
Daddy.

✳

What happened to Frankenstein's
stupid son?
He had so much wax in his ears
that he became a permanent
contributor to Madame Tussaud's.

✳

Why did Dr Frankenstein have his
telephone cut off?
Because he wanted to win the
Nobel prize!

✳

Dr Frankenstein: Igor, have you
seen my latest invention? It's a new
pill consisting of 50 per cent glue
and 50 per cent aspirin.
Igor: But what's it for?
Dr Frankenstein: For monsters with
splitting headaches.

✳

Igor: Only this morning Dr
Frankenstein completed another
amazing operation. He crossed an
ostrich with a centipede.
Dracula: And what did he get?
Igor: We don't know – we haven't
managed to catch it yet.

✳

What happened when Dr
Frankenstein swallowed some
uranium?
He got atomic ache.

✳

Monster: Someone told me Dr Frankenstein invented the safety match.
Igor: Yes, that was one of his most striking achievements.

French

What is the Guillotine?
A French chopping centre.

※

Did you hear about the Frenchman who jumped into the river in Paris?
He was declared to be in Seine.

French fries

Spooky happenings at the supermarket! A customer was just leaning over the freezer looking for some frozen French fries when ten fish fingers crept up and pulled him in. . .

※

A tourist walked into a fish and chip shop in Ireland. "I'll have fish and chips twice," he orders.
"Sure, I heard you the first time," came the reply.

Fridge

Why did Ken keep his trumpet in the fridge?
Because he liked cool music.

※

A woman went to the fridge to get some milk and all she found was a disembodied hand there. It was all fingers and thumbs.

Friend

What did the mouse say when his friend broke his front teeth?
Hard cheese.

※

"What shall we play today?" said Theresa to her best friend Emma.
"Let's play schools," said Emma.
"OK!" said Theresa. "But I'm going to be absent."

※

My friend is so stupid that he thinks twice before saying nothing.

※

My friend is so stupid he thinks that an autograph is a chart showing sales figures for cars.

※

A friend in need is – someone to avoid!

Frog

Where does a ten-ton frog sleep?
Anywhere it wants to!

※

134

What do you call a
frog spy?
A croak and
dagger agent.

How do frogs manage to lay so
many eggs?
They sit eggsaminations.

❋

What did the bus conductor say to
the frog?
Hop on.

❋

What do you say to a hitch-hiking
frog?
Hop in!

❋

What do you get if you cross a frog
with a ferry?
A hoppercraft.

❋

Why do frogs have webbed feet?
To stamp out forest fires.

❋

What is a frog's favorite dance?
The Lindy Hop.

❋

What happens to illegally-parked
frogs?
They get toad away.

❋

What did the croaking frog say to
his friend?
I think I've got a person in my
throat.

❋

Why was the frog down-in-the-
mouth?
He was un-hoppy.

❋

What would you get if you crossed
a frog with a little dog?
A croaker spaniel.

❋

What is a frog's favorite game?
Croak-et.

❋

What do frogs drink?
Hot croako.

❋

What kind of shoes do frogs like?
Open toad sandals.

❋

What do you call an eighty-year-old frog?
An old croak.

✳

What do you call a girl with a frog on her head?
Lily.

✳

What's white on the outside, green on the inside and comes with relish and onions?
A hot frog.

✳

What happens if you eat a hot frog?
You croak in no time.

✳

Where do you get frogs' eggs?
In a spawn shop.

✳

What do you get if you cross a werewolf with a frog?
A creature that can bite you from the other side of the road.

✳

Waiter, waiter! There's a frog in my soup.
Don't worry, ma'am, there's not enough there to drown him.

✳

First witch: I'm so unlucky.
Second witch: Why?
First witch: Last night I went to a party and met a handsome prince.
Second witch: What's unlucky about that?
First witch: When I kissed him he turned into a frog.

✳

Where do frogs keep their coats?
In the croakroom.

✳

Teacher: Why did you put that frog in Melinda's case?
Boy: Because I couldn't find a mouse.

Frogs' Legs
Waiter, waiter! Have you got frogs' legs?
No, sir, I always walk like this.

✳

Waiter, waiter, do you have frogs' legs?
Yes sir.
Well then hop into the kitchen for my soup.

✳

Waiter, waiter, can I have frogs' legs?
Well I suppose you could but you'd need surgery!

※

What do you call an ant with frogs' legs?
An ant-phibian.

Fruit

What's red and green and wears boxing gloves?
A fruit punch.

What is Dracula's favorite fruit?
Neck-tarines.

※

Teacher: If you saw me standing by a witch, what fruit would it remind you of?
Pupil: A pear.

※

First boy: She had a beautiful pair of eyes, her skin had the glow of a peach, her cheeks were like apples and her lips like cherries – that's my girl.
Second boy: Sounds like a fruit salad to me.

※

Why is history like a fruit cake?
Because it's full of dates.

※

Cookery teacher: Helen, what are the best things to put in a fruit cake?
Helen: Teeth!

Funeral

Did you hear about the Do-It-Yourself funeral?
They just loosen the earth and you sink down by yourself.

Fur

What's big, heavy, furry, dangerous and has sixteen wheels?
A monster on roller-skates.

※

Lady: I'd like a fur coat, please.
Store assistant: Certainly, madam, what fur?
Lady: To keep myself warm, of course.

※

Boy: Did you know you can get fur from a three-headed mountain monster?
Girl: Really? What kind of fur?
Boy: As fur away as possible!

Furniture

Where did the witch get her furniture?
From the Ideal Gnome Exhibition.

💥

What's the longest piece of furniture in the school?
The multiplication table.

💥

A country lad on one of his rare visits to the market town saw a music stool in the window of a shop. He went in, bought it, and took it home. Two weeks later he was back in the shop in a furious rage. "I bin sittin' on this darn stool for two weeks," he told the manager, "and I ain't got a note out of it!"

💥

Doctor! Doctor! I think I'm a dog!
Sit down, please.
Oh no – I'm not allowed on the furniture.

💥

HIC!

Gambling

Little Tommy was the quietest boy in school. He never answered any questions but his homework was always quite excellent. If any one said anything to him he would simply nod, or shake his head. The staff thought he was shy and decided to do something to give him confidence. "Tommy," said his teacher. "I've just bet Miss Smith $5 I can get you to say three words. You can have half."

Tommy looked at her pityingly and said, "You lose."

"I want you to help me stop my son gambling," an anxious father said to his boy's principal. "I don't know where he gets it from but it's bet, bet, bet."

"Leave it to me," said the principal. A week later he phoned the boy's father. "I think I've cured him," he said.

"How?"

"Well, I saw him looking at my beard and he said, 'I bet that's a false beard.' 'How much?' I said, and he said '$5'"

"What happened?" asked the father.

"Well, he tugged my beard, which is quite natural, and I made him give me $5. I'm sure that'll teach him a lesson."

"No, it won't," said the father. "He bet me $10 this morning that he'd pull your beard with your permission by the end of the week."

Game

What game do ants play with monsters?
Squash.

What is the favorite game at a ghost's Halloween party?
Hide and Shriek.

Brian: Let's play a game of wits.
Diane: No, let's play something you can play, too.

Gangster

Who is the biggest gangster in the sea?
Al Caprawn.

Garbage

The garbage men were just about to leave the street when a woman came running out of the house carrying some cardboard boxes.

"Am I too late for the garbage?" she called.

"No, lady," replied one of the men, "Jump right in!"

✳

A garbage man was walking along whistling while balancing a bin on his head and one on each shoulder.

"How do you manage to do that?" asked Jane.

"It's easy," he replied. "Just put your lips together and blow."

Garlic

First vampire: I live on garlic alone.

Second vampire: Anyone who does that *should* live alone.

✳

First witch: Why do you keep throwing bunches of garlic out of the window?

Second witch: To keep the vampires away.

First witch: But there aren't any vampires round here.

Second witch: See, it works doesn't it.

✳

Did you hear about the man who ate 106 cloves of garlic a day?

He was taken to hospital in a coma. Doctors said it was from inhaling his own breath.

Gas

A monster goes to a gas station and says: Fill me up.

The gas man replies: You have to have a car for me to do that!

The monster replies to the gas man: But I had a car for lunch!

✳

What did the angry monster do when he got his gas bill?

He exploded.

✳

Two old friends met, ten years after the end of the Second World War. One said, "Is that your face or are you still wearing your gas mask?"

✳

General

At a diplomatic reception, the Mexican general appeared in a magnificent uniform, liberally bespattered with medals and decorations. "That's most impressive," said the US ambassador. "Tell me, general, what did you get all those for?"

"In your money," replied the Mexican general, "about five dollars!"

✳

Where does a general keep his armies?
Up his sleevies.

Geography

Did you hear about the brilliant geography teacher?
He had abroad knowledge of his subject.

✳

"Alec," groaned his father when he saw his son's school report. "Why are you so awful at geography?"
"It's the teacher's fault, Dad. He keeps telling us about places I've never heard of."

✳

On her holidays, the geography teacher explained that she went to the Himalayas, visiting remote mountain areas. "In fact," she said, "we went where the hand of man has never set foot."

✳

Simple Simon was writing a geography essay. It began, The people who live in Paris are called parasites . . .

✳

Jennifer: How come you did so badly in history? I thought you had all the dates written on your sleeve?
Miriam: That's the trouble, I put on my geography blouse by mistake.

Geometry

Teacher: What's the best way to pass this geometry test?
Boy: Knowing all the angles?

Ghost

How did the ghost song-and-dance act make a living?
By appearing in television spooktaculars.

※

What kind of street does a ghost like best?
A dead end.

※

What did the papa ghost say to the baby ghost.
Fasten your sheet belt.

※

What do you call a ghost that stays out all night?
A fresh air freak.

※

Why did the ghost go to the funfair.
He wanted to go on the rollerghoster.

※

Why did the ghost work at Scotland Yard?
He was the Chief In-Spectre.

※

What do you call the ghost who is a child-rearing expert?
Dr Spook.

※

Which ghost ate too much porridge?
Ghouldilocks.

※

What happened when a ghost asked for a brandy at his local pub?
The landlord said "Sorry, we don't serve spirits."

※

What is a ghost boxer called?
A phantomweight.

※

What happened to the ghost who went to a party?
He had a wail of a time.

※

The Ghost of the Witch – by Eve L. Spirit

※

A Ghost in My House – by Olive N. Fear

※

Did you hear about the ghost comedian?
He was booed off stage.

※

Did you hear about the ghost who learnt to fly?
He was pleased to be back on terror-firma.

※

Did you hear about the ghost who wore glasses?
They were spooktacles.

Did you hear about the ghost who enjoyed doing housework?
He used to go round with the oooo-ver.

※

A man was staying in a big old house and in the middle of the night he met a ghost. The ghost said, "I have been walking these corridors for 300 years."
The man said, "In that case, can you tell me the way to the toilet?"

※

Why did the ghost go trick-or-treating on the top floor?
He was in high spirits.

※

Who did the ghost invite to his party?
Anyone he could dig up.

※

What are pupils at ghost schools called?
Ghoulboys and ghoulgirls.

※

What do you get is you cross a ghost with a packet of potato chips?
Snacks that go crunch in the night.

※

What do you call a ghost who only haunts the Town Hall?
The nightmayor.

✳

Woman in bed: Aaagh! Aaagh! A ghost just floated into my room!
Ghost: Don't worry, ma'am, I'm just passing through.

✳

What did one ghost say to another?
I'm sorry, but I just don't believe in people.

✳

What do you call a ghost who's always sleeping?
Lazy bones.

✳

Who said "Shiver me timbers!" on the ghost ship?
The skeleton crew.

Ghoul
How did the glamorous ghoul earn her living?
She was a cover ghoul.

✳

What kind of ghoul has the best hearing?
The eeriest.

✳

What's a ghost's favorite Beatles' song?
The Ghoul on the Hill.

✳

It is a terrible night and Greg the Ghoul is out playing in it. There's thunder and lightning and all the graves are opening and all the nasty things that ever there were are wandering the earth.
Question: What did Greg's mother say?
Answer: Come in, Greg.

✳

Knock knock.
Who's there?
Ghoul.
Ghoul who?
Ghoulpost painter.

✳

Knock knock.
Who's there?
Harry.
Harry who?
Harry up! There's a ghoul after us!

Giant
A Very Hungry Giant – by Ethan D. Lot

✳

Where do you find giant snails?
On the end of a giant's fingers.

Gift
What parting gift did a mommy werewolf give to her son when he left home?
A comb.

Giraffe
What's worse than a giraffe with a sore throat?
A centipede with athlete's foot.

Girl
Why did the wizard turn the naughty girl into a mouse?
Because she ratted on him.

※

There was a young girl from Hyde
Who fell down a hole and died
Her unfortunate mother
Tripped up on another
And now they're interred side by side.

※

First witch: My, hasn't your little girl grown?
Second witch: Yes, she's certainly gruesome.

※

Did you hear about the girl monster who wasn't pretty and wasn't ugly?
She was pretty ugly.

※

On a coach trip to Washington a little girl kept sniffing. "Haven't you got a hankie, dear?" asked a little old lady across the aisle.
"Yes," replied the little girl. "But I'm not supposed to talk to strangers, so I certainly can't lend you my handkerchief."

※

She's the kind of girl that boys look at twice – they can't believe it the first time.

What kind of girl does a mummy take on a date?
Any old girl he can dig up.

My sister's going out with David.
Any girl who goes out with David must be able to appreciate the simpler things in life.

Belinda: James told me last night that he'd met the most beautiful girl in the world.
Barbara: Oh, dear, I'm so sorry. I thought he was going to marry you.

Handsome Harry: Every time I walk past a girl she sighs.
Wisecracking William: With relief!

Val: Girls are smarter than boys, you know!
Alec: I didn't know that.
Val: See what I mean.

Two teenage boys were talking in the classroom. One said, "I took my girlfriend to see The Bride of Dracula," last night.
"Oh yeah," said the other, "what was she like?"
"Well, she was about six foot six, white as a ghost and she had big red staring eyes and fangs."
The other said, "Yes, but what was the Bride of Dracula like?"

Glass
How can you tell if a monster has a glass eye?
Because it comes out in conversation

Anne: Ugh! The water in my glass is cloudy.
Dan, trying to impress his new girlfriend: It's all right, it's just the glass that hasn't been washed.

Doctor, doctor, I think I've been bitten by a vampire.
Drink this glass of water.
Will it make me better?
No, but I'll be able to see if your neck leaks.

Pa was taking Danny around the museum when they came across a magnificent stuffed lion in a glass case. "Pa," asked the puzzled Danny, "how did they shoot the lion without breaking the glass?"

Dad, there's a man at the door collecting for the new swimming pool.
Give him a glass of water!

Glasses

A monster went to see the doctor because he kept bumping into things. "You need glasses," said the doctor.

"Will I be able to read with them?" asked the monster.
"Yes."
"That's brilliant," said the monster. "I didn't know how to read before."

Glove

Why do elephants have trunks?
Because they don't have glove compartments.

Two people went into a very dark, spooky cave. "I can't see a thing," said one.
"Hold my hand," said the other.
"All right." The first man reached out. "Take off that horrible bristly glove first, though."
"But I'm not wearing a glove. . ."

What makes an ideal present for a monster?
Five pairs of gloves – one for each hand.

Did you hear about the witch who was ashamed of her long black hair?
She always wore long gloves to cover it up.

Gnome
What did the little demon do when he bought a house? He called it Gnome Sweet Gnome.

Goal
Did you hear about the idiotic goalkeeper who saved a penalty but let it in on the action replay?

Goat
Did you hear about the man who tried to cross the Loch Ness Monster with a goat?
He had to get a new goat.

God
"What are you drawing?" asked the teacher.
"God," the little girl replied firmly.
"But nobody knows what God looks like," said the teacher.
"They will when I've finished."

Gold
Where do frogs keep their treasure?
In a croak of gold at the end of the rainbow.

He has a heart of gold.
And teeth to match!

Monster: Doctor, I have this irrepressible urge to paint myself all over in gold.
Doctor: Don't worry, it's just a gilt complex.

Goldfish
One goldfish to his tankmate: "If there's no God, who changes the water?"

What smells of fish and goes round and round at a hundred miles an hour?
A goldfish in a blender.

What did Dr Frankenstein get when he put his goldfish's brain in the body of his dog?
I don't know, but it is great at chasing submarines.

Golf

Two ants were watching a useless golfer swing wildly, trying to hit the ball. One said to the other, "Come on, lets get on the ball before he hits us."

※

"Let me inform you, young man," said the slow elderly golfer, "I was playing this game before you were born."
"That's all very well, but I'd be obliged if you'd try to finish it before I die."

※

"What are the elements, Andrew?" asked the science teacher.
"Er . . . earth . . . air . . . fire . . ."
"Well done," said the teacher.
"There's one more."
"Er . . . oh, yes. Golf."
"Golf! Yes, I heard my mom say that dad's in his element when he plays golf."

※

My wife says that if I don't give up golf she'll leave me.
Say, that's tough, old man.
Yeah, I'm going to miss her.

※

Happily innocent of all golfing lore, Sam watched with interest the efforts of the man in the bunker to play his ball. At last it rose amid a cloud of sand, hovered in the air, and then dropped on the green and rolled into the hole. "Oh my," Sam chuckled, "he'll have a tough time getting out of that one!"

※

"Can ye see your way to letting me have a golf ball, Jock?" Ian asked his old friend.
"But Ian, you said you were going to stop playing golf," said Jock, reluctantly handing over an old spare.
"By degrees, Jock. By degrees," replied Ian pocketing the ball. "I've stopped buying balls as a first step."

Gooseberry

What's the difference between a worm and a gooseberry?
Ever tried eating worm pie?

※

Why is King Kong big and hairy?
So you can tell him apart from a gooseberry.

Gorilla

What should you do if you find a gorilla sitting at your school desk? Sit somewhere else.

Gossip

She's such a gossip it doesn't take her long to turn an earful into a mouthful.

❉

She's such a gossip she tells you what you were going to say to her before you have the chance to tell her.

Grandfather

When the picture of the vampire's grandfather crashed to the floor in the middle of the night what did it mean? That the nail had come out of the wall.

❉

Are you writing a thank-you letter to Grandpa like I told you to?
Yes Mom.
Your handwriting seems very large.
Well, Grandpa's very deaf, so I'm writing very loudly.

❉

How old is your Grandad?
I dunno, but we've had him a long time.

❉

Boy: Grandad, do you know how to croak.
Grandad: No, I don't think so. Why?
Boy: Because Daddy says he'll be a rich man when you do.

Grandmother

Pete: I haven't slept a wink for the past two nights.
Jimmy: Why's that?
Pete: Granny broke her leg. The doctor put it in plaster and told her she shouldn't walk upstairs. You should hear the row when she climbs up the drainpipe.

❉

Grape

What did the grape do when the elephant sat on it?
It let out a little wine.

✳

Why do grape harvesters have noses?
So they have something to pick during the growing season.

Grass

Why is grass so dangerous?
Because it's full of blades.

Grasshopper

What is green and can jump a mile a minute?
A grasshopper with hiccups.

HIC!

What do you call a grasshopper with no legs?
A grass-hovver.

Graveyard

Sergeant: Officer, I want you to stand guard outside the graveyard tonight.
Officer: But what do I do if I see some body snatchers?
Sergeant: Just keep calm and don't get carried away.

✳

Why is the graveyard such a noisy place?
Because of all the coffin!

✳

When can't you bury people who live opposite a graveyard?
When they're not dead.

Greece

Dave: What did you have for supper?
Maeve: It was what I call an Eastern Mediterranean dish.
Dave: What do you mean?
Maeve: Full of Greece.

✳

Green

Did you hear about the snooker-mad monster? He went to the doctor because he didn't feel well.
"What do you eat?" asked the doctor.
"For breakfast I have a couple of red snooker balls, and at lunchtime I grab a black, a pink and two yellows. I have a brown with my tea in the afternoon, and then a blue and another pink for dinner."
"I know why you are not feeling well," exclaimed the doctor.
"You're not getting enough greens."

Guitar

Why did Silly Sue throw her guitar away?
Because it had a hole in the middle.

Sign on the school noticeboard: Guitar for sale, cheap, no strings attached.

Guillotine

During the French Revolution a Frenchman, an Englishman and an Irishman were condemned to the guillotine. The Frenchman was called first and he very calmly put his head on the block. The executioner released the blade, but halfway down it stuck. The tradition in France was that if this happened, the condemned man was set free. So the Frenchman was saved. The Englishman laid his head on the block and the executioner released the blade. The same thing happened and the Englishman was set free. The Irishman was led from the cart kicking and screaming. "I'm not going near that thing until you get it fixed!"

Gun

A little boy ran home from school on the first day and pestered his mother into taking him into a toy shop. When they got there he insisted that she buy him a gun.
"But why do you need a gun?" asked his mother.
"Because teacher told us she was going to teach us to draw tomorrow."

Farmer Giles, why do you have two barrels on your shotgun?
So that if I miss the fox with the first I can get him with the other.
Why not fire with the other first, then?

※

Knock knock.
Who's there?
Ghana.
Ghana who?
Ghana get me a gun and shoot that werewolf.

※

There was a fierce chief of the Sioux
Who into a gun barrel blioux
To see if it was loaded;
The rifle exploded –
As he should have known it would dioux!

※

Two men were out hunting when one of them saw a rabbit. "Quick," said the first, "shoot it."
"I can't," said the second. "My gun isn't loaded."
"Well," said the first," you know that, and I know that, but the rabbit doesn't."

※

Hag

What do you call a hag that stops cars with her thumb?
A witch hiker.

✳

What is another term for a witch?
A hag lady.

Hair

How do warty witches keep their hair out of place?
With scare spray.

Did you hear about the monster who lost all his hair in the war?
He lost it in a hair raid.

✳

Janet came home from school and asked her mother if the aerosol spray in the kitchen was hair lacquer. "No," said Mom. "It's glue."
"I thought so," said Janet. "I wondered why I couldn't get my beret off today."

✳

Teacher: I see you don't cut your hair any longer.
Jason: No sir, I cut it shorter.

✳

Bill: Gilly has lovely long red hair all down her back.
Will: Pity it's not on her head!

✳

Is that your face or are you wearing your hair back to front today?

Hairdresser

What do you get if you cross a hairdresser with a werewolf?
A monster with an all-over perm.

Halloween

Why did the wizard wear a yellow robe to the Halloween party?
He was going as a banana.

✳

Why are teachers happy at Halloween parties?
Because there's lots of school spirit.

✳

What happened to the girl who wore a mouse costume to her Halloween party?
The cat ate her.

✳

What did the really ugly man do for a living?
He posed for Halloween masks.

✷

What happened when the girl dressed as a spoon left the Halloween party?
No one moved. They couldn't stir without her.

✷

Why was the boy unhappy to win the prize for the best costume at the Halloween party?
Because he just came to pick up his little sister.

✷

Where do ghoulies go to on the day before Halloween party?
To the boo-ty parlour.

✷

Doctor, doctor, I'm so ugly. What can I do about it?
Hire yourself out for Halloween parties.

Hamburger
Why did the teacher have her hair in a bun?
Because she had her nose in a hamburger.

✷

What do you get if you cross a bee with a quarter of a pound of ground beef?
A humburger.

Hammer
No, Billy, you can't play with the hammer. You'll hurt your fingers.
No, I won't, Dad. Sis is going to hold the nails for me.

✷

I don't think much of that new doctor.
Why not?
Old Charlie Evans went to see him the other week. He tapped Charlie's knee with that little hammer and his leg fell off!

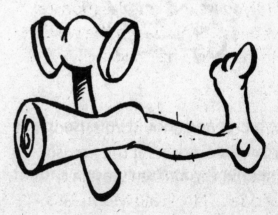

What's the safest way to use a hammer?
Get someone else to hold the nails.

✷

An apprentice blacksmith was told by his boss to make a hammer. The lad had not the slightest idea how to begin, so he thought he'd be crafty and nip out and buy one. He duly showed the new hammer to his boss, who said, "That's excellent boy! Now make fifty more just like it!"

Hand

Teacher: Dennis! When you yawn you should put your hand to your mouth.
Dennis: What, and get it bitten?

Which hand should you use to stir your tea?
Neither – you should use a spoon!

What did the big, hairy monster do when he lost a hand?
He went to the second-hand shop.

Did you hear about the monster who had an extra pair of hands?
Where did he keep them?
In a handbag.

Which hand would you use to grab a poisonous snake?
Your enemy's.

Knock knock.
Who's there?
Grub.
Grub who?
Grub hold of my hand and let's go!

"Waiter, waiter," called a diner at the Monster Cafe. "There's a hand in my soup."
"That's not your soup, sir, that's your finger bowl."

"Can I have some two-handed cheese, please?" a man in a restaurant asked the waiter.
"What do you mean, 'two-handed cheese'?" asked the waiter.
"You know, the kind you eat with one hand and hold your nose with the other."

Doctor: You seem to be in excellent health, Mrs Brown. Your pulse is as steady and regular as clockwork.
Mrs Brown: That's because you've got your hand on my watch.

Hat

Does she have something on her mind?
Only if she's got a hat on.

✳

First Woman: Whenever I'm down in the dumps I buy myself a new hat.
Second Woman: Oh, so that's where you get them.

✳

What happened to the witch with an upside down nose?
Every time she sneezed her hat blew off.

✳

Why did the witch lose her way?
Because her hat was pointing in the wrong direction.

✳

While visiting close friends, a gnat,
Decided to sleep in a hat.
But an elderly guest
Decided to rest
Now the gnat and the hat are quite flat.

✳

My grandad has so many wrinkles he has to screw his hat on.

A police officer was escorting a prisoner to jail when his hat blew off. "Shall I run and get it for you?" asked the prisoner obligingly.
"You must think I'm daft," said the officer. "You stand here and I'll get it."

Haunting

Did you hear about the musical ghost?
He wrote haunting melodies.

✳

First Ghost: I find haunting castles really boring these days.
Second Ghost: I know what you mean. I just don't seem to be able to put any life into it.

✳

Why was the ghost arrested?
He didn't have a haunting licence.

Knock knock.
Who's there?
Olive.
Olive who?
Olive in a haunted house

Hawaii
Knock, knock.
Who's there?
Hawaii.
Hawaii who?
I was fine until you turned up!

Head
Why was the monster standing on his head?
He was turning things over in his mind.

What does the school principal and a bullfrog have in common?
Both have a big head that consists mostly of mouth.

I feel sorry for your little mind – all alone in that great big head.

Did you hear about the headless horseman who got a job in a department store?
He's the head buyer.

Monster: Doctor, doctor, I need to lose 30 pounds of excess flab.
Doctor: All right, I'll cut your head off.

Witch: Doctor, I've got a head like a turnip, three ears, two noses and a mouth the wrong way round.
What am I?
Doctor: Ugly.

How does your head feel today?
As good as new.
It should be as good as new – it's never been used.

When you leave school, you should become a bone specialist. You've certainly got the head for it.

What did the two acrobats say when they got married?
We're head over heels in love!

Why does a witch wear a pointed black hat?
To keep her head warm.

☀

Every time I take my girlfriend out for a meal she eats her head off.
She looks better that way.

☀

How do you cure a headache?
Put your head through a window, and the pane will disappear.

Headache
She could give a headache to an aspirin!

Heart
What kind of bandage do people wear after heart surgery?
Ticker tape.

Why didn't the skeleton want to go to school?
Because his heart wasn't in it.

☀

Girl: My teacher's a peach.
Mother: You mean she's sweet.
Girl: No, she has a heart of stone.

Heaven
An angel in heaven was welcoming a new arrival. "How did you get here?" he asked.
And the new angel replied, "Flu . . ."

Hell

A warning to any young sinner,
Be you fat or perhaps even thinner.
If you do not repent,
To Hell you'll be sent.
With nothing to eat but school
dinner.

Hiccups

What's fearsome, hairy and drinks
from the wrong side of a glass?
A werewolf with hiccups.

Highwayman

What do you call
a highwayman
who is ill?
Sick Turpin.

Hindu

"So glad to meet you," said the
Hindu politely.
"Charmed, I'm sure," replied the
snake.

Hippie

Teacher: Who knows what a hippie
is?
Clever Dick: It's
something
that holds
your leggy
on.

Did you hear about the hippie
ghost?
He was ghoul man, really ghoul.

History

Why is history the sweetest lesson?
Because it's full of dates.

Boy to Friend: My dad is so old,
when he was at school, history was
called current events.

Hobo

Wife: Shall I give that hobo one of my cakes?
Husband: Why, what harm has he ever done us?

※

A hobo knocked on the back door of a house and asked for a bite to eat. "Go away," said the lady of the house, "I never feed hobos."
"That's all right, lady," said the hobo, "I'll feed myself."

Hole

Why did the golfer wear an extra pair of trousers?
In case he got a hole in one.

An idiotic laborer was told by an equally idiotic foreman to dig a hole in the road. "And what shall I do with the earth, sir?" asked the laborer.
"Don't be daft, man," he replied. "Just dig another hole and bury it."

※

Rebecca, you've been a long time putting salt in the salt-cellar.
Well, Mom, you can't get much at a time through that little hole in the top.

Holiday

Did you hear about the monster who went to a holiday camp?
He won the ugly mug and knobbly knees competition and he wasn't even entered.

Homework

Arthur: It's true that there is a connection between television and violence.
Martha: What makes you think that?
Arthur: Because I told my teacher I had watched television instead of doing my homework, and she hit me.

※

What do young ghosts write their homework in?
Exorcise books.

※

I enjoy doing my homework
Even at weekends,
But my best friend's just told me
He thinks I'm round the bend.

※

Teacher: Andrew, your homework looks as if it is in your father's handwriting.
Andrew: Well, I used his pen, Sir.

※

Boy: Why did you throw my homework in the garbage?
Teacher: Because it was trash.

※

Father: Would you like me to help you with your homework?
Son: No, thanks, I'd rather get it wrong by myself.

Honey
What did the spider say to the bee?
Your honey or your life.

Why do bees have sticky hair?
Because of the honey combs.

※

If bees make honey what do wasps make?
Waspberry jam.

※

First man: I've just been stung by a bee.
Second man: How was that?
First man: I was charged $50 for a pot of honey.

Horse
What do ghosts like about riding horses?
Ghoulloping.

※

Why was Dracula so happy at the races?
His horse won by a neck.

※

A mean horseman went into a saddler's shop and asked for one spur. "One spur?" asked the saddler. "Surely you mean a pair of spurs, sir?"
"No, just one," replied the horseman. "If I can get one side of the horse to go, the other side is bound to come with it!"

※

"I asked you to draw a horse and trap," said the art teacher. "You've only drawn the horse. Why?"

"Well, sir. I thought the horse would draw the trap."

Hospital

"Your students must miss you a lot," said the woman in the next bed to the teacher in hospital.

"Not at all! Their aim's usually good. That's why I'm here."

❊

Why did the vampire go to hospital?

He wanted his ghoulstones removed.

Hotel

A man arrived at a seaside hotel where he had made a reservation rather late at night. All the lights were out, so he knocked on the door. After a long time a light appeared in an upstairs window and a woman called out, "Who are you? What do you want?"

"I'm staying here!"

"Stay there, then," she retorted, and slammed the window shut!

❊

There was a little old lady from a small town in America who had to go to Texas. She was amazed at the size of her hotel and her suite. She went into the huge cafe and said to the waitress, who took her order for a cup of coffee, that she had never before seen anything as big as the hotel or her suite.

"Everything's big in Texas ma'am," said the waitress. The coffee came in the biggest cup the old lady had ever seen. "I told you, ma'am, that everything is big in Texas," said the waitress. On her way back to her suite, the old lady got lost in the vast corridors. She opened the door of a darkened room and fell into an enormous swimming pool. "Please!" she screamed. "Don't flush it!"

❊

165

Did you hear about the ghoul's favorite hotel?
It had running rot and mould in every room.

What do witches ring for in a hotel?
B-room service.

Teacher: I'd like a room, please.
Hotel Receptionist: Single, Sir?
Teacher: Yes, but I am engaged.

House
How to Keep Vampires From Your House – by Dora Steel

There's a large crack in the sitting room of Jimmy's house so he goes around telling everyone that he's from a broken home.

Knock knock.
Who's there?
Alistair.
Alistair who?
Alistairs in this house creak really spookily.

A stupid man was struggling out of his house with a big table. His neighbor said to him, "Hello, Harry. Where are you going with that then?"
And Harry replied, "I'm taking it to the store to have it measured for a new tablecloth."

Humans
What kind of beans do cannibals like best?
Human beans.

Hil: Who was the fastest runner in history?
Bill: Adam. He was first in the human race.

Hunter

Commissioned by a zoo to bring them some baboons, the big game hunter devised a novel scheme to trap them – his only requirements being a sack, a gun, and a particularly vicious and bad-tempered dog. Once in the jungle he explained to his assistant, "I'll climb this tree and shake the branches; if there are any baboons up there, they will fall to the ground – and the dogs will bite their tail and immobilise them so that you can pick them up quite safely and put them in the sack."
"But what do I need the gun for?" asked the assisant.
"If I should fall out of the tree by mistake, shoot the dog."

※

The big game-hunter was showing his friends his hunting trophies. Drawing their attention to a lion skin rug on the floor he said, "I shot this fellow in Africa. Didn't want to kill such a magnificent beast, of course, but it was either him or me."
"Well," said a guest, "he certainly makes a much better rug than you would!"

※

When to go Monster-Hunting – by Mae B. Tomorrow.

※

I Caught the Loch Ness Monster – by Janet A. Big-Wun

Husband

Mrs Brown was always complaining about her husband. "If things go on like this I'll have to leave him," she moaned to Mrs Jenkins.
"Give him the soft-soap treatment," said Mrs Jenkins.
"I tried that," replied Mrs Brown, "it didn't work. He spotted it at the top of the stairs."

※

First cannibal: I don't know what to make of my husband these days.
Second cannibal: How about a curry?

※

When Wally Witherspoon proposed to his girlfriend she said, "I love the simple things in life, Wally, but I don't want one of them for a husband."

※

Two friends were discussing the latest scandalous revelations about a Hollywood actress. "They say she likes her latest husband so much she's decided to keep him for another month," said one to the other.

※

Mr and Mrs Weinstock were always fighting. Then one morning as Mrs Weinstock was going to the bank she was knocked down by a hit and run driver. A police officer rushed up and asked her if she'd taken the car's number. "I didn't need to," replied Mrs Weinstock. "It was my husband in that car."

"Did you see him?" asked the officer.

"No," said Mrs Weinstock, "but I'd know that laugh anywhere."

Woman: If you were my husband I'd poison your coffee.
Man: And if you were my wife, I'd drink it.

A salesman was trying to persuade a housewife to buy a life assurance policy. "Just imagine, if your husband were to die," he said. "What would you get?"

"Oh a sheepdog, I think," replied the wife. "They're so well-behaved."

Ice

How do ghosts like their drinks?
Ice ghoul.

❋

What happened when the Ice
Monster ate a curry?
He blew his cool.

Ice cream

Knock, knock.
Who's there?
Ice.
Ice who?
Ice cream, we all scream.

❋

Waiter, waiter! What's this fly doing
in my ice cream?
Maybe he likes winter sports.

❋

A fat girl went into a cafe and
ordered two slices of apple pie with
four scoops of ice cream covered
with lashings of raspberry sauce
and piles of chopped nuts. "Would
you like a cherry on the top?"
asked the waitress.
"No, thanks," said the girl, "I'm on
a diet."

Icicle

What lives in the winter, dies
in the summer and
grows with its roots
upwards?
An icicle.

Igloo

What's an Igloo?
An icicle made for two.

Idiot

How does an idiot call for his dog?
He puts two fingers in his mouth and then shouts Rover.

❄

Did you hear about the idiot who made his chickens drink boiling water?
He thought they would lay hard boiled eggs.

❄

Did you hear about the village idiot buying bird seed?
He said he wanted to grow some birds.

Knock, knock.
Who's there?
Howard.
Howard who?
Howard you like to stand out here in the cold while some idiot keeps saying "Who's there?"

❄

I can't understand the critics saying that only an idiot would like that television program. I really enjoyed it.

❄

What do you get when you cross an idiot with a watch?
A cuckoo clock.

❄

Why did the idiot plant nickels in his garden?
He wanted to raise some hard cash.

❄

Did you hear about the village idiot buying bird seed?
He said he wanted to grow some birds.

Illness

What illness did everyone on the Enterprise catch?
Chicken
Spocks.

Incredible

What's large and green and sits in a corner on its own all day?
The Incredible Sulk.

Infection

What is the best way of stopping infection from witch bites?
Don't bite any witches.

Ink

Mom, do you think the baby would like some blotting paper to eat?
No, dear, I don't think he would.
Why?
He's just swallowed a bottle of ink...

When is ink like a sheep?
When it's in a pen

What is an inkling?
A baby fountain pen.

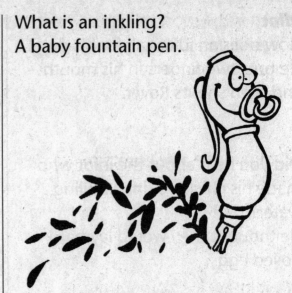

What do you get if you cross a tall green monster with a fountain pen?
The Ink-credible Hulk.

Insect

What is the insect family's favorite game?
Cricket.

Which is the most religious insect in the Middle East?
A mosque-ito.

✺

What did one stick insect say to another?
Stick around.

✺

What insect lives on nothing?
A moth, because it eats holes.

✺

What do you get if you cross a moth with a firefly?
An insect that can find its way around a dark wardrobe.

✺

Knock knock.
Who's there?
Insect.
Insect who?
Insect your name and address here.

✺

What is a grasshopper?
An insect on a pogo stick.

✺

How do you start an insect race?
One, two, flea, go!

Insult

Hugh: I didn't come here to be insulted.
Sue: Oh really, where do you usually go?

Intruder

How did the intruder get in the house?
Intruder window.

Invention

What did the musical skeleton do?
Invented the trombone.

✺

Igor: Dr Frankenstein's just invented a new kind of glue.
Dracula: I hope it doesn't make him stuck up.

✺

Did you hear about the mad scientist who invented a gas so strong it burns its way through anything?
No, what about him?
Now he's trying to invent something to keep it in!

Invisible
Doctor, doctor, I keep thinking I'm an invisible ghost.
Did someone say something?

※

How did the invisible boy upset his mother?
He kept appearing.

※

What is even more invisible than the invisible ghost?
His shadow.

※

Have you any invisible ink?
Certainly, sir.
What color?

※

Doctor, doctor! I'm becoming invisible!
Yes, I can see you're not all there.

※

Who was that at the door?
The Invisible Man.
Tell him I can't see him.

Irish

Did you hear about the Irish schoolboy who was studying Greek Mythology?
When the teacher asked him to name something that was half-man and half-beast he replied "Buffalo Bill."

Did you hear about the Irish boy who had a soft spot for his math teacher?
It was a bog in the middle of Ireland.

Did you hear about the Irish monster who went to night school to learn to read in the dark?

Did you hear about the Irish kamikaze pilot? He flew ninety-nine missions . . .

An Irishman went into a post office to see if there were any letters for him. "I'll see, sir," said the clerk. "What is your name?"
"You're having me on now because I'm Irish," said the Irishman. "Won't you see the name on the envelope?"

Did you hear about the Irishman who spent an hour in a big store looking for a cap with a peak at the back?

Did you hear about the Irishman who was stranded for an hour when the escalator broke down?

Iron

Did you hear about the man who tried to iron his curtains?
He fell out of the window.

Doctor: Now tell me, Granny Perkins, how you happened to burn both your ears.
Granny Perkins: I was doing the ironing when the telephone rang, and I picked up the iron and put that to my ear by mistake.
Doctor: But you burnt both your ears!
Granny Perkins: Yes, well as soon as I put the phone down it rang again!

Why are most monsters covered in wrinkles?
Have you ever tried to iron a monster?

Island

Why is an island like the letter T?
Because they're both in the middle of water.

Italian

How can you tell an Italian witch from an English one?
By her suntan.

Did you hear about the Italian ghost?
He liked spooketti.

Ivy

What is a witch with poison ivy called?
An itchy witchy.

Knock knock.
Who's there?
Ivy.
Ivy who?
Ivy cast a spell on you.

Jack

What do you call a man with a car on his head?
Jack.

Jack Frost

How does Jack Frost get to work?
By icicle.

Jail

Paddy and Mick were sent to jail in a high security prison, but they developed an ingenious method of communicating with each other by means of a secret code and banging on the pipes. However, their scheme broke down when they were transferred to different cells.

Biology Teacher: What kinds of birds do we get in captivity?
Mary: Jail birds, Miss!

Jam

What do traffic wardens like for tea?
Traffic jam sandwiches.

Jelly

Two boys were walking through a churchyard one dark and stormy night. As one stopped to do up his shoelaces they heard an eerie voice coming from behind one of the tombs saying "Now that I've got you, I'm going to eat your legs first, then your arms, then you head and finally I'll gulp down your body." Terrified, the boys ran for the exit but before they could get out of the gate a figure in black loomed before them. "I thought I heard someone," said the minister, "would you boys like a jelly baby?"

※

Jimmy was caught by his mother in the pantry. "And what do you think you're up to?" she asked furiously. "I'm up to my seventh jelly tart," said Jimmy.

※

What's red and dangerous?
Raspberry and tarantula jelly.

Jellyfish

Why did the jellyfish's wife leave him?
He stung her into action.

※

Did you hear about the stupid jellyfish?
It set!

※

What fish tastes best with cream?
A jellyfish.

※

What do you get if you cross a jellyfish with an elephant?
Jelly the Elephant.

※

What is slimy and wobbly, tastes of raspberry and lives in the seas?
A red jellyfish.

There once was a lonely young jellyfish.
Who then met a sweet, loving shellyfish.
They went with the motion
Of waves in the ocean.
And became better known as the jollyfish.

※

What happened when one jellyfish met another?
They produced jelly babies.

Jet

Is the squirt from an elephant's trunk very powerful?
Of course – a jumbo jet can keep 500 people in the air for hours at a time.

Job

"You never get anything right," complained the teacher. "What kind of job do you think you'll get when you leave school?"
"Well, I want to be the weather girl on TV."

A teacher was being interviewed for a new job and asked the principal what the hours were. "We try to have early hours you know. I hope that suits."
"Of course," said the teacher. "I don't mind how early I leave."

Old witch: Now I know you want a job with me. Do you tell lies?
Young witch: No, but I can pick it up.

Did you hear about the man who left his job at the mortuary?
It was a dead end job.

You should get a job in the meteorology office.
Why?
Because you're an expert on wind.

Who has the most dangerous job in Transylvania?
Dracula's dentist.

Good morning, sir. I'm applying for the job as handyman.
I see. Well, are you handy?
Couldn't be more so. I only live next door.

Wilberforce Witherspoon saw a notice outside a police station which read: MAN WANTED FOR ROBBERY. So he went in and applied for the job!

Jockey

The P.E. teacher, Miss Janet Rockey
Wanted to train as a jockey.
But, sad to recall,
She grew far too tall.
So now she teaches us hockey.

Joke

Have you heard the joke about the slippery eel?
You wouldn't grasp it.

＊

Boy: A Vampire told me a joke yesterday.
Girl: Was it good?
Boy: It was a scream.

＊

Have you heard the joke about the wall?
You'd never get over it.

＊

How do you make a thicko laugh on Friday?
Tell him a joke on Monday.

＊

Cary: There's no point in telling you a joke with a double meaning.
Mary: Why not?
Cary: You wouldn't get either of them.

Judge

Who is the most powerful ghoul?
Judge Dread.

＊

As the judge said to the dentist: Do you swear to pull the tooth, the whole tooth, and nothing but the tooth?

When is an English teacher like a judge?
When she hands out long sentences.

Juggler

What has two eyes like a juggler, two arms like a juggler, two hands like a juggler, but isn't a juggler?
A photo of a juggler.

Jump

Can the Abominable Snowman jump very high?
Hardly – he can only just clear his throat!

☀

Why did the wizard jump off the top of the Empire State Building?
He wanted to make a hit on Broadway.

☀

Did you hear about the man who jumped in the Hudson River?
He committed sewercide.

☀

Did you hear about the skeleton who couldn't jump out of the plane?
He had no guts.

☀

What do you do if you see a skeleton running across the road?
Jump out of your skin and join him.

☀

Why did the monster jump up and down?
Because he'd just taken his medicine and he'd forgotten to shake the bottle.

☀

Bungee Jumping with Monsters – by Wade R. Go

☀

The plane was circling at 5,000 meters and the Killarney Green Berets paratroop squad were about to make their first jump. "Hold everything!" shouted the commanding officer. "You're not wearing your parachute, O'Leary."
"It's all right, sir," replied O'Leary. "Sure, it's only a practice jump we're doing."

Jumper

What do you get if you cross a kangaroo with a sheep?
A woolly jumper.

Jungle

Why did the egg go into the jungle?
Because it was an eggsplorer.

☀

Kangaroo

Why was the mother kangaroo cross with her children?
Because they ate potato chips in bed.

Why was the young kangaroo thrown out by his mother?
For smoking in bed.

What's the difference between a kangaroo, a lumberjack and a bag of peanuts?
A kangaroo hops and chews and a lumberjack chops and hews.
Yes, but what's the bag of peanuts for? For monkeys like you.

Karate

Did you hear about the idiotic karate champion who joined the army?
The first time he saluted, he nearly killed himself.

Ketchup

Waiter, waiter, could I have a mammoth steak please?
With pleasure, sir.
No, with ketchup, please.

Kettle

Girl: Shall I put the kettle on?
Boy: No, I think you look alright in the dress you're wearing.

Key

Why is it difficult to open a piano?
Because all the keys are inside.

What key went to university?
A Yale.

Doctor, come quickly!
What's the matter?
We can't get into our house!
That's scarcely my concern, is it?
Yes, it is. The baby's swallowed the
front door key!

Kick
A blind man was waiting to cross
the road when a dog stopped and
cocked its leg against him. The
blind man felt in his pocket for a
sweet, bent down, and offered it to
the dog. A passer-by remarked
what a very kind act that was
considering what the dog had
done. "Not at all," said the blind
man. "I only wanted to find out
which end to kick."

Bob had just missed a shot at goal,
which meant the other team won.
"I could kick myself," he groaned,
as the players came off the pitch.
"Don't bother," said the captain, "
you'd miss."

Kid
Mother: Did you get a good place
in the geography test?
Daughter: Yes, Mum, I sat next to
the cleverest kid in the class.

Boy: Where does the new kid come
from?
Girl: Alaska.
Boy: Don't bother – I'll ask her
myself.

A naughty child was irritating all the passengers on the flight from London to New York. At last one man could stand it no longer. "Hey kid," he shouted. "Why don't you go outside and play?"

Kidney

The kidneys are infernal organs.

☀

A pound of kiddies, please, butcher.
You mean a pound of kidneys.
That's what I said, diddie I?

Kill

What is green, has four legs and can kill you if it falls onto you out of a tree?
A snooker table.

☀

What is pretty and delicate and carries a sub-machine gun?
A killer butterfly.

☀

Jailer: Come on, son, you're in for the chop.
Convicted killer: Oh no! I ordered steak and fries.

☀

What do you call a witch who kills her mother and father?
An orphan.

☀

What's another word for a murderer who kills old ladies?
A Killergran.

☀

Waiter, waiter! There's a dead fly in my soup.
Yes sir, it's the heat that kills them.

☀

"Why are you crying Alec?" asked the teacher.
"'Cos my parrot died last night. I washed it in Wisk . . ."
"Alec," said the teacher. "You must have known that Wisk's bad for parrots."
"Oh it wasn't the Wisk that killed it, sir. It was the tumble drier."

☀

Teacher: And did you see the Catskill Mountains on your visit to New York State?
Jimmy: No, but I saw them kill mice.

☀

Why was the sword-swallowing monster put in prison?
He coughed and killed two people.

☀

186

Andrew: I'm too tired to mow the lawn.

Father: You're just lazy. Hard work never killed anyone.

Andrew: I don't want to be the first!

King

Who is the king of all the mice?
Mouse Tse Tung.

※

Who is the smelliest, hairiest monarch in the world?
King Pong.

※

The cannibal king was having dinner when a servant came running in. "Your Majesty," he said, "the slaves are revolting!"

"You don't have to tell me," said the king. "I'm trying to eat them. "Where did we get these slaves anyway?"

"From the country next door," replied the servant.

"We must get a new butcher," said the king. "Bring me Delia Smith."

"We can't, Your Majesty, she's still cooking for you."

"Well, bring her to me once she's crispy enough," said the king.

King Kong

Why is King Kong big and hairy?
So you can tell him apart from a gooseberry.

※

What's brown and furry on the inside and clear on the outside?
King Kong in plastic wrap.

※

Why didn't King Kong go to Hong Kong?
He didn't like Chinese food.

※

What do you get if King Kong sits on your best friend?
A flat mate.

What should you do if you are on a picnic with King Kong?
Give him the biggest bananas.

＊

What do you get if you cross King Kong with a frog?
A gorilla that catches airplanes with its tongue.

＊

Where does King Kong sleep?
Anywhere he wants to.

＊

What happened when King Kong swallowed Big Ben?
He found it time-consuming.

＊

What do you get if you cross King Kong with a parrot?
A messy cage.

＊

What do you get if King Kong sits on your piano?
A flat note.

＊

First man: I can trace my ancestors back to royalty.
Second man: Yeah, right – to King Kong!

＊

Knock knock.
Who's there?
King Kong.
King Kong who?
King Kong's now part of China.

＊

Two policemen in New York were watching King Kong climb up the Empire State Building. One said to the other, "What do you think he's doing?"
"It's obvious," replied his colleague. "He wants to catch a plane."

＊

Kippers

I say! Did you hear about the taxi driver who found a pair of kippers in the back of his cab?

No! Tell me about it!

The police told me that if no one claimed them within six months, he could have them back.

Kiss

What's it called when a vampire kisses you goodnight?

Necking.

Two elderly teachers were talking over old times and saying how much things had changed. "I mean," said the first, "I caught one of the boys kissing one of the girls yesterday."

"Extraordinary," said the second. "I didn't even kiss my wife before I married her, did you?"

"I can't remember. What was her maiden name?"

"Do you know the difference between roast chicken and a long, lingering kiss?" a boss asked his secretary one day.

"No, I don't," she said.

"Great!" said the boss. "Let's have chicken for lunch."

Bill: What would it take to make you give me a kiss?

Gill: An anaesthetic.

Jonah: Did you hear about Jim Jenkins' wife?

Mona: No, what about her?

Jonah: She's so ugly that when they got married everyone kissed him.

Kitchen

Waiter, waiter, are there snails on the menu?

Oh yes, sir, they must have escaped from the kitchen.

Kitten

Witch: Doctor, doctor, I keep thinking I'm my own cat.
Doctor: How long have you thought this?
Witch: Since I was a kitten.

Why is a witch's kitten like an unhealed wound?
Both are a little pussy.

Knee

What do you call a short vampire?
A pain in the knee.

Did you hear about the monster who went to summer camp?
He won the ugly mug and knobbly knees competition and he wasn't even entered.

Knife

Why was Mac the Knife so amusing?
He had a very sharp wit.

A woman was in court charged with wounding her husband. "But why did you stab him over a hundred times?" asked the judge. "Oh, your Honor," replied the defendant, "I didn't know how to switch off the electric carving knife."

Knight

What do you get if you cross a mosquito with a knight?
A bite in shining armor.

Knit

How did the teacher knit a suit of armor?
She used steel wool.

Why did the monster knit herself three socks.
Because she grew another foot.

Knitting

Ronald had broken a rib playing football. He went to the doctor, who asked how he was feeling. "I keep getting a stitch in my side," he replied.
"That's good," said the doctor. "It shows the bone is knitting."

Knot

Why was the villain on the gallows smiling?
He was knot-happy.

Doctor, doctor, how can I stop my cold going to my chest?
Tie a knot in your neck.

Knowledge

What keeps ghouls cheerful?
The knowledge that every shroud has a silver lining.

Kung Fu

What lives in a pod and is a Kung Fu expert?
Bruce Pea.

Ladder

Sign outside the school caretaker's hut:

> WILL THE PERSON WHO BORROWED THE LADDER FROM THE CARETAKER PLEASE RETURN IT IMMEDIATELY OR FURTHER STEPS WILL BE TAKEN.

What is a snake's favorite game?
Snakes and Ladders.

Two men were painting a house.
Pat: Have you got a good hold on that paint brush, Mick?
Mick: Yes, I have, Pat. Why?
Pat: Well, hold on tight, because I'm taking this ladder away.

Lady

Knock, knock.
Who's there?
Little old lady.
Little old lady who?
I didn't know you could yodel.

Did you hear about the lady ghost who did the can-can?
Oooooo-la-la!

Little Johnny and his mother were on a train. Johnny leant over and started to whisper in his mother's ear. "Johnny, how many times have I told you," said his mother, "it's rude to whisper. If you have something to say, say it out loud." "All right," said Johnny. "Why does the lady opposite look like an ugly, haggard old witch?"

The Lady Ghost – by Sheila Peer

"Please, ma'am!" said a little boy at kindergarten. "We're going to play elephants and circuses, do you want to join in?"
"I'd love to," said the teacher.
"What do you want me to do?"
"You can be the lady that feeds us peanuts!"

What do you get if you cross a zombie with a boy scout?
A creature that scares old ladies across the road.

Ladybird

Which fly captured the ladybird?
The dragon-fly.

Why was the ladybird kicked out of the forest?
Because she was a litter bug.

Lake

Why were the ghosts wet and tired?
They had just dread-ged the lake.

*

Teacher: What do you know about Lake Erie?
Rose: It's full of ghosts, sir.

*

Lamb

"Mary," said her teacher. "You can't bring that lamb into school. What about the smell?"
"Oh, that's all right, ma'am," said Mary. "It'll soon get used to it."

Lampshade

What circles a lampshade at 200 mph?
Stirling Moth.

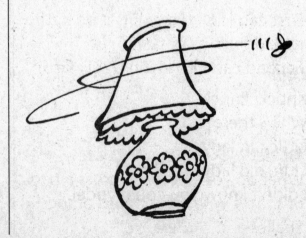

Landing

Why did the stupid pilot land his plane on a house?
Because the landing lights were on.

Language

Why do zombies learn Latin and Greek?
Because they like dead languages.

Lap

Did you hear about the idiot who won the Tour de France?
He did a lap of honor.

First cat: How did you get on in the milk-drinking contest?
Second cat: Oh, I won by six laps!

Larder

What do you get if you cross a bag of snakes with a cupboard of food?
Snakes and Larders.

Laser

What does Luke Skywalker shave with?
A laser blade.

Late

Teacher: Why are you late, Penelope?
Penelope: I was obeying the sign that says "Children – Dead Slow," ma'am.

First Ghost: Am I late for dinner?
Second Ghoul: Yes, everyone's been eaten.

Mossop! Why are you late this morning?
I got married, sir.
Very well, but see that it doesn't happen again.

Laugh

What did the owls do when one of them had a punk haircut?
They hooted with laughter.

How do you make a skeleton laugh?
Tickle his funny bone.

What do you get if you cross a werewolf with a hyena?
I don't know, but if it laughs I'll join in.

A boa with coils uneven
Had the greatest trouble in breathing
With jokes she was afflicted
For her laughs got constricted
And her coils started writhing and wreathing.

What do you do if you split your sides laughing?
Run until you get a stitch.

Cheryl: They say I have an infectious laugh.
Meryl: In that case don't laugh near me!

Law
What sort of sentence would you get if you broke the law of gravity?
A suspended one.

Why was the man arrested for looking at sets of dentures in a dentist's window?
Because it was against the law to pick your teeth in public.

Lawn
What has four legs, a tail, whiskers and cuts grass?
A lawn miaower.

Two men were out walking together, when they saw a truck pass by laden with grassy sods of earth for the laying of a lawn. "Do you know, Mick," said one of them to the other, "if I ever get rich that's what I'll have done – send away my lawn to be cut."

What did the gardener say when he saw his non-too-bright assistant laying the lawn at a new house?
Green on top!

Lawyer
Why did J.R. see his lawyer?
Because he wanted to Sue Ellen.

Lazy
Did you hear about Lenny the Loafer?
He is so lazy that he sticks his nose out of the window so that the wind will blow it for him.

Did you hear about the competition to find the laziest spook in the world?
All the competitors were lined up on stage. "I've got a really nice, easy job for the laziest person here," said the organizer. "Will the laziest spook raise his hand?" All the spooks put up their hands – except one. "Why didn't you raise your hand?" asked the presenter. "Too much trouble," yawned the spook.

Roger is so lazy that when he drops something he waits till he has to tie his shoelaces before he'll pick it up.

Leaf
What does a caterpillar do on New Year's Day?
Turns over a new leaf.

Leaning Tower of Pisa
What makes the Tower of Pisa lean?
It doesn't eat much.

Leap Frog
Why doesn't Kermit like elephants?
They always want to play leap-frog with him.

Learning
A little monster was learning to play the violin.
"I'm good, aren't I?" he asked his big brother.
"You should be on the radio," said the brother.
"You think I'm that good?"
"No, I think you're terrible, but at least if you were on the radio, I could switch you off."

Waiter, waiter! What's this spider doing in my alphabet soup?
Probably learning to read, sir.

Leg
Why are snake's hard to fool?
They have no leg to pull.

What has a bottom at its top?
A leg.

What happened when the werewolf chewed a bone for an hour?
When he got up he only had three legs.

First cannibal: Come and have dinner in our hut tonight.
Second cannibal: What are you having?
First cannibal: Hard-boiled legs.

Did you hear about the witch who went in for the lovely legs competition?
She was beaten by the microphone stand.

What do you call a witch with one leg?
Eileen.

Knock knock.
Who's there?
Thumping.
Thumping who?
Thumping green and slimy is creeping up your leg.

Doctor, I've just been bitten on the leg by a werewolf.
Did you put anything on it?
No, he seemed to like it as it was.

What has fifty legs but can't walk?
Half a centipede.

My uncle must be the meanest man in the world. He recently found a crutch – then he broke his leg so he could use it.

What is green and sooty and whistles when it rubs its back legs together?
Chimney Cricket.

What do you call a guard with a hundred legs?
A sentrypede.

※

What happened to the skeleton that was attacked by a dog?
It ran off with some bones and left him without a leg to stand on.

※

I can't understand why people say my girlfriend's legs look like matchsticks.
They do look like sticks – but they certainly don't match.

※

Dad, when I get old will the calves of my legs be cows . . . ?

Lemon
My Mother uses lemon juice for her complexion.
Maybe that is why she always looks so sour.

Lemonade
Jimmy: Is that lemonade OK?
Timmy: Yes. Why do you ask?
Jimmy: I just wondered if it was as sour as your face.

※

Why do vampires drink blood?
Lemonade makes them burp.

Letter
Which two letters are rotten for your teeth?
D K

※

Why is the letter "t" so important to a stick insect?
Without it would be a sick insect.

※

Have you ever seen a duchess?
Yes – it's the same as an English "s"!

※

What do snakes write on the bottom of their letters?
With love and hisses.

※

What's the definition of a school report?
A poison pen letter from the principal.

※

Why did the young witch have such difficulty writing letters?
She had never learned to spell properly.

※

199

What kind of letters did the snake get from his admirers?
Fang mail.

What's a zombie say when he gets a letter from his girlfriend?
It's a dead-letter day.

How does a ghost start a letter?
Tomb it may concern.

Last night I wrote myself a letter. But I forgot to sign it and now I don't know who it's from.

What did the werewolf write at the bottom of the letter?
Best vicious . . .

Midge was scribbling industriously over some paper with a pencil when her mother asked her what she was drawing. "I'm not drawing, Mom," she said indignantly, "I'm writing a letter to Jenny."
"But you can't write," Mom pointed out.
"That's all right," said Midge, "Jenny can't read."

How did skeletons send each other letters in the days of the Wild West?
By Bony Express.

Teacher: Alan, give me a sentence starting with "I."
Alan: I is . . .
Teacher: No, Alan. You must always say "I am."
Alan: Oh, right. I am the ninth letter of the alphabet.

Liar
Wizard: Doctor, doctor, everyone thinks I'm a liar.
Doctor: I don't believe you

Library
Why did the sparrow fly into the library?
It was looking for bookworms.

A frog walked into a library and asked the librarian what he would recommend. "How about this sir?" asked the librarian, showing him Toad of Toad Hall.
"Reddit, reddit," said the frog.

※

Found in the school library: The Broken Window – by Eva Brick

※

Did you hear about the schoolgirl who was so excited about a book she found in the library called How to Hug?
It turned out to be volume eight of an encyclopedia.

Lice

What do you call a top pop group made up of nits?
The Lice Girls.

Lick

Doctor: How is your husband's lumbago?
Wife: Not too good. I rubbed his neck with whiskey like you told me to and he broke his neck trying to lick it off!

※

What's the most important thing to remember in Chemistry?
Never lick the spoon.

Lid

How can you tell if a corpse is angry?
It flips its lid.

※

How can you tell if a vampire's been at the tomato juice?
There are teeth marks on the lid.

A huge hairy monster went to the doctor to ask for help because he was becoming very weak. The doctor prescribed some pills and a tonic to build him up. A few days later the monster went back to the surgery. "Are you feeling stronger?" asked the doctor.
"No," said the monster. "The medicine isn't working – you see, I can't get the lids off the bottles!"

※

If King Kong went to Hong Kong to play ping-pong and died, what would they put on his coffin?
A lid.

Lie

Jan: I Can't stop telling lies.
Dan: I don't believe you.

✳

Why does the Hound of the Baskervilles turn round and round before he lies down for the night?
Because he's the watchdog and he has to wind himself up.

✳

Doctor, doctor, I think I'm a witch!
You'd better lie down for a spell.

✳

What lies at the bottom of the sea and shivers?
A nervous wreck.

✳

Why are ghosts bad at telling lies?
Because you can see right through them.

✳

Does he tell lies?
Let's just say his memory exaggerates.

✳

Doctor, doctor, I keep thinking I'm a spider.
What a web of lies!

✳

How did the midget monster get into the police force?
He lied about his height.

✳

What do you call a skeleton that's always telling lies?
A boney phony.

✳

It's a note from the teacher about me telling lies – but it's not true.

Life

First Ghost: I saw The Phantom of the Opera last night, on television.
Second Ghost: Was it frightening?
First Ghost: Yes, it half scared the life into me!

Lifejacket

Why did the teacher wear a lifejacket at night?
Because he liked sleeping on a water bed, and couldn't swim!

Light

First vampire: Are you a light sleeper?
Second vampire: No, I sleep in the dark.

A man went to the dentist's and saw a man hanging by one arm from the center of the ceiling.
"What's he doing there?" he asked the dentist.
"Oh, pay no attention," said the dentist, "he thinks he's a lightbulb."
"Well, why don't you tell him he isn't?" asked the startled customer.
"What?" replied the dentist, "and work in the dark?"

Knock knock.
Who's there?
Brighton.
Brighton who?
Brightonder the light of the full moon.

Why did the monster eat a lightbulb?
Because he was in need of light refreshment.

What makes a glow-worm glow?
A light meal.

What did the traffic light say to the motorist?
Don't look now, I'm changing.

Mr Timpson noticed his neighbor, Mr Simpson, searching very hard for something in his front yard.
"Have you lost something, Mr Simpson?" asked Mr Timpson.
"Yes," replied Mr Simpson. "I've mislaid my spectacles."
"Oh dear," said Mr Timpson. "Where did you last see them?"
"In my sitting-room," said Mr Simpson.
"In your sitting room?" asked Mr Timpson. "So why are you looking for them in your front yard?"
"Oh," replied Mr Simpson, "there's more light out here!"

He's so thick that after he'd watched a gardening program on TV he started watering the light bulbs.

Joe: What does "opaque" mean?
Jose: Something light can't pass through – like your head!

He's a light eater.
Yes, as soon as it's light he starts eating!

What do you get if you cross a glow-worm with a python? A twenty-foot long strip-light that can squeeze you to death.

Lighthouse
Why did the toad become a lighthouse keeper?
He had his own frog-horn.

Lightning
Witch: Doctor, doctor, each time I put my bra on I get thunder and lightning on my stomach.
Doctor: That's all right, it's just a storm in a C-cup.

A woodpecker was pecking a hole in a tree. All of a sudden a flash of lightning struck the tree to the ground. The woodpecker looked bemused for a moment and then said, "Gee, I guess I don't know my own strength."

Line
What did the snake say to the cornered rat?
Hiss is the end of the line, buddy!

What's a devil's picket line called?
A demon-stration.

Don't you like being a telegraph linesman?
No, it's driving me up the pole.

Lion
Boy: I once met a lion who had been bitten by a snake.
Girl: What did he say?
Boy: Nothing, silly, lions don't talk!

Did you hear about the boy who was told to do 100 lines?
He drew 100 cats on the paper. He thought the teacher had said lions.

A huge lion was roaring through the jungle when he suddenly saw a tiny mouse . He stopped and snarled at it menacingly. "You're very small," he growled fiercely. "Well, I've been ill," replied the mouse piteously.

There was once a puppy called May who loved to pick quarrels with animals who were bigger than she was. One day she argued with a lion. The next day was the first of June. Why? Because that was the end of May!

*

First lion: Every time I eat, I feel sick.
Second lion: I know. It's hard to keep a good man down.

Lisp
What's long and green and goes hith?
A snake with a lisp.

List
Doctor: I'm sorry madam, but I have to tell you are a werewolf.
Patient: Give me a piece of paper.
Doctor: Do you want to write your will?
Patient: No, a list of people I want to bite.

Listen
Reg: I keep talking to myself.
Roger: I'm not surprised – no one else would listen to you!

Little
Girl: Why do you call me pilgrim?
Teacher: Because you're making so little progress.

*

Teacher: I wish you'd pay a little attention.
Girl: I'm paying as little as possible.

Lizard
What powerful reptile is found in the Sydney Opera House?
The Lizard of Oz.

*

What happened to the lizard in the wizard's garden pond?
He had him newt-ered.

Why did the lizard go on a diet?
It weighed too much for its scales.

Loaf
This loaf is nice and warm!
It should be – the cat's been sitting on it all day!

Lobster
Waiter, waiter, this lobster's only got one claw.
It must have been in a fight, sir.
Then bring me the winner.

Local
At our local restaurant you can eat dirt cheap – but who wants to eat dirt?

Locust
What do you get if you cross an elephant with some locusts?
I'm not sure, but if they ever swarm – watch out!

Lock
Heard about the vampire who was locked up in an asylum?
He went bats.

Why don't you get locks on cemetery gates?
There's no point – all the ghosts have skeleton keys.

Please sir! Please sir! Why do you keep me locked up in this cage?
Because you're the teacher's pet.

What if you can't work the lock on your door?
Sing until you get the right key.

What does the music teacher do when he's locked out of the classroom?
Sings until he gets the right key.

* * *

"What is your occupation?" asked the judge.
"I'm a locksmith, your Honor."
"And what were you doing in the jeweler's shop at three in the morning when the police officers entered?"
"Making a bolt for the door!"

London

A man telephoned London Airport. How long does it take to get to New York?
Just a minute.
Thanks very much.

* * *

Visitor: How do I get to the London Palladium?
Musician: Practice.

Lonely

Why did the tadpole feel lonely?
Because he was newt to the area.

* * *

Did you hear about the monster who sent his picture to a lonely hearts club?
They sent it back saying they weren't that lonely!

Lone Ranger

What do you get if you cross the Lone Ranger with an insect?
The Masked-quito.

Long

How would you measure the height of the Eiffel Tower with an aneroid barometer, Alec?
I'd tie a long piece of string to it, and throw it off the top. When it hit the ground, I'd measure the string.

* * *

Why did the math teacher take a ruler to bed with him?
He wanted to see how long he would sleep.

* * *

Why did the stupid person give up his attempt to cross the English Channel on a plank?
He couldn't find a plank that was long enough.

* * *

What is the best way to speak to a monster.
From a long distance.

✳

Harry's very good for other people's health. Whenever they see him coming they go for a long walk!

Lord

Kelly: Is God a doctor, ma'am?
Teacher: In some ways, Kelly. Why do you ask?
Kelly: Because the Bible says that the Lord gave the tablets to Moses.

✳

"Can anyone think of a vegetable that's mentioned in the Bible?" asked the English teacher.
"Lettuce, sir," said Melissa.
"I don't think so, Melissa," the teacher said.
"Oh, yes, sir," protested Melissa.
"Lettuce with a gladsome mind praise the Lord for he is kind."

Lost

What is green and slimy and is found at the North Pole?
A lost frog.

✳

There was a young yeti from Gloucester
Whose granny and grandfather lost 'r.
Next day she was found
In the snow-covered ground
But they didn't know how to defrost her.

✳

Did you hear about the sick werewolf?
He lost his voice but it's howl right now.

✳

Two witches lost their brooms and crashlanded on an iceberg. "Do you think we'll be here long?" asked the first.
"No," said the second, "here comes the Titanic."

✳

What did Enormous Eric win when he lost 50 pounds in weight?
The No-Belly Prize.

Love

What happened when the young wizard met the young witch?
It was love at first fright.

✳

What's a vampire's favorite love song?
How Can I Ignore the Girl Necks Door.

※

Witch: Will you love me when I'm old and ugly?
Wizard: Darling, of course I do.

※

Knock, knock.
Who's there?
Yule.
Yule who?
Yule never know just how much I love you.

※

Who were the smallest people to fall in love?
Gnomeo and Juliet.

※

Harry was madly in love with Betty, but couldn't pluck up enough courage to pop the question face to face. Finally he decided to ask her on the telephone. "Darling!" he blurted out, "will you marry me?"
"Of course, I will, you silly boy," she replied, "who is it speaking?"

※

Did you hear about the short-sighted monster who fell in love with a piano?
It had such wonderful white teeth, how could he resist it?

※

Freda: Boys whisper they love me.
Fred: Well, they wouldn't admit it out loud, would they?

※

Luck
Which is the unluckiest monster in the world?
The Luck Less Monster.

※

What did the doctor say to the witch in hospital?
With any luck you'll soon be able to get up for a spell.

※

This morning I felt that today was going to be my lucky day. I got up at seven, had seven dollars in my pocket, there were seven of us at lunch and there were seven horses in the seven o'clock race – so I backed the seventh.
Did it win?
No, it came seventh.

※

Lump

There was an old monster with humps
Who was terribly down in the dumps
He was frumpy and grumpy
And jumpy and stumpy
Because of his terrible lumps.

Lunch

Waiter, waiter! My lunch is talking to me!
Well you asked for a tongue sandwich, sir.

✳

Jared, we're having very important guests for lunch today, so clean yourself up and make yourself presentable, please.
Why – they're not going to eat me, are they?

✳

How does Batman's mother call him in for lunch?
Batman, din-ner, din-ner, din-ner, din-ner, din-ner, Bat-man!

✳

Mad

What happened to the two mad vampires?
They both went a little batty.

⁂

Witch: Doctor, Doctor, my sisters think I'm mad because I like peas.
Doctor: There's nothing wrong with that, I like peas, too.
Witch: Oh, good, come back to my hovel and I'll show you my collection.

Maggot

What did one maggot say to another?
What's a nice girl like you doing in a joint like this?

⁂

Waiter, waiter! I can't eat this meat, it's crawling with maggots.
Quick, run to the other end of the table, you can catch it as it goes by.

⁂

What did the cowboy maggot say when he went into the saloon bar?
Gimme a slug of whiskey.

Magic

Black Magic – by Sue Pernatural

⁂

What do you get if you cross a snake with a magic spell?
Addercadabra.

Magician

What do you get if you cross a snake with a magician?
Abra da cobra.

⁂

What would you get if you crossed a bat with a magician?
A flying sorcerer.

⁂

What did one magician say to another?
Who was that girl I sawed you with last night?

Magnifying glass

Bacon discovered the magnifying glass. At our local cafe you need a magnifying glass to discover the bacon.

⁂

How can a teacher increase the size of her pay check?
By looking at it through a magnifying glass.

Maid

What's the difference between Noah's Ark and Joan of Arc?
One was made of wood and the other was Maid of Orleans.

Mail

What does the mailman take to vampires?
Fang mail.

What do you get if you cross King Kong with a watchdog?
A terrified mailman.

Man

What happened to the man who turned into an insect?
He beetled off.

What happened when the man who was about to be shot was offered a cigarette.
He refused it on health grounds.

Knock knock.
Who's there?
Arnold.
Arnold who?
Arnold man who looks like a wizard.

Did you hear about the man who stole some rhubarb?
He was put into custardy.

Manners

What do you call a python with a great bedside manner?
A snake charmer.

How can you tell you are talking to an undertaker?
By his grave manner.

Young Jimmy was having supper with his Gran. "Would you like a cookie?" she asked.
"Yes, please," replied Jimmy.
"What good manners you have," said his Gran. "I do like to hear young people say 'please' and 'thank you'."
"I'll say them both if I can have a big slice of that cake," replied Jimmy.

213

Manure

How do you keep flies out of the kitchen?

Put a bucket of manure in the lounge.

Marriage

My Peter keeps telling everyone he's going to marry the most beautiful girl in the world.

What a shame! And after all the time you've been engaged!

A man and a woman from Rye
Courted for years side by side.
He said, "Dear we've tarried
Why don't we get married?"
"'Cos no one would have us," she cried.

"In some countries," said the geography teacher, "men are allowed more than one wife. That's called polygamy. In others, women are allowed more than one husband. That's called polyandry. In this country, men and women are allowed only one married partner. Can anyone tell me what that's called?"

"Monotony, sir!"

Why did the science teacher marry the school cleaner?

Because she swept him off his feet.

Mask

Why do surgeons wear masks in the operating theater?

So that if they make a mistake no one will know who did it.

Witch: I've never been so insulted in my life! I went to a Halloween party, and at midnight they asked me to take my mask off.
Spook: Why are you so angry?
Witch: I wasn't wearing a mask.

Match

This match won't light.
That's funny – it did this morning.

❋

Why did the idiots' tug-o'-war team lose the match?
They pushed.

Math

A blind rabbit and a blind snake ran into each other on the road one day. The snake reached out, touched the rabbit and said, "You're soft and fuzzy and have floppy ears. You must be a rabbit." The rabbit reached out, touched the snake and said "You're slimy, beady-eyed and low to the ground. You must be a math teacher."

❋

Did you hear about the math teacher who fainted in class?
Everyone tried to bring her 2.

❋

What's black and white and horrible?
A math examination paper.

❋

In the summer vacation the math teacher collected information for a national opinion poll. But after a week she was fired. Her vital statistics were wrong.

❋

The math teacher and the English teacher went out for a quick pizza after school. "How long will the pizzas be?" asked the math teacher.
"Sorry, sir," replied the waiter, "we don't do long pizzas, just ordinary round ones."

❋

Girl: Mom, you know you're always worried about me failing math?
Mother: Yes.
Girl: Well, your worries are over.

❋

"Frank," said the weary math teacher, "if you had seven dollars in your pocket, and seven dollars in another pocket, what would you have?"
"Someone else's pants!"

❋

Mother: Do you know a girl named Jenny Simon?
Daughter: Yes, she sleeps next to me in math.

Mattress

How does a Smart Alec spend hours on his homework every night, and yet get twelve hours sleep?
He puts his homework underneath his mattress.

Mayfly

What do you call a mayfly with a machine gun?
Baddy-long-legs.

Meat

What did the cannibal say to the explorer?
Nice to meat you!

✳

Why do some witches eat raw meat?
Because they don't know how to cook.

✳

Waiter, waiter! There's a fly in my soup.
Yes, ma'am, it's the bad meat that attracts them.

✳

Waiter, waiter! What's this dead fly doing on my meat?
I don't know, ma'am, it must have died after tasting it.

✳

Waiter: And how did you find your meat, sir?
Customer: Oh, I just lifted a potato and there it was.

Medal

What did the zombie get his medal for?
Deadication.

Medical

My son's just received a scholarship to medical school – but they don't want him while he's alive.

Medicine

Parent to Doctor: Will those pills really cure my little Amy?
Doctor: Well, no one I've given them to has ever come back.

Did you know that Dr Jekyll has created a new medicine?
One sip and you're a new man

What kind of medicine does Dracula take for a cold?
Coffin medicine.

First monster: What is that son of yours doing these days?
Second monster: He's at medical school.
First monster: Oh, what's he studying?
Second monster: Nothing, they're studying him.

What medicine do you give a sick ant?
Antibiotics.

Meeting

Why did the wooden monsters stand in a circle?
They were having a board meeting.

Memory

Man: Doctor, doctor, I think I'm losing my memory.
Doctor: When did this happen?
Man: When did what happen?

Menu

Mr Smooth was ordering a meal in a restaurant and was horrified to see that the waiter was covered with pimples. "Have you got acne?" he asked.
"No," replied the waiter, "just what you can see on the menu."

At a restaurant which prided itself on its wide selection of dishes, a customer was inspecting the menu. "You'll find, sir," said the waiter proudly, "that everything is on the menu. Absolutely everything!"
"Yes, so I see," said the customer tartly, "so take it back and bring me a clean one!"

Mercy

Rich Lady: That painting you did of me doesn't do me justice.

Artist: It's not justice you want, it's mercy!

Meringue

What's the fastest cake in the world?

Meriiiiiiiiiiiiiiinnnnnnnnnnnnngue.

Mermaid

What is a mermaid?

A deep-she fish.

Metal

Did you hear about the monster who ate bits of metal every night? It was his staple diet.

Mexican

Did you hear about the Mexican who threw his wife over a cliff? When the police officer asked him why he'd done it he said, "Tequila! Tequila!"

Mexico

What kind of cans are there in Mexico?

Mexicans.

Mice

Hickory dickory dock
The mice ran up the clock.
The clock struck one,
And the rest got away with minor injuries.

*

How do mice celebrate when they move house?
With a mouse-warming party.

*

Why do mice need oiling?
Because they squeak.

*

Knock knock.
Who's there?
Caterpillar.
Caterpillar who?
Caterpillar a few mice for you.

Mickey Mouse

Why did Mickey Mouse
take a trip to outer
space?
He wanted to find
Pluto.

Middle

What is Smokey the Elephant's
middle name?
The.

Harry: I've a soft spot for you.
Mary: Really?
Harry: Yes, in the middle of a
swamp!

Milk

When should you feed witch's milk
to a baby?
When it's a baby witch.

What is a skeleton's favorite drink?
Milk – it's so good for the bones.

Did you hear about the witch who
was so poisonous she could make
her own yoghurt just by staring at
a carton of milk for a couple of
minutes?

Mary had a bionic cow,
It lived on safety pins.
And every time she milked that
cow.
The milk came out in tins.

What do we get from naughty
cows?
Bad milk!

What do ghosts like in their coffee?
Evaporated milk.

＊

What happened at the badly organized milking contest?
There was udder chaos.

Millionaire
What do you get if you cross a sorceress with a millionaire?
A very witch person.

＊

Can I borrow that book of yours – How To Become A Millionaire?
Sure. Here you are.
Thanks – but half the pages are missing.
What's the matter? Isn't half a million enough for you?

Mind
The stupid monster went to the mind reader's and paid $5 to have his thoughts read. After half an hour the mind reader gave him his money back.

＊

She has a mind of her own.
Of course she does. No one else would want it."

＊

You can read his mind in his face.
Yes, it's usually a complete blank.

＊

In one way Julian is lucky. If he went out of his mind no one would notice the difference.

＊

Don't let your mind wander. It's not old enough to be allowed out on its own.

＊

First monster: I've just changed my mind.
Second monster: Does it work any better?

Mirror
What does a vampire say to the mirror?
Terror, terror on the wall.

I Saw a Witch in the Mirror – by Douglas Cracked

Did you hear about the witch who was so ugly she kept sending her mirror back for repairs?

Did you hear about the witch who looked in the mirror?
It was a shattering experience.

Do you look in the mirror after you've washed?
No, I look in the towel!

Husband: Why have you put a mirror on the television set. dear?
Wife: Because I wanted to see what my family looks like.

Missionary
What did the cannibal mom say to her son who was chasing a missionary?
Stop playing with your food!

What happened when the cannibal bit off a missionary's ear?
He had his first taste of Christianity.

Cannibal: Mom, mom, I've been eating a missionary and I feel sick.
Mom: Well, you know what they say – you can't keep a good man down.

Mistake
Teacher: Your books are a disgrace, Archibald. I don't see how anyone can possibly make as many mistakes in one day as you do.
Archibald: I get here early, sir.

Billy and Bobby were watching a John Wayne film on TV. In one scene John Wayne was riding madly towards a cliff. "I bet you $10 he falls over that cliff," said Billy.
"Done," said Bobby. John Wayne rode straight over the cliff. As Mick handed over his $10, Billy said, "I feel a bit guilty about this, I've seen the film before."
"So have I," said Bobby, "but I didn't think he'd be fool enough to make the same mistake twice."

What do you call a ghost's mistake?
A boo-boo.

First Undertaker: I've just been let go.
Second Undertaker: Why?
First Undertaker: I buried someone in the wrong place.
Second Undertaker: That was a grave mistake.

Model
Did you hear about the ghostly model who got into magazines?
She was a cover ghoul!

Why does a model smile at lightning?
She thinks she's getting her picture taken!

Mole
What purrs along the road and leaves holes in the lawn?
A Moles-Royce.

Money
Why is money called dough?
Because we all knead it.

Where do bees keep their money?
In a honey-box.

Why did the mean teacher walk around with her purse open?
She'd read there was going to be some change in the weather.

Make Money from Rich Men – by Marie Mee

Johnny collected lots of money from trick-or-treating and he went to the candy store to buy some chocolate. "You should give that money to charity," said the sales girl.
Johnny thought for a moment and said, "No, I'll buy the chocolate. You give the money to charity."

What happened when the puss swallowed a nickel?
There was money in the kitty.

How can a teacher double his money?
By folding it in half.

✳

What do vampires gamble with?
Stake money.

✳

Three animals were having a drink in a cafe, when the owner asked for the money. "I'm not paying," said the duck. "I've only got one bill and I'm not breaking it."
"I've spent my last buck," said the deer.
"Then the duck'll have to pay," said the skunk. "Getting here cost me my last scent."

✳

Dad, would you like to save some money?
I certainly would, son. Any suggestions?
Sure. Why not buy me a bike, then I won't wear my shoes out so fast.

✳

I hate paying my income tax.
You should be a good citizen – why don't you pay with a smile?
I'd like to but they insist on money . . . !

✳

What happened when Dumbo went to a mind-reader?
They gave him his money back.

✳

The best way of saving money is to forget who you borrowed it from.

✳

Owen: Thank you so much for lending me that money. I shall be everlastingly in your debt.
Lenny: That's what I'm afraid of!

Monk
What do you get if you cross a janitor with a monk who smokes large cigars?
A caretaker with a bad habit.

Monkey
What do you do if you find King Kong in the kitchen?
Just don't monkey with him.

✳

What business is King Kong in?
Monkey business.

✳

How can you mend King Kong's arm if he's twisted it?
With a monkey wrench.

✳

What's the difference between a sigh, a car and a monkey?
A sigh is oh, dear. A car is too dear. A monkey is you, dear.

Monster
What do you call a mouse that can pick up a monster?
Sir.

Why did the monster stop playing with his brother?
He got tired of kicking him around.

What do you call a monster with a wooden head?
Edward.

What does a polite monster say when he meets you for the first time?
Pleased to eat you!

How do you tell a good monster from a bad one?
If it's a good one you will be able to talk about it later!

What do you call a monster with two wooden heads?
Edward Woodward.

What does a monster do when he loses his head?
He calls a head hunter.

How did the monster cure his sore throat?
He spent all day gargoyling.

What do you call a monster with four wooden heads?
I don't know but Edward Woodward would.

※

On which day do monsters eat people?
Chewsday.

※

What kind of monster can sit on the end of your finger?
The bogeyman.

※

Tracking Monsters – by Woody Hurt

※

Little monster: Mom, I've finished. Can I leave the table?
Mommy monster: Yes, I'll save it for your supper.

※

First monster: I have a hunch.
Second monster: I thought you were a funny shape.

※

Did you hear the joke about the two monsters who crashed?
They fell off a cliff, boom, boom.

※

How do you address a monster?
Very politely.

※

Knock knock.
Who's there?
Turner.
Turner who?
Turner round, there's a monster breathing down your neck.

※

Knock knock.
Who's there?
Oliver.
Oliver who?
Oliver lone and I'm frightened of monsters.

※

Knock knock.
Who's there?
Aida.
Aida who?
Aida whole village 'cos I'm a monster.

※

Knock knock.
Who's there?
Teheran.
Teheran who?
Teheran very slowly – there's a monster behind you.

※

Did you hear about the monster who had twelve arms and no legs? He was all fingers and thumbs.

❋

Why did the monster lie on his back?
To trip up low-flying aircraft.

❋

One day a boy was walking down the street when he saw a sea monster standing on the corner looking lost. The boy put a lead on the sea monster and took him to the police station. "You should take him to the museum," said the police officer. The next day the police officer saw the boy in the town still with the monster on a lead. "I thought I told you to take him to the museum," said the policeman.
"I did," said the boy, "and today I'm taking him to the cinema."

❋

How do you keep monster in suspense?
I'll tell you tomorrow . . .

❋

What do you get if you cross a plum with a man-eating monster?
A purple people-eater.

❋

Knock knock.
Who's there?
Kenya.
Kenya who?
Kenya save me from the monsters?

❋

Where is the monster's temple?
On the side of his head.

❋

How do you communicate with the Loch Ness Monster at 20,000 fathoms?
Drop him a line.

❋

What should you call a polite, friendly, kind, good-looking monster?
A failure.

Months
The headmaster was interviewing a new teacher. "You'll get $10,000 to start, with $15,000 after six months."
"Oh!" said the teacher. "I'll come back in six months then."

❋

You're only as old as you act. That means you're about six months old.

❋

Waiter, how long have you worked here?
Six months, sir.
Well, it can't have been you who took my order.

✳

Andy: What's the difference between a wage and a salary, sir?
Teacher: If you earn a wage, you are paid every week, if you earn a salary, you are paid every month. Teachers, for example, get paid salaries because they are paid monthly.
Andy: Please, sir, where do they work?

Moon
Knock knock.
Who's there?
Turin.
Turin who?
Turin to a werewolf under a full moon.

✳

Knock knock.
Who's there?
Athens.
Athens who?
Athenshadow over the moon.

Moose
What has antlers and sucks your blood?
A moose-quito.

✳

Who has large antlers, has a high voice and wears white gloves?
Mickey Moose.

✳

A Scotsman paying his first visit to the zoo stopped by one of the cages. "An' whut animal would that be?" he asked the keeper.
"That's a moose from Canada," came the reply.
"A moose!" exclaimed the Scotsman, "Hoots – they must ha' rats like elephants over there!"

Morning

Did you hear about the teacher whose students were such swots that when she walked into the classroom and said "Good morning" they wrote it in their notebooks?

✳

My dad is rather tired this morning. Last night he dreamed he was working.

✳

You're ugly!
And you're drunk!
Yes, but in the morning I'll be sober!

Moses

In which Biblical story is tennis mentioned?
When Moses served in Pharoah's court...

Mosquito

Why did the mosquito go to the dentist?
To improve his bite.

What has six legs, bites and talks in code?
A morse-quito.

✳

How do you know if you have a tough mosquito?
If you slap him, he slaps you back.

✳

What do you call A Tale of Two Mosquitoes?
A bite-time story.

✳

Why is it best to be bitten quickly by one mosquito?
Because an itch in time saves nine.

✳

Why are mosquitoes religious?
They prey on you.

✳

Why are mosquitoes annoying?
Because they get under your skin.

✳

What's the mosquitoes' favorite song?
I've Got You Under My Skin

✳

Collecting Mosquitoes – by Lara Bites

✳

What's the difference between a lawyer and a mosquito?
A mosquito drops off you when you die.

✳

What did one mosquito say to another when they came out of the cinema?
Fancy a bite?

✳

What do you call a mosquito on vacation?
An itch-hiker.

✳

Knock knock.
Who's there?
Mosquito.
Mosquito who?
Mosquito smoking soon.

✳

Knock knock
Who's there?
Anna.
Anna who?
Anna-nuther mosquito.

✳

Doctor, doctor, I keep thinking I'm a mosquito.
Go away, sucker.

✳

Collecting Mosquitoes – by Ethan Alive

✳

Waiter, waiter! There's a mosquito in my soup.
Don't worry sir, mosquitoes have very small appetites.

✳

Two mosquitoes were buzzing round when they saw a drunken man. One said to the other, "You bite him – I'm driving."

Moth
Knock knock.
Who's there?
Moth.
Moth who?
Motht people know the anthwer.

✳

A mother moth was telling her baby moth off saying, "If you don't eat all your cotton, you won't get any satin."

Mothballs
How can you make a moth ball?
Hit it with a fly-swatter.

✳

Why wouldn't they let the butterfly into the dance?
Because it was a moth ball.

Mother

What do you call a ghost's mother and father?
Transparents.

✳

Mrs Monster: Try to be nice to Mother when she comes to stay this weekend, dear.
Mr Monster: How can I do that?
Mrs Monster: Well, fall down when she hits you.

✳

Terry: When my mother was young she had a coming-out party.
Gerry: When they saw her they probably sent her back in again.

✳

My mother gets migraines. Probably because her halo's too tight.

Motorbike

I wouldn't say he's thick-headed – but he's the only person I know who's allowed to ride a motorbike without a helmet.

Motto

The principal was very proud of his school's academic record.
"It is very impressive," said one parent who was considering sending his son there. "How do you maintain such high standards?"
"Simple," said the head. "The school motto says it all."
"What's that?" asked the parent.
"If at first you don't succeed, you're expelled."

Mountain

Why did the witch go over the mountain?
She couldn't go under it.

✳

Mouse

What goes "eek, eek, bang?"
A mouse in a minefield.

Which mouse was a Roman
emperor?
Julius Cheeser.

What's grey and furry on the inside
and white on the outside?
A mouse sandwich.

What goes "dot, dot, dash,
squeak?"
Mouse code.

How do you save a drowning
rodent?
Use mouse to mouse resuscitation.

What kind of musical instrument
do rats play?
Mouse organ.

Mouth

What happened to the wizard who
brushed his teeth with
gunpowder?
He kept shooting his mouth off.

Foaming at the Mouth – by Dee
Monic

What has four eyes and a mouth?
The Mississippi.

This morning my dad gave me
soap flakes instead of corn flakes
for breakfast!
I bet you were mad.
Mad? I was foaming at the mouth!

Does he have a big mouth?
Put it this way, he can sing a duet
by himself.

Did you say he had a big mouth?
Put it this way, he's the only person
I know who can eat a banana
sideways!

Movies

Did you hear about the witch's
child who was so ugly they hired
an actress to play her in their home
movies?

A man in a movie theater notices what looks like a bear sitting next to him. "Are you a bear?" he asks. "Yes."
"What are you doing at the movies?"
"Well, I liked the book."

※

Which space movie stars Count Dracula?
The Vampire Strikes Back.

※

A man sat playing chess with a huge hairy purple monster in a pub. A stranger came in and sat down and in amazement watched them playing. When they had finished the game he came over. "I'm a movie producer," he explained as he introduced himself. "Your monster could make a fortune in Hollywood."
The man just shrugged. "He's not that clever," he said dismissively. "I've just beaten him three times in the last four games."

Moving
Attendant in the Chamber of Horrors: Could you keep moving on, please, ma'am, we're stock-taking today.

Mud
How do vampire football players get the mud off?
They get in the bat-tub.

※

Teacher: Fred! Wipe that mud off your shoes before you come in the classroom.
Fred: But, sir, I'm not wearing any shoes.

Multiply
Why did some snakes disobey Noah when he told them to "go forth and multiply?"
They couldn't – they were adders.

※

Rabbits can multiply – but only a snake can be an adder.

Mummies
Where do mummies go if they want to swim?
The Dead Sea.

※

How can you tell when a mummy is angry?
He flips his lid.

Muscles

Who's stronger than a muscleman who can tear up a telephone directory?
Someone who can tear up a street.

Mushroom

Which vegetable goes best with jacket potatoes?
Button mushrooms.

Music

When is the water in the shower room musical?
When it's piping hot.

Why is a pupil learning to sing like someone opening a tin of sardines?
Because they both have trouble with the key.

So you want to play the banjo?
Why pick on that . . . ?

Why don't skeletons play music in church?
They have no organs.

The music teacher could not control her class. A deafening noise always came from her room. One day when it was worse than usual the science teacher could bear it no longer. She ran into the music room where she found the music teacher sitting at her piano and the boys and girls raising Cain. "Do you know my students can't concentrate for the din in here?" the science teacher said.
"No!" said the music teacher, "but if you hum it I'll try and follow."

Modern music isn't as bad as it sounds.

Piano Tuner: I've come to tune the piano.
Music Teacher: But we didn't send for you.
Piano Tuner: No, but the people who live across the street did.

Why did the music student have a piano in the bathroom?
Because he was practicing Handel's Water Music.

Henry: I'd like to learn to play a drum, Sir.
Music Teacher: Beat it!

What is musical and handy in the supermarket. A Chopin Lizst.

What musical instrument never tells the truth? A lyre.

Why did they arrest the musician? He got into treble.

Nail

What's the difference between a nail and a boxer?
One gets knocked in, the other gets knocked out.

Nailbiting

What did the vampire do to stop his son biting his nails?
He cut all his fingers off.

※

Doctor, doctor, Cuthbert keeps biting his nails!
That's not serious in a child.
But Cuthbert bites his toe nails.

※

First cannibal: Your son's very full of himself isn't he?
Second cannibal: Yes, that's because he bites his nails.

※

"I'm very worried about my little boy's nailbiting habit," a woman said to her doctor.
"Nailbiting is very common in youngsters," said the doctor.
"What! Six inch rusty ones?"

Names

A new porter in Paris was instructed by the manager that it was important to call the guests by their names, in order to make them feel welcome, and that the easiest way to find out their name was to look at their luggage. Armed with this advice, the porter took two guests up to their rooms, put down their bags and said, "I hope you have a very 'appy stay 'ere in Paris, Mr and Mrs Genuine Cowhide."

※

"Your daughter's only five and she can spell her name backwards? Why, that is remarkable." The headmistress was talking to a parent who was trying to impress her with the child's academic prowess so that she would be accepted into the school.
"Yes, we're very proud of her," said the mother.
"And what is your daughter's name?"
"Anna."

※

"What's your first name?" the teacher asked a new kid.
"It's Orson, ma'am. I was named after Orson Welles, the film star."
"Just as well your last name's not Cart. Isn't it?"
"Yes ma'am. It's Trapp."

A little girl was next in line. "My name's Curtain," she said.
"I hope your first name's not Annette?"
"No. It's Velvet."

Napoleon
Doctor, doctor, I think I'm Napoleon.
How long have you felt like this?
Ever since Waterloo.

Who was the most famous French ant?
Napoleant.

Narrow
What is the definition of a narrow squeak?
A thin mouse.

Nasty
Knock knock.
Who's there?
Scott.
Scott who?
Scott a nasty look about it, has this place. Is it haunted?

Knock knock.
Who's there?
Dora.
Dora who?
Dora steel is needed to ward off the nasty witches.

I always think twice before speaking.
I expect it gives you time to think up something really nasty.

Neck

What happened when a vicar saw a zombie with nothing on his neck?
He made a bolt for it.

What happened to the lovesick vampire?
He became a neck-romancer.

What happened at the vampires' race?
They finished neck and neck

What do romantic vampires do?
Neck.

Witch: You should keep control of your little boy. He just bit me on the ankle.
Vampire: That's only because he couldn't reach your neck.

Why do people hate being bitten by vampires?
Because it's a drain in the neck.

What did the vampire say when he saw the neck of the sleeping man?
Ah! Breakfast in bed!

What is red, sweet and bites people in the neck?
A jampire.

First Vampire: I don't think much of your sister's neck.
Second Vampire: Never mind – eat the vegetables instead.

Necktie

Waiter, waiter, your necktie is in my soup!
That's all right, sir. It won't shrink.

What did the necktie say to the hat?
You go on ahead and I'll hang around.

Needle

Teacher: Spell the word "needle," Kenneth.

Kenneth: N-e-i-

Teacher: No, Kenneth, there's no "i" in needle.

Kenneth: Then it's a rotten needle, sir!

Nelson's Column

Why did the witch climb Nelson's Column?

To get her cat back.

Nerves

Two girls were talking in the corridor. "That boy over there is getting on my nerves," said Clarrie. "But he's not even looking at you," replied Clara.

"That's what's getting on my nerves," retorted Clarrie.

Did you hear about the man who took up monster-baiting for a living?

He used to be a teacher but he lost his nerve.

Nervous

What's the definition of a nervous breakdown?

A chameleon on a tartan rug.

What do you call a nervous witch?

A twitch.

Nest

Where do vultures meet for coffee?

In a nest-cafe.

News

Good news – two boys went out one day climbing trees.

Bad news – one of them fell out.

Good news – there was a hammock beneath him.

Bad news – there was a rake beside the hammock.

Good news – he missed the rake.

Bad news – he missed the hammock, too.

Good news! At school today there will be free Coca-Cola for everyone . . . the bad news is that straws are 50 cents each!

Newspaper

Moths: when will they learn that if a light is bright then it probably isn't the moon? And when it's my head they're smacking into then they'll soon meet a rolled up newspaper.

Why do you get a charge out of reading a newspaper?
Because it's full of current events.

New Year

What do vampires sing on New Year's Eve?
Auld Fang Syne.

New Zealand

Teacher: Matthew, what is the climate of New Zealand?
Matthew: Very cold, sir.
Teacher: Wrong.
Matthew: But sir! When they send us meat, it always arrives frozen!

Night

A catcall is when someone goes out at night saying "Puss, puss, puss."

✳

Did you hear about the Irish monster who went to night school to learn to read in the dark?

✳

Did you hear about the woman who was so keen on road safety that she always wore white at night?
Last winter she was knocked down by a snow plow.

Nits

What's the difference between head lice and nits?
A real nit is too stupid to find your head.

Noah

Why didn't the two worms go into Noah's Ark in an apple?
Because everyone had to go in pairs.

✳

Just before the Ark set sail, Noah saw his two sons fishing over the side. "Go easy on the bait, guys," he said. "Remember I've only got two worms."

✳

What was Noah's occupation?
Preserving pears.

✳

Knock, knock.
Who's there?
Noah
Noah who?
Noah good place to eat?

Noble

Why are pianos so noble?
Because they're either upright or grand.

Nobody

Why did the ant-elope?
Nobody gnu.

Noise

Why was the horrible big monster making a terrible noise all night?
After eating Madonna he thought he could sing.

﹡

What can you make that can't be seen?
A noise.

﹡

Two boys camping out in a back garden wanted to know the time, so they began singing at the top of their voices. Eventually a neighbor threw open his window and shouted down at them, "Hey! Less noise! Don't you know what the time is? It's three o'clock!"

Noose

The sheriff looked at the man with a noose around his neck and said, "I'll tell you what, I'm going to give you a suspended sentence."
The man said, "Thank you, thank you, thank you."
The sheriff said, "Right boys, hang him!"

﹡

Why was the murderer hanged in the evening?
Because it was the six o'clock noose.

﹡

Why did the villain start thinking about the old times when he was on the gallows?
He felt noose-talgic.

﹡

Did you hear about the considerate hangman?
He said, "Now, is the noose too tight?"

What do you call a Scottish sea monster who hangs people?
The Loch Noose Monster.

North Pole

What is green and slimy and is found at the North Pole?
A lost frog.

Northern

Which is the most dangerous animal in the Northern Hemisphere?
Yak the Ripper.

Nose

How do you know when there's a monster under your bed?
Your nose touches the ceiling.

Why did the viper viper nose?
Because the adder adder handkerchief.

❋

What usually runs in witches' families?
Noses.

❋

There was a big monster from Leek
Who, instead of a nose, had a beak.
It grew quite absurd
Till he looked like a bird.
He migrates at the end of the next week.

❋

Did you hear about the boy who got worried when his nose grew to eleven inches long?
He thought it might turn into a foot.

❋

Why did the monster take his nose apart?
To see what made it run.

What do you do if your nose goes on strike?
Picket.

What is it that even the most careful person overlooks?
His nose.

Visitor: You're very quiet, Jennifer.
Jennifer: Well, my mom gave me 10 cents not to say anything about your red nose.

Simon: I was going to buy you a handkerchief for your birthday.
Sarah: That was a kind thought. But why didn't you?
Simon: I couldn't find one big enough for your nose.

Note
Did you hear about the stupid kidnapper?
He enclosed a stamped, self-addressed envelope with the ransom note.

Novel
What is the bees' favorite novel?
The Great Gats-bee.

Nude
What's the difference between a Peeping Tom and someone who's just got out of the bath?
One is rude and nosey. The other is nude and rosy.

Numbers
Nick and Mick were at a bingo session and one of them kept on looking over the other's shoulder and telling him when his numbers were being called. Mick got annoyed and said, "Look, why don't you fill in your own card?"
"I can't," said Nick, "it's full."

Numbskull

Why did the skeleton stay out in the snow all night?
He was a numbskull.

Nun

What's black and white, black and white, black and white?
A nun rolling down a hill.

What do you get if you cross a nun and a chicken?
A pecking order.

A motorist ran into a shop. "Do you own a black and white cat?" he asked.
"No," replied the manager.
"Oh dear," said the motorist, "I must have run over a nun."

Nurse

"What do you do?" a young man asked the beautiful girl he was dancing with.
"I'm a nurse."
"I wish I could be ill and let you nurse me," he whispered in her ear.
"That would be miraculous. I work on the maternity ward."

Did you hear what happened when there was an epidemic of laryngitis at school?
The school nurse sent everyone to

the croakroom.

Nursery

"Welcome to school, Simon," said the nursery school teacher to the new boy. "How old are you?"

"I'm not old," said Simon. "I'm nearly new."

Nut

How do you catch a squirrel?
Climb up a tree and act like a nut.

The domestic science teacher was in a delicatessen buying nuts for the afternoon's cake baking. "What kind of nuts would you like?" asked the salesgirl.

"Cashew," replied the teacher.

"Bless you," said the salesgirl. "What kind of nuts would you like?"

Oat

What do you get if you cross a monster with a cow and an oat field?
Lumpy porridge.

Ocean Liner

Waiter on ocean liner: Would you like the menu, sir?
Monster: No, thank you. Just bring me the passenger list.

Octopus

Girl: Do you know what family the octopus belongs to?
Boy: No one in our street.

What do you get if you cross an octopus with a skunk?
An octopong.

What do you call a neurotic octopus?
A crazy, mixed-up squid.

What does an octopus wear when it's cold?
A coat of arms.

How do eels get around the seabed?
They go by octobus.

What's wet and wiggly and says how do you do sixteen times?
Two octopuses shaking hands.

What is an octopus?
An eight-sided cat.

What do octopuses play in their spare time?
Name that tuna.

Office

The new office-boy came into his boss's office and said, "I think you're wanted on the phone, sir."
"What d'you mean, you think?" demanded the boss.
"Well, sir, the phone rang, I answered it and a voice said 'Is that you, you old fool?'"

Where is Dracula's American office?
The Vampire State Building.

A butler came running into his important master's office. "Sir, sir, there's a ghost in the corridor. What shall I do with him?"
Without looking up from his work the master said, "Tell him I can't see him."

Officer

Police officer: And what do you think you are doing on this road, Dracula?
Dracula: Looking for the main artery, officer.

What did the police officer say to his stomach?
I've got you under a vest.

What nickname did the police give to the new blonde woman police officer?
A fair cop.

Oil

What's thick, black, floats on water and shouts "Knickers!"?
Crude oil.

What is black, gushes out of the ground and shouts "Excuse me?"
Refined oil.

Ointment

Jake: That ointment the vet gave me for the dog makes my fingers smart.

Blake: Why don't you rub some on your head then?

Old

How can you tell an old person from a young person?

An old person can sing and brush their teeth at the same time.

Omen

The Omen – by B. Warned

Onion

When Lee ate raw onions for a week what did he become?

Lone Lee.

Why are fried onions like a xerox machine?

They keep repeating themselves.

Opera

Music Teacher: Do you like opera, Francesca?

Francesca: Apart from the singing, yes.

What is a snake's favorite opera?
Wriggletto.

Operation

Doctor, doctor, I'm at death's door!
Don't worry, Mrs Jenkins. An
operation will soon pull you
through.

✸

"I'm sorry," said the surgeon. "But I
left a sponge in you when I
operated last week."
"Oh," said the patient, "I was
wondering why I was so thirsty all
the time."

✸

What kind of ghosts haunt
operating
theatres?
Surgical
spirits.

Opposite

At graduation day to mark the end
of a particularly trying year the
principal said, "A parent said to me
recently that half the teachers do
all the work and the other half
nothing at all. I'd like to assure all
the parents here this afternoon that
at this school the opposite is the
case."

Optician

A very shy young man went into an
optician's one day to order a new
pair of spectacles. Behind the
counter was an extremely pretty
young girl, which reduced the
customer to total confusion. "Can I
help you, sir?" she asked with a
ravishing smile.
"Er – yes – er – I want a pair of rim-
speckled hornicles . . . I mean I
want a pair of heck-rimmed
spornicles . . . er . . . I mean . . .
At which point the optician himself
came to the rescue. "It's all right,
Miss Jones. What the gentleman
wants is a pair of
rim-sporned
hectacles."

Orange

What do you get if you cross an orange with a comedian?
Peels of laughter.

Why did the orange stop rolling down the hill?
It ran out of juice.

Orbit

What did the astronaut say to the author?
I took your book into orbit and I couldn't put it down.

Orchestra

What do you call a Mammoth who conducts an orchestra?
Tuskanini.

Why did the school orchestra have bad manners?
Because it didn't know how to conduct itself.

Did you hear about the vampire who joined an orchestra?
He stood on the roof and conducted lightning.

Ostrich

Why does an ostrich have such a long neck?
Because its head is so far from its body.

Outlaw

What's furry, has whiskers and chases outlaws?
A posse cat.

✳

What happened at the outlaws' party?
The chief outlaw's mother-in-law turned up because she thought it was an in-laws party.

Oven

Did you hear about the time Eddy's sister tried to make a birthday cake?
The candles melted in the oven.

Owl

What do two lovesick owls say when it's raining?
Too-wet-to-woo!

✳

What sits in a tree and says "Hoots mon, hoots mon?"
A Scottish owl.

✳

Why were the mommy and daddy owls worried about their son?
Because he didn't seem to give a hoot anymore.

✳

What did the owl say to his friend as he flew off?
Owl be seeing you later.

What does an educated owl say?
Whom.

✳

Why did the owl 'owl?
Because the Woodpecker would peck 'er.

✳

What do confused owls say?
Too-whit-to-why?

✳

What did the baby owl's parents say when he wanted to go to a party?
You're not owld enough.

✳

What do Scottish owls sing?
Owld Lang Syne.

✳

What did the scornful owl say?
Twit twoo.

✳

How do you know that owls are cleverer than chickens?
Have you ever heard of Kentucky Fried Owl?

✳

Knock knock.
Who's there?
Owl.
Owl who?
Owl I can say is knock knock!

✳

Knock knock
Who's there?
Owl.
Owl who?
Owl be sad if you don't let me in.

✳

Knock knock.
Who's there?
Owl.
Owl who?
Owl aboard!

✳

Two owls were playing pool. One said, "Two hits."
The other replied, "Two hits to who?"

✳

Paddy

What do you call a big Irish spider?
Paddy-long-legs.

✳

Two Irishmen looking for work saw a sign which read TREE FELLERS WANTED. "Oh, now, look at that," said Paddy. "What a pity there's only de two of us!"

Pain

What's the difference between a vampire with toothache and a rainstorm?
One roars with pain and the other pours with rain.

Paint

What is the best way to get paint off a chair?
Sit on it before the paint's dry.

✳

Did you hear what Dumb Donald did when he offered to paint the garage for his Dad in the summer holidays?
The instructions said put on three coats, so he went in and put on his blazer, his raincoat and his parka.

Painter

Who is a bee's favorite painter?
Pablo Beecasso.

Paper

First witch: Have you tried one of these new paper cauldrons?
Second witch: Yes.
First witch: Did it work?
Second witch: No, it was tearable.

✳

Teacher: What happened to your homework?
Boy: I made it into a paper plane and someone hijacked it.

✳

Girl: You think you're clever but really you're just stupid.
Her enemy: You are like a piece of blotting paper. You soak everything in – but you get it all backwards!

Parachute

Did you hear about the man who hijacked a submarine?
He demanded a million dollars and a parachute.

A pilot flying over the jungle was having trouble with his plane and decided to bail out before it crashed. So he put on his parachute, jumped, pulled the rip-cord, and drifted gently down to land. Unfortunately, he landed right in a large cooking pot which a tribal chief was simmering gently over a fire. The chief looked at him, rubbed his eyes, looked again, and asked, "What's this flier doing in my soup?"

Pardon

"I beg your pardon," said the man, returning to his seat in the theater, "but did I step on your toe as I went out?"

"You certainly did," the woman replied.

"Oh, good," said the man, "that means I'm in the right row."

❊

The acoustics in this hall are marvelous, aren't they?
Pardon?

❊

Parent

What do young ghosts call their parents?

Deady and Mummy.

Park

In the park this morning I was surrounded by lions.

Lions! In the park?

Yes – dandelions!

Parrot

Why wouldn't the parrot talk to the Frenchman?

Because he only spoke pigeon English.

※

My parrot lays square eggs.

That's amazing! Can it talk as well?

Yes, but only one word.

What's that?

Ouch!

※

How do you know you are haunted by a parrot?

He keeps saying "Oooo's a pretty boy then?"

※

What do you get if you cross a centipede with a parrot?

A walkie-talkie.

※

"I'd like a cheap parrot, please," an old lady said to a pet shop owner. "This one's cheap and it sings The Star-Spangled Banner."

"Never mind that," said the customer. "Is it tender?"

Miss: Why do we put a hyphen in a bird-cage?

Stella: For a parrot to perch on, miss.

Party

Ghost: Are you coming to my party?

Spook: Where is it?

Ghost: In the morgue – you know what they say, the morgue the merrier.

※

What should you do if you find yourself surrounded by Dracula, Frankenstein, a zombie and a werewolf?
Hope you're at a costume party.

Tom: Did you got to Ann's party?
Max: No, the invitation said "from five to nine", and I'm ten.

Passenger
What did the monster say when he saw a rush-hour train full of passengers?
Oh good! A chew-chew train!

Peach
James: I call my girlfriend Peach.
John: Because she's beautiful?
James: No, because she's got a heart of stone!

Peace
What do you call a warlock who tries to stop fights?
A Peacelock.

Peanuts
How can you tell if an elephant has been sleeping in your bed?
The sheets are wrinkled and the bed smells of peanuts.

Pear
Harry: Please may I have another pear, Miss?
Teacher: Another, Harry? They don't grow on trees, you know.

Peas
"Any complaints?" asked the teacher during school lunch.
"Yes, sir," said one bold lad, "these peas are awfully hard, sir."
The master dipped a spoon into the peas on the boy's plate and tasted them. "They seem soft enough to me," he declared.
"Yes, they are now, I've been chewing them for the last half hour."

Pedestrian

Why did the witch have pedestrian eyes?
They looked both ways before they crossed.

Pelican

What do a vulture, a pelican and a taxman have in common?
Big bills!

Pen

What does an executioner do with a pen and paper?
Writes his chopping list.

Pencil

Vincent, why have you got a sausage stuck behind your ear?
Eh? Oh, no, I must have eaten my pencil for lunch!

Why is a pencil the heaviest thing in your bag?
Because it's full of lead.

Why did the man take a pencil to bed?
To draw the curtains . . . I'd tell you another joke about a pencil, but it hasn't any point.

Pencil Sharpener

What do witches use pencil sharpeners for?
To keep their hats pointed.

Penguin

What do you get if you cross a giant, hairy monster with a penguin?
I don't know but it's a very tight-fitting tuxedo.

Perfume

What perfume do lady snakes like to wear?
"Poison" by Dior.

✴

What happened when the monster stole a bottle of perfume?
He was convicted of fragrancy.

✴

"What's your new perfume called?" a young man asked his girlfriend.
"High Heaven," she replied.
"I asked what it was called, not what it smells to!"

✴

Jerry: Is that a new perfume I smell?
Kerry: It is, and you do!

Permission

Teacher: I'd like to go through one whole day without having to punish you.
Girl: You have my permission, sir.

Pet

Why did a man's pet vulture not make a sound for five years?
It was stuffed.

✴

What is the difference between a poisonous snake and a school principal?
You can make a pet out of the snake.

✴

Keeping Pet Snakes – by Sir Pent

✴

A woman walked into a pet shop and said, "I'd like a frog for my son."
"Sorry, ma'am," said the manager, "we don't do part exchange."

✴

What pet makes the loudest noise?
A trum-pet.

✴

Did you hear about the witch who fed her pet vulture on sawdust?
The vulture laid ten eggs and when they hatched, nine chicks had wooden legs and the tenth was a woodpecker.

✴

Caspar: I was the teacher's pet last year.
Jaspar: Why was that?
Caspar: She couldn't afford a dog.

✴

Advertisement: Dog for sale. Really gentle. Eats anything. Especially fond of children.

※

Did you hear about the man who took his pet skunk to the cinema? During a break in the film, the woman sitting in front, who had been most affected by the animal's smell, turned round and said in a very sarcastic voice, "I'm surprised that an animal like that should appreciate a film like this."

"So am I," said the man. "He hated the book."

※

Waiter, waiter! There's a slug in my lettuce.
Sorry, madam, no pets allowed here.

Phantom
What do ghosts write with?
Phantom pens.

※

What do ghosts see at the theatre?
A phantomime.

※

Ghost: Do you believe in the hereafter?
Phantom: Of course I do.
Ghost: Well, hereafter leave me alone.

Phone
What do you call a Yeti in a phone box?
Stuck.

What do ghosts use to phone home?
A terror-phone.

※

Vampire: Doctor, doctor, I keep thinking I'm a telephone.
Doctor: Why's that?
Vampire: I keep getting calls in the night.

※

At three o'clock one morning a veterinary surgeon was woken from a deep sleep by the ringing of his telephone. He staggered downstairs and answered the phone. "I'm sorry if I woke you," said a voice at the other end of the line.

"That's all right," said the vet, "I had to get up to answer the telephone anyway."

I see you've burnt your ear. Were you doing the ironing when the phone rang?

Photographs
One day Tony's girlfriend wrote to him to say their friendship was off and could she have her photograph back? Tony sent her a pile of pictures of different girls with the message: I can't remember what you look like. Could you please take out your photo and return the rest.

What do you think of this photograph of me?
It makes you look older, frankly.
Oh, well, it'll save the cost of having another one taken later on.

Poor old Stephen sent his photograph off to a Lonely Hearts Club. They sent it back saying that they weren't that lonely.

Piano
What happened when a monster fell in love with a grand piano?
He said, "Darling, you've got lovely teeth."

Why was the piano player arrested?
Because he got into treble.

Do you think, Professor, that my wife should take up the piano as a career?
No, I think she should put down the lid as a favor.

What do you call an ant who can't play the piano?
Discord-ant.

Waiter, waiter, does the pianist play requests?
Yes, sir.
Then ask him to play tiddlywinks until I've finished my meal.

Picture

Some girls who are the picture of health are just painted that way.

What did the picture say to the wall?
I've got you covered.

Pie

Waiter, waiter, why is my apple pie all mashed up?
You did ask me to step on it, sir.

What is a ghost's favorite dessert?
Boo-berry pie with I-scream.

A tramp knocked at a door and asked for some food. "Didn't I give you some pie a week ago?" asked the lady of the house.
"Yeah, lady," said the tramp, "but I'm all right again now."

Piece

Did you hear about the idiot who invented the one-piece jigsaw puzzle?

Mom, can I have two pieces of cake, please?
Certainly – take this piece and cut it in two!

Bernie: Why have you given me this piece of rope?
Ernie: They say if you give someone enough rope they'll hang themselves!

Pig

Doctor, doctor, I've got a little sty.
Then you'd better buy a little pig.

What happened when the nasty monster stole a pig?
The pig squealed to the police.

Why did the pig run away from the pig-sty?
He felt that the other pigs were taking him for grunted.

The teacher was furious with her son. "Just because you've been put in my class, there's no need to think you can take liberties. You're a pig." The boy said nothing.
"Well! Do you know what a pig is?"
"Yes, Mom," said the boy. "The offspring of a swine."

Why didn't the piglets listen to the father pig?
Because he was an old boar.

Where do pigs go when they die?
To the sty in the sky.

Pigeons
Why did the teacher put corn in his shoes?
Because he had pigeon toes.

Pill
Doctor, doctor, these pills you gave me for BO . .
What's wrong with them?
They keep slipping out from under my arms!

Bill and Gill make a perfect pair, don't they?
They certainly do. She's a pill and he's a headache.

Pirates
What did everyone say about the kind-hearted pirate?
That his barque was worse than his bite.

Pixie
How do pixies eat?
By gobblin'.

Place
Knock knock.
Who's there?
Glasgow.
Glasgow who?
Glasgow away from this place – it's scary!

Witch: Doctor, doctor, I've broken my arm in two places.
Doctor: Well don't go back to those places again.

❊

The Stock Market is a place where sheep and cattle are sold.

❊

What did the teacher say after spending thousands in the expensive hotel?
I'm sorry to leave, now that I've almost bought the place.

❊

Geography teacher: What is the coldest place in the world?
Ann: Chile.

❊

They say he's going places.
The sooner the better!

Planet
Wizard from Another Planet – by A. Lee-En

❊

On her annual visit to another planet, an old lady turns to the cabin steward and says.
"I hope this spaceship doesn't travel faster than sound.
"Why?" replies the cabin steward.
"Because my friend and I want to talk, that's why."

Play
Why is Hollywood full of vampires?
They need someone to play the bit parts.

❊

Why did the vampire sit on a pumpkin?
It wanted to play squash.

❊

What do vampires play poker for?
High stakes.

❊

"You play fair with me and I'll play fair with you," said the boss to the new worker. "Just remember: you can't do too much for a good employer."
"Don't worry, I won't."

❊

Plumber
What happens when plumbers die?
They go down the drain.

✷

What do you call a highly skilled plumber?
A drain surgeon.

Poetry
Why did the bee start spouting poetry?
He was waxing lyrical.

Pogo
What is big, hairy and bounces up and down?
A monster on a pogo stick.

What happened when the skeletons rode pogo sticks?
They had a rattling good time.

Poison
What's the best thing about deadly snakes?
They've got poisonality.

✷

What do witches sing at Christmas?
Deck the halls with poison ivy . . .

✷

How do you poison a woman with a pair of scissors?
Give her arseanick!

Pole
What kind of pole is short and floppy?
A tadpole.

✷

What do you get if you cross a frog with a decathelete?
Someone who pole vaults without a pole.

Police
How can you tell if you are looking at a police glow-worm?
He has a flashing light.

✷

What happened to the wizard who ran away with the circus?
The police made him bring it back again.

※

Did you hear about the cannibal who joined the police force?
He said he wanted to grill his suspects.

Popeye
Who makes suits and eats spinach?
Popeye the Tailorman.

※

What happens when Popeye tries to cook his dinner. There's Olive Oyl all over the place.

Porcupine
What's a porcupine's favorite food?
Prickled onions.

Pork
Cooking with Pork – by Chris P. Bacon

※

Diner to Waiter: A pork chop, please and make it lean.
Waiter: Certainly, ma'am, which way?

Porridge
Which ghost ate too much porridge?
Ghouldilocks.

※

What happened to the man who couldn't tell the difference between porridge and putty?
All his windows fell out.

Pot
What should you expect if you drop in on a witch's home unexpectedly?
Pot luck.

Potato
Sid: Mom, all the boys at school call me Big Head.
Mom: Never mind, love, just pop down to the greengrocer's for me and collect the 14 lbs of potatoes I ordered in your cap.

※

Why did the farmer plow his field with a steamroller?
Because he planned to grow mashed potatoes.

Poverty
What happened to the poverty-stricken ghost?
He was dread-bare.

Power
How do you save power?
Kill a watt today.

Why did the vampire's girlfriend break up with him?
Because he had such a powerful crush on her.

Pram
Did you hear about the witch who had the ugliest baby in the world?
She didn't push the pram – she pulled it.

Prescription
Patient: Doctor, doctor, I feel terrible. I can hardly breathe, I can't walk, I keep having palpitations and my skin is covered in nasty blotches.

Doctor: Oh, dear.
Patient: Are you writing me a prescription?
Doctor: No, a note for the undertaker.

Present
Mother: How was your first day at school?
Little Boy: OK, but I haven't got my present yet.
Mother: What do you mean?
Little Boy: Well, the teacher gave me a chair, and said, "Sit there for the present."

What did you get for Christmas?
A mouth-organ. It's the best present I ever got.
Why?
My mom gives me fifty cents a week not to blow it.

Bill: Do you like the dictionary I bought you for your birthday?
Ben: Sure. It's a great present but I just can't find the words to thank you enough.

Prince

Did you hear about the skeleton who wore a kilt?
He was called Boney Prince Charlie.

Princess

Who is the most royal ant?
Princess Ant.

Printer

When George left school he was going to be a printer.
All the teachers said he was the right type.

Prize

What did Enormous Eric win when he lost 50 pounds in weight?
The No-Belly Prize.

Did you hear about the new prize for people who cure themselves of BO?
It's called the No-Smell Prize.

Professor

"Eureka!" shouted the famous scientist when he made an important discovery.
"Sorry, professor," said his assistant. "I didn't have time to shower this morning."

Promise

I'll lend you a dollar if you promise not to keep it too long.
Oh, I won't. I'll spend it right away.

Psychiatry

Why did the witch go to the psychiatrist?
Because she thought everybody loved her.

Psychiatrist: Well, what's your problem?
Patient: I prefer brown shoes to black shoes.
Psychiatrist: There's nothing wrong with that. Lots of people prefer brown shoes to black shoes. I do myself.
Patient: Really? How do your like yours – fried or boiled?

What happens if you tell a psychiatrist you are schizophrenic?
He charges you double.

"The trouble is," said the entertainer to the psychiatrist, "that I can't sing, I can't dance, I can't tell jokes, I can't act, I can't play an instrument or juggle or do magic tricks or do anything!"
"Then why don't you give up show-business?"
"I can't – I'm a star!"

Patient: Doctor, you have to help me stop talking to myself.
Doctor: Why is that?
Patient: I'm a salesman and I keep selling myself things I don't want.

Puffin

Which bird is always out of breath?
A puffin.

Punch

Father: This report gives you a D for conduct and an A for courtesy. How on earth did you manage that?
Son: Easy. Whenever I punch someone, I apologize.

Punishment

"I have decided to abolish all corporal punishment at this school," said the principal at morning assembly. "That means that there will be no physical punishment."
"Does that mean that we don't have to eat school meals any more, sir?"

Tracy: Would you punish someone for something they haven't done?
Teacher: Of course not.
Tracy: Oh good, because I haven't done my homework.

*

Mother: Why are you spanking Tom?
Father: Because his school report is due tomorrow and I won't to be here.

Puppy

Mandy had a puppy on a leash. She met Sandy and said, "I just got this puppy for my little brother."
"Really?" said Sandy. "Whoever did you find to make a swap like that?"

Python

What do most people do when they see a python?
They re-coil.

*

What did the python say to the viper?
    I've got a crush on you.

What is a snake's favorite comedy show?
Monty Python.

*

Doctor, doctor, I keep thinking I'm a python.
Oh, you can't get round me like that, you know.

*

QUACK!

QE2

What happened when the cannibal crossed the Atlantic on the QE2? He told the waiter to take the menu away and bring him the passenger list.

Quack

What's the difference between a gymnastics teacher and a duck? One goes quick on its legs, the other goes quack on its legs.

QUACK!

Quarter

The night-school teacher asked one of his students when he had last sat an exam. "1945," said the lad. "Good lord! That's more than 40 years ago." "No, Sir! An hour and half, it's quarter past nine now."

Quartet

What has eight feet and sings? The school quartet.

Quebec

A gym teacher who came from
Quebec,
Wrapped both legs around his
neck.
But sad, he forgot
How to untie the knot.
And now he's a highly-strung
wreck.

Queen

What does a queen do when she
burps?
She issues a royal pardon.

A boastful American from Texas was being shown the sights of London by a taxi-driver. "What's that building there?" asked the Texan.

"That's the Tower of London, sir," replied the taxi-driver.

"Say, we can put up buildings like that in two weeks," drawled the Texan. A little while later he said, "And what's that building we're passing now?"

"That's Buckingham Palace, sir, where the Queen lives."

"Is that so?" said the Texan. "Do you know back in Texas we could put a place like that up in a week?" A few minutes later they were passing Westminster Abbey. The American asked again, "Hey cabbie, what's that building over there?"

"I'm afraid I don't know, sir," replied the taxi-driver. "It wasn't there this morning."

Queen Bee

How does a queen bee get around the hive?
She's throne.

※

What did the drone say to the queen bee?
Swarm in here isn't it?

※

Which queen can never wear a crown?
A queen bee.

Why did the queen bee kick all the other bees out of the hive?
Because they kept droning on and on.

Question

When doing exams Dick knows all the answers.
It's the questions that get him confused.

※

Knock, knock.
Who's there?
Sacha.
Sacha who?
Sacha lot of questions in this exam!

Queue

A man was walking behind a hearse with a big vampire's cat on a lead. Behind them stretched a long line of mourners. "What happened?" asked a passer-by.
"The vampire's cat bit my wife, and she died of fright."
"Can I borrow it?" the passer-by asked.
The man pointed behind him, "Get in the queue."

Quickly

A farmer was showing a schoolboy round his farm when they came to a field where the farmer's sheep were grazing. "How many sheep do you reckon there are?" the farmer asked proudly.

"Seven hundred and sixty-four," replied the boy after a few seconds. The farmer gaped.

"That's exactly right, boy. How did you count them so quickly?"

"Simple," said the boy genius. "I just counted the legs and divided by four!"

Quick Sand

Why is the school swot like a quick sand?
Because everything in school sinks into him.

Quiet

Mr Monster: Oi, hurry up with my supper.
Mrs Monster: Oh, do be quiet – I've only got three pairs of hands.

Knock, knock.
Who's there?
Quiet Tina.
Quiet Tina who?
Quiet Tina classroom.

What did the Pharaohs use to keep their babies quiet?
Egyptian dummies.

Knock knock.
Who's there?
Paris.
Paris who?
Paris by the vampire very quietly.

Quietly

Teddy came thundering down the stairs, much to his father's annoyance. "Teddy," he called, "how many more times have I got to tell you to come downstairs quietly? Now, go back upstairs and come down like a civilized human being." There was a silence, and Teddy reappeared in the front room. "That's better," said his father, "now in future will you always come down stairs like that." "Suits me," said Teddy. "I slid down the railing."

Quitter

Penny: No one could call your dad a quitter.
Kenny: No, he's been sacked from every job he's ever had.

Rabbit

What do you get if you pour hot water down a rabbit hole?
Hot cross bunnies!

How can you tell when it's rabbit pie for dinner?
It has hares in it.

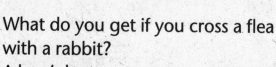

What do you get if you cross a flea with a rabbit?
A bug's bunny.

Racing cars

Why did the stupid racing car driver make ten pit stops during the Grand Prix?
He was asking for directions.

Railroad

What's the difference between a teacher and a conductor on the railroad?
One trains the mind, the other minds the train.

Rain

"Gosh, it's raining cats and dogs," said Suzie looking out of the kitchen window.
"I know," said her mother who had just come in. "I've just stepped in a poodle!"

Zoe: I'm sure I'm right.
Chloe: You're as right as rain – all wet!

Raincoat

English Teacher: Now give me a sentence using the word "fascinate."
Clara: My raincoat has ten buttons but I can only fasten eight.

Recipe

What ghost is handy in the kitchen?
A recipe spook.

Recognize

I didn't recognize you for a minute. It was one of the happiest minutes of my life.

✳

A lady put a lonely hearts ad in the paper and had a reply which said, "I would love to meet you, but I have to tell you that I am eight feet tall, covered in matted fur, with large fangs and slobbering lips. If you still want to meet me then I'll be under the clock in Penn Station at six o'clock next Saturday."
The lady replied, "I would be interested in meeting you but please will you wear a red carnation and carry a rolled-up copy of The New York Times so that I can recognize you?"

✳

What did Tarzan say when he saw the monsters coming?
Here come the monsters.
And what did he say when he saw the monsters coming with sunglasses on?
Nothing – he didn't recognize them!

Record

What is a mouse's favorite record?
Please cheese me.

✳

What's a rat's least favorite record?
What's up Pussycat.

Red

When should you stop for a glow-worm?
When he has a red light.

✳

Barber: Did you come in with a red scarf on?
Man: No.
Barber: Oh dear, I must have cut your throat.

✳

My girlfriend is a beautiful redhead – no hair, just a red head.

✳

Teacher: You seem to be exceedingly ignorant, Williams. Have you read Dickens?
Williams: No, sir.
Teacher: Have you read Shakespeare?
Williams: No, sir.
Teacher: Well, what have you read?
Williams: Er . . . er . . . I've red hair, sir.

Red Indian

I bet I can make you speak like a Red Indian.
How?
That's right!

Reference

Did your previous employer give you a reference?
Yes, but I left it at home.
What does it say?
Er, well, it says I was one of the best employers that he had ever turned out . . .

Reforms

Why did the witches go on strike?
Because they wanted sweeping reforms.

Reincarnation

Did you hear about the man who believed in reincarnation?
In his will he left his money to himself.

Reindeer

I don't care who you are, get those reindeer off my roof.

Relation

What happened at the vampires' reunion?
All the blood relations went.

Religion

How do Religious Education teachers mark exams?
With spirit levels.

Reptile

What do you call a rich frog?
A gold-blooded reptile.

⁕

Collecting Reptiles – by Ivor Frog

Rescue

A mountaineer fell down a very deep crevasse, breaking both his arms. Another member of the party managed to lower a rope until it was just within reach of the man's head. "Quick!" he shouted. "Get hold of the rope with your teeth and I'll pull you up." Inch by painful inch, the mountaineer was dragged back up the crevasse. When he only had two feet to go, his rescuer called out, "Are you all right?"
"Yes, aaaaaaarrrrrrgggggghhhhh!" came the reply.

Restaurant

Why was the restaurant called "Out of this World"?
Because it was full of Unidentified Frying Objects.

⁕

Jane's father decided to take all the family out to a restaurant for a meal. As he'd spent quite a lot of money for the meal he said to the waiter, "Could I have a bag to take the leftovers home for the dog?"
"Gosh!" exclaimed Jane, "Are we getting a dog?"

⁕

Customer to friend: This is a wonderful restaurant. I ordered salad and I got the freshest salad in the world, I ordered coffee, and I got the freshest coffee in the world.
Friend: I know – I ordered a small steak and got a calf.

Retire

Why did the janitor take early retirement?
Because he realized that grime doesn't pay.

⁕

The wonderful Wizard of Oz
Retired from business becoz
What with up to date science
To most of his clients
He wasn't the wiz that he woz.

Revolution

What happened when the wheel
was invented?
It caused a revolution.

Revolving

Did you hear about the girl who
met the boy in a revolving door?
They've been going round
together ever since.

✳

Why are you covered in bruises?
I started to walk through a
revolving door and then I changed
my mind.

Rice

What do witches eat for breakfast?
Rice Krispies because they snap at
them.

Rich

Two weevils came to town from
the country. One worked hard and
became very rich. The other
became the lesser of two weevils.

✳

Did you hear about the exclusive
school where all the pupils smelt?
It was for filthy rich kids only.

✳

The Rich Man's Guide to Good
Living by Ivor Lot

Riddle

What gets wetter the more it dries?
A towel.

✳

What is found in the middle of both America and Australia?
The letter R.

※

What goes up but never comes down?
Your age.

※

If the green house is on the right side of the road and the red house is on the left side of the road, where is the white house?
In Washington.

※

What travels round the world but stays in a corner?
A stamp.

※

What can be right, but never wrong?
An angle.

River
What do you get if you cross a river with an inflatable wizard?
To the other side.

※

What do you call a hairy beast in a river?
A weir-wolf.

Road
What do you call a witch by the side of the road with her thumb out?
A witch-hiker.

What do you call a witch who drives really badly?
A road hag.

Robin
Teacher: What's a robin?
John: A bird that steals, ma'am.

Robinson Crusoe
Why is a janitor nothing like Robinson Crusoe?
Because Robinson Crusoe got all his work done by Friday.

※

Two fleas were sitting on Robinson Crusoe's back as he lay on the beach in the sun. "Well, so long," said one to the other, "I'll see you on Friday."

Robot

Why did the robot turn into a ghost?
Because he couldn't rust in peace.

※

Why did the robot act stupid?
Because he had a screw loose.

Rock

Where do geologists go for entertainment?
To rock concerts.

Rocking Chair

Why did the principal put wheels on her rocking chair?
She liked to rock and roll.

Roller Skates

What's big, heavy, furry, dangerous and has sixteen wheels?
A monster on roller-skates.

※

What is black and has eight wheels?
A witch on roller skates.

Rolls Royce

What do you get if you cross a Rolls Royce with a vampire?
A monster that attacks expensive cars and sucks out their gas tanks.

Roman

The great Roman emperor Caesar was watching Christians being thrown to the lions. "One good thing about this sport," he said to one of his aides, "we're never bothered with spectators running onto the field."

Rome

How do we know that Rome was built at night?
Because all the books say it wasn't built in a day!

Romeo

Some girls think I'm handsome, said the young Romeo, and some girls think I'm ugly. What do you think, Sheila?
A bit of both. Pretty ugly.

Room

What do you call two witches who share a room?
Broom-mates.

※

Laurie: We should all do our bit to clean up the environment.
Mom: I agree. You could start with your room.

What room has no floor, ceiling, windows or doors?
A mushroom.

Rope

If a dog is tied to a rope 15 feet long, how can it reach a bone 30 feet away?
The rope isn't tied to anything!

Rose

What do you get if you cross a tarantula with a rose?
I don't know but I wouldn't try smelling one.

Rowing

A large sailing ship was at anchor off the coast of Mauritius, and two dodos watched the sailors rowing ashore. "We'd better hide," said the first dodo.
"Why?" asked the second.
"Because," said the first, "we're supposed to be extinct, silly!"

Rowing boat

Boat attendant: Come in number 9, your time is up.
Assistant: But sir, we only have eight rowing boats.
Boat attendant: Oh, dear, number 6 must be in trouble then.

Rubbish

"Sir!" said Alexander. "Empty Coke cans, hamburger cartons, plastic bags, used kleenex, broken bottles, empty boxes . . ."

"Alexander!" snapped the teacher. "You're talking rubbish again!"

✻

What training do you need to be a rubbish collector?
None, you pick it up as you go along.

Run

What should you do if a monster runs through your front door?
Run through the back door.

✻

How did the witch feel when she got run over by a car?
Tired.

✻

Is it true that a witch won't hurt you if you run away from her?
It all depends on how fast you run!

✻

Knock knock.
Who's there?
Mecca.
Mecca who?
Mecca run for it!

✻

Why did the skeleton run up a tree?
Because a dog was after its bones.

Sports coach: Come on, Sophie. You can run faster than that.
Sophie: I can't, sir. I'm wearing run-resistant panty-hose.

✻

A driver approached the principal one afternoon and said, "I'm awfully sorry, but I think I've just run over the school cat. Can I replace it?"
The principal looked him up and down and replied, "I doubt if you'd be the mouser she was."

Running

Will: Why do you call that new player Cinderella?
Bill: Because he's always running away from the ball.

Rush

What did one slug say to another who had hit him and rushed off?
I'll get you next slime!

Russian

Knock, knock.
Who's there?
Russia.
Russia who?
Russiaway from this place – quick!

What do you call a flea that lives in Russia?
A Moscow-ito.

Saint

What did the dragon say when he saw Saint George in his shining armor?
Oh no, not more tinned food!

Salad

Waiter, waiter! There's a maggot in my salad.
Don't worry, he won't live long in that stuff.

Waiter, waiter! There's a spider in my salad.
Yes sir, the chef's using Webb lettuces today.

Why did the tomato blush?
Because it saw the salad dressing.

Mommy, Mommy, I don't like Daddy!
Well, just eat the salad then dear.

Sandwich

What do vampires make sandwiches out of?
Self-raising dead.

Knock knock.
Who's there?
Crispin.
Crispin who?
Crispin crunchy frog sandwich.

Two monsters were working on a construction site. When lunchtime came, one of them took out a box of sandwiches. "Rat paste and tomato," he moaned, as he bit into the first. "More rat paste and tomato," he muttered as he ate the second.
"Rat paste and tomato?" his friend asked as he picked up the third sandwich.
"Yes," sighed the monster. "I hate rat paste and tomato."
"Why don't you ask your wife to make you something different?"
The monster looked at him strangely. "I don't have a wife – I make my sandwiches myself."

A little demon came home from school one day and said to his mother, "I hate my sister's guts." "All right," said his mother, "I won't put them in your sandwiches again."

❋

Girl: Can you eat spiders?
Boy: Why?
Girl: One's just crawled into your sandwich.

❋

Bring me a crocodile sandwich immediately.
I'll make it snappy, sir.

Santa
What do you get if you cross a witch's cat with Father Christmas?
Santa Claws

❋

Who carries a sack and bites people?
Santa Jaws.

Satisfy
Why is a complaining teacher the easiest to satisfy?
Because nothing satisfies them.

Saucer
How do witches on broomsticks drink their tea?
Out of flying saucers.

❋

How do you get milk from a witch's cat?
Steal her saucer.

❋

What do you call an alien starship that drips water?
A crying saucer.

Sausage
Waiter, waiter! There are two worms on my plate.
Those are your sausages, sir.

❋

What kind of sausages do vampires like best?
Fang-furters.

❋

What is the most popular food served at a nudist camp?
Skinless sausages.

❋

How do you make a sausage roll?
Push it.

Scaffolding

A worker on a construction site rushed up to the man in charge. "Boss!" he cried. "Someone's just dropped a trowel from the top of the scaffolding and sliced my ear off!" Immediately, his boss organized a search party to find the ear in the hope that surgeons might be able to sew it back on. "Here it is!" cried one of the searchers, waving an ear.

"No, that's not it," said the injured workman. "Mine had a pencil behind it!"

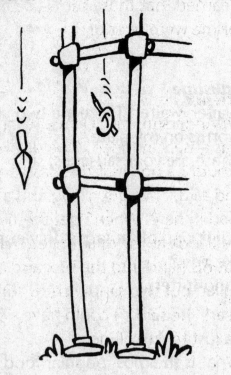

School

What school subject are snakes best at?

Hiss-tory.

Mother: Did you enjoy the school outing, dear?

Jane: Yes. And we're going again tomorrow.

Mother: Really? Why's that?

Jane: To try and find the kids we left behind.

※

Teacher: You weren't at school last Friday, Robert. I heard you were at the movie theater.

Robert: That's not true, sir. And I've got the tickets from the football game to prove it.

※

"I hope you're not one of those boys who sits and watches the school clock," said the principal to a new boy.

"No, Sir. I've got a digital watch that bleeps at half past three."

※

There was once a lad called Willy Maufe. When he went to school for the first time the teacher asked him his name. "I'm Maufe," said Willy. "Don't be silly, boy," said the teacher. "You'll stay here till 3.30 like the rest of us."

※

Why do vampires like school lunches?
Because they know they won't get stake.

✳

When I was at school I was as smart as the next fellow. What a pity the next fellow was such an idiot.

✳

My dad is a real jerk. I told him I needed an encyclopedia for school and he said I'd have to walk just like everyone else!

✳

What should you do if you find a gorilla sitting at your school desk?
Sit somewhere else.

✳

A school inspector was talking to a student. "How many teachers work in this school?" he asked.
"Only about half of them, I reckon," replied the student.

✳

Why is school like a shower?
One wrong turn and you're in hot water.

✳

Knock knock.
Who's there?
Ida.
Ida who?
Ida nawful time at school today.

✳

Mother: What did you learn at school today?
Son: Not enough. I have to go back tomorrow.

✳

What did you learn in school today, son?
I learned that those sums you did for me were wrong!

Science
Mr Anderson, the science teacher, was absent-minded. One day he brought a box into the classroom and said, "I've got a frog and a toad in here. When I get them out we'll look at the differences." He put his hand into the box and pulled out two sandwiches. "Oh dear!" he said. "I could have sworn I'd just had my lunch."

✳

Trixie: When I die I'm going to leave my brain to science.
Tracey: I suppose every little bit helps.

✳

"Now don't forget, boys," the science teacher droned on. "If it wasn't for water we would never learn to swim. And if we'd never learned to swim, just think how many people would have drowned!"

Scientist
Who was the most famous scientist ant?
Albert Antstein.

Wife to Husband: I think Spencer may grow up to be a space scientist. I was talking to his teacher today and she said he was taking up space.

Scratch
Did you hear about the bloke who set up a flea circus?
He started it from scratch.

How do you find out where a flea has bitten you?
Start from scratch.

Why did the flea fail his exams?
He wasn't up to scratch.

Teacher: Peter! Why are you scratching yourself?
Peter: 'Cos no one else knows where I itch.

Did you hear that Dumb Donald got splinters in his fingers?
He'd been scratching his head!

Screw
Why did the man go out and buy a set of tools?
Because everyone kept telling him he had a screw loose.

Seconds
Doctor, doctor, I've only got 50 seconds to live.
Just sit over there a minute.

Secret
What do you mean by telling everyone I'm an idiot?
I'm sorry. I didn't know it was supposed to be a secret.

Secretary
Boss: Are you willing to do an honest day's work?
Secretary: Yes, as long as you give me an honest week's pay for it.

Did you hear about the really high-powered business tycoon?
He had a tall secretary for taking dictation in longhand, a small secretary for taking dictation in shorthand, and a tiny secretary for taking footnotes!

Security
Why was the robber so secure?
He was a safe robber.

Knock knock.
Who's there?
Max.
Max who?
Maximum security is needed in these parts.

Shadow
What is as big as King Kong but doesn't weigh anything?
King Kong's shadow.

It was so hot when we went on holiday last year that we had to take turns sitting in each other's shadow.

Sheep
What do you get if you cross a sheep and a rainstorm?
A wet blanket.

What happened to the vampire who swallowed a sheep? He felt baaaaaaaaaaaaaad.

Sherlock Holmes
What do you get if you cross a skeleton with a famous detective?
Sherlock Bones.

Shoe
What runs about all day and lies down at night with its tongue hanging out?
A training shoe.

We're so poor that Mom and Dad can't afford to buy me shoes. I have to polish my feet and lace my toes together.

Shop

Is this a second-hand shop?
Yes, sir.
Good. Can you fit one on my watch, please?

※

She's so stupid she thinks a shoplifter is a very strong person who goes round picking up shops.

※

The manager of a shop observed one of his customers in a furious argument with a junior assistant. As he hurried over, the customer finally yelled, ". . . and I shall never come into this place again!" And he stalked out, slamming the door behind him.
"Hicks," said the manager severely, "how many more times must I tell you that the customer is always right."
"As you wish, sir," said the junior. "He was saying you were a lop-eared, bald-headed, brainless idiot!"

※

Notice (in a new shop window):
Don't go elsewhere and be robbed – try us!

※

Laura: Whenever I go to the corner shop the sales assistant shakes my hand.
Lionel: I expect it's to make sure you don't put it in the till.

※

When is a shop like a boat?
When it has sales.

Shopping

Where do ghosts go shopping?
In boo-tiques.

※

Gone Shopping – by Carrie R. Bag

Short

The Short Break – by T.N. Cookies

※

How do you fix a short circuit?
Lengthen it.

※

298

Teacher: Carol, what is "can't" short for?
Carol: Cannot.
Teacher: And what is "don't" short for?
Carol: Doughnut!

Show
What happened to the entertainer who did a show for an audience of cannibals?
He went down really well.

Shy
What did the shy pebble monster say?
I wish I was a little boulder.

What makes people shy?
Coconuts.

Sick
The transatlantic liner was experiencing particularly heavy weather, and Mrs Amberly wasn't feeling well. "Would you care for some more supper, ma'am?" asked the steward.
"No, thanks," replied the wretched passenger. "Just throw it overboard to save me the trouble."

What do you give a sick snake?
Asp-rin.

"Teacher reminds me of the sea," said Alec to Billy.
"You mean she's deep, sometimes calm, but occasionally stormy?"
"No! She makes me sick."

Why did the zombie go to hospital?
He wanted to learn a few sick jokes.

Did you hear about the sick ghost?
He had oooooo-ping cough.

Did you hear about the sick werewolf?
He lost his voice but it's howl right now.

Sign
A police officer was amazed to see a hiker walking along the road carrying a sign which read "To Seattle."
"What are you doing with that?" asked the police officer.
"I'm walking to Seattle," said the hiker, "and I don't want to lose my way."

Sign at a health food store:
Closed on account of sickness.

Sign at hairdresser's:
We curl up and dye for you.

Sign at composer's studio:
Out Chopin, Bach in a minuet.

Silver Shovel

What did they say about the
aristocratic monster?
That he was born with a silver
shovel in his mouth.

Sing

Why didn't the witch sing at the
concert?
Because she had a frog in her
throat.

Singer

At a concert, the boring singer with
the tuneless voice announced, "I
should now like to sing Over The
Hills and Far Away."
"Thank goodness for that,"
whispered someone in the
audience. "I thought he was going
to stay all evening."

When is a singer not a singer?
When he's a little hoarse.

Singing

What do you call singing insects?
Humbugs.

Why did the singing teacher have
such a high-pitched voice?
She had falsetto teeth.

Dan: Can you sing top C?
Sam: No, I sing low-sy!

Sister

Witch: Doctor, doctor, my sister
here keeps thinking she's invisible.
Doctor: Which sister?

Jim: My sister wants to be an actress.
Tim: Is she pretty?
Jim: Well, put it this way, she'd be perfect on radio.

※

Michael: It's hard for my sister to eat.
Maureen: Why?
Michael: She can't bear to stop talking.

※

My sister went on a crash diet.
Is that why she looks a wreck?"

Skate
What does a cannibal call a skateboarder?
Meals on wheels.

Skeletons
What happened when the ghosts went on strike?
A skeleton staff took over.

※

If a skeleton rings your doorbell is he a dead ringer?

※

How does a skeleton call his friends?
On a telebone.

How did the skeleton know it was going to rain?
He could feel it in his bones.

※

What do you call a skeleton that won't get up in the morning?
Lazy bones.

※

What do you call a skeleton snake?
A rattler.

※

Did you hear about the skeleton who couldn't jump out of the plane?
He had no guts.

※

Why wasn't the naughty skeleton afraid of the police?
Because he knew they couldn't pin anything on him.

※

What kind of plate does a skeleton eat off?
Bone china.

What did the old skeleton complain of?
Aching bones.

Skunk

What's black and white, stinks and hangs from a line?
A drip-dry skunk.

What do you get if you cross a skunk with a bee?
Something that stinks and stings.

What do you get if you cross a skunk and an owl?
A bird that smells but doesn't give a hoot!

What's wet, smells and goes ba-bump, ba-bump?
A skunk in the spin-drier.

Sky

Why is the air so clean and healthy on Halloween?
Because so many witches are sweeping the sky.

Two men were walking down the street when one turned to the other and said, "Look, there's a dead pigeon."
"Where? Where?" said his friend looking up at the sky.

Sled

Billy: I never had a sled when I was a kid. We were too poor.
Milly, feeling sorry for him: What a shame! What did you do when it snowed?
Billy: Slid down the hills on my cousin.

Sledgehammer

Why did the child take a sledgehammer to school?
It was the day they broke up.

Sleep

What knocks you out each night but doesn't harm you?
Sleep.

✳

First vampire: Are you a light sleeper?
Second vampire: No, I sleep in the dark.

✳

I'm not saying our teacher's fat, but every time he falls over he rocks himself to sleep trying to get back up.

✳

My dad is so short-sighted he can't get to sleep unless he counts elephants.

✳

Why is it not safe to doze on trains?
Because they run over sleepers.

Slippers

A doctor visited his patient in the hospital ward after the operation. "I've got some bad news – we amputated the wrong leg. Now the good news – the man in the next bed wants to buy your slippers."

Slug

Waiter, waiter! There's a slug in my dinner.
Don't worry, sir, there's no extra charge.

✳

What did the slug say as he slipped down the window very fast?
How slime flies!

✳

Waiter, waiter! There's a fly in my soup?
And what's the problem sir?
I ordered slug soup.

✳

How do you know your kitchen is filthy?
The slugs leave trails on the floor that read "Clean me."

✳

Waiter, waiter! There's a slug in my salad.
I'm sorry, sir, I didn't know you were a vegetarian.

✳

"What's the secret of living to be 100?" the reporter asked the old man.
"Slugs!" replied the centenarian.
"Slugs?"
"Yes! I've never eaten one in my entire life!"

Smell

Ding dong bell,
Pussy's down the well,
But we've put some disinfectant down
And don't mind about the smell.

❋

A man walked into a chemist shop and asked for a spray that filled a room with the smell of rotten eggs, stale socks and sour milk. "What on earth do you want something like that for?" asked the chemist.
"I've got to leave my flat this morning, and it states in the lease that I must leave it exactly as I found it!"

Smoking

What's the result of smoking too much?
Coffin.

❋

Snails

What do you do when two snails have a fight?
Leave them to slug it out.

How do snails get their shells all shiny?
They use snail polish.

❋

What gas do snails prefer?
Shell.

❋

Waiter, waiter! Do you serve snails.
Sit down, sir, we'll serve anyone.

❋

A snail starts a slow climb up the trunk of an apple tree. He is watched by a sparrow who can't help laughing and eventually says "Don't you know there aren't any apples on the tree yet?"
"Yes," said the snail, "but there will be by the time I get up there."

Snake

What do you get if you cross a
serpent and a trumpet?
A snake in the brass.

What's green and slimy and goes
hith?
A snake with a lisp.

What do you call a snake that is
trying to become a bird?
A feather boa.

What is a snake's favorite
dance?
Snake, rattle and roll.

What do you get if you cross a
snake with a pig?
A boar constrictor.

What did one snake say to
another?
Hiss off!

What did the snake say to the
cornered rat?
Hiss is the end of the line, buddy!"

What did one snake say when the
other snake asked him the time?
Don't asp me!

What would you get if you crossed
a new-born snake with a basket-
ball?
A bouncing baby boa.

There once was a snake named
Drake
Who started a fight with a rake
It cut off his tail
Drake went very pale
And that's the short end of my tale.

Doctor, doctor, I keep thinking I'm
a snake about to shed its skin.
Just slip into something more
comfortable.

Knock knock.
Who's there?
Snake.
Snake who?
Snake a run for it!

First person: I've just been bitten by
A snake on one arm.
Second person: Which one?
First person: I don't know, one
snake looks very much like the next
one.

Snoring

Wizard: Doctor, doctor, I snore so
loudly I keep myself awake!
Doctor: Sleep in another room
then.

Do men always snore?
No. Only when they're asleep.

Why didn't the banana snore?
'Cos it was afraid to wake up the
rest of the bunch.

Snowman

What do you get if you cross King
Kong with a
snowman?
Frostbite.

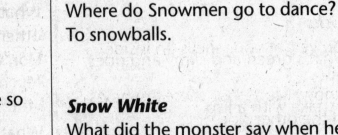

What do Snowmen call their
offspring?
Chill-dren.

Where do Snowmen go to dance?
To snowballs.

Snow White

What did the monster say when he
saw Snow White and the Seven
Dwarfs?
Yum, yum!

Soap

What do you get if you cross a
mouse with a packet of
soap powder?
Bubble and
Squeak.

Why did the stupid sailor grab a
bar of soap when his ship sank?
He thought he could wash himself
ashore.

How did your mom know you hadn't washed your face?
I forgot to wet the soap.

Socks

You've got your socks on inside out.
I know, Mom, but there are holes on the other side.

✳

Andy was late for school. "Andy!" roared his mother. "Have you got your socks on yet?"
"Yes, Mom," replied Andy. "All except one."

Soldiers

What do ghostly soldiers say to strangers?
Who ghost there?

✳

Which soldiers smell of salt and pepper?
Seasoned troopers.

Son

Was the carpenter's son a chip off the old block?

✳

Thought for the day: Where do fathers learn all the things they tell their sons not to do?

✳

Teacher: That's the stupidest boy in the whole school.
Mother: That's my son.
Teacher: Oh! I'm so sorry.
Mother: *You're* sorry?

Song

How do ghosts learn songs?
They read the sheet music.

✳

What song to snakes like to sing?
Viva Aspana.

✳

What song does a ghost sing to warn people that he's around?
Beware My Ghoulish Heart.

Soup

What sort of soup do skeletons like?
One with plenty of body in it.

✳

How do you make gold soup?
Put 14 carrots in it.

✳

Hey, Waiter, you've got your thumb in my bowl of soup!
Don't worry, sir, the soup isn't hot.

Mommy, Mommy, what's a vampire?
Be quiet, dear, and drink your soup before it clots.

Customer: Waiter, this soup tastes funny.
Waiter: So laugh, sir.

Space cadet
Why was Harold called the space cadet when he was at school?
Because he had a lot of space between his ears.

Spade
How do you stop a monster digging up your garden?
Take his spade away.

How do you confuse an idiot?
Give him two spades and ask him to take his pick.

Spaghetti
I'd say he was spineless.
Yes, about as spineless as cooked spaghetti.

Spain
In Spain they use a garotte. It's pretty g'rotty.

Spectacles
"No, no, no!" said the enraged businessman to the persistent salesman. "I cannot see you today!"
"That's fine," said the salesman, "I'm selling spectacles."

Doctor: You need spectacles.
Patient: How do you know?
Doctor: I could tell as soon as you walked through the window.

Spell
What happened to the naughty little witch at school?
She was ex-spelled.

Why did the witch keep turning people into Mickey Mouse?
She was having Disney spells.

What do you call a bee who's had a spell put on him?
Bee-witched.

Have you heard about the good-weather witch?
She's forecasting sunny spells.
Why aren't we getting any sun then?
Because she can't spell "sunny."

First Witch: I'm going to cast a spell and make myself beautiful. I'll have hundreds of men at my feet.
Second witch: Yes, chiropodists.

Knock knock.
Who's there?
Marie.
Marie who?
Marie me or I'll cast a spell on you.

Why was the student witch so bad at essays?
Because she couldn't spell properly.

Spelling

"Please, ma'am! How do you spell ichael?"
The teacher was rather bewildered.
"Don't you mean Michael?" she asked.
"No, ma'am. I've written the 'M' already."

School Doctor: Have you ever had trouble with appendicitis?
Naomi: Only when I tried to spell it.

How do you spell wrong?
R-o-n-g.
That's wrong.
That's what you asked for, isn't it?

First witch: Here's a banana if you can spell it.
Second witch: I can spell banana. I just don't know when to stop.

The young lad had applied for a job, and was asked his full name.
"Aloysius Montmorency Geoghan," he replied.
"How do you spell that?" asked the manager.
"Er – sir – er – can't you just put it down without spelling it?"

Knock knock.
Who's there?
Edwin.
Edwin who?
Edwin a spelling contest if I were a better witch.

※

What's the favorite subject of young witches at school?
Spelling.

Spiders

Little Miss Muffet
Sat on a tuffet
Eating a bowl of stew
Along came a spider
And sat down beside her.
Guess what? She ate him up too!

※

What did the spiders say to the fly?
We're getting married. Do you want to come to the webbing?

※

Why do spiders enjoy swimming?
They have webbed feet.

※

Why are spiders like tops?
They're always spinning.

※

Where do spiders go for fun?
To Webley.

What kind of doctors are spiders like?
Spin doctors.

※

What do you call a hundred spiders on a tyre?
A spinning wheel.

※

Two spiders were sitting on a web.
One of them said, "See that fly up there. He's never flown before."
The other one said, "What's that got to do with you?"
The first one said, "I'm trying to talk him down."

※

What did the "just married" spiders call their new home?
Newlywebs.

※

Waiter, waiter! There's a spider in my soup.
It's hardly deep enough to drown him sir.

Spirit

How do you get a ghost to lie perfectly flat?
You use a spirit level.

Sponge

What is full of holes but can hold water?
A sponge.

Spooks

What did the mother ghost say to the naughty baby ghost?
Spook when you're spooken to.

Did you hear about the little spook who couldn't sleep at night because his brother kept telling him human stories?

Did you hear about the spook who went on a high fiber diet?
He had beans on ghost twice a day.

Sport

What is a mosquito's favorite sport?
Skin-diving.

How many vampires can you fit into an empty sports stadium?
One – after that it's not empty.

Squash

What happened to the firefly who was squashed?
He was de-lighted.

What do monsters play when they are in the bus?
Squash.

Why did the vampire sit on a pumpkin?
It wanted to play squash.

What game do ants play with monsters?
Squash.

Squirrel

An old lady was considering buying a squirrel fur coat. "But will it be all right in the rain?" she asked anxiously. "Oh certainly, ma'am," said the manager smoothly. "After all, you've never seen a squirrel with an umbrella have you?"

311

Statue

Bertie: You remind me of a Greek statue.

Gertie: Do you mean you think I'm beautiful?

Bertie: Yes, beautiful, but not all there.

Steal

Why did the firefly keep stealing things?

He was light-fingered.

* * *

Mom and Dad are in the iron and steel business. She does the ironing and he does the stealing.

* * *

Why did you leave your last employment?

The boss accused me of stealing a ten dollar bill.

But why didn't you make him prove it?

He did.

* * *

I'm learning to steal pets – a cat burglar is teaching me how.

* * *

Two small-time thieves had been sent by the Big Boss to steal a van-load of goods from a bathroom suppliers. One stayed in the van as look-out and the other went into the storeroom. Fifteen minutes went by, then half an hour, then an hour – and no sign of him. The look-out finally grew impatient and went to look for his partner. Inside the store the two came face to face. "Where have you been?" demanded the worried look-out.

"The boss told me to take a bath, but I couldn't find the soap and a towel."

Stomach

Please Sir. There's something wrong with my stomach.

Well, button up your jacket and no one will notice.

* * *

Spook: Should you eat spiders and slugs and zombie slime on an empty stomach?

Witch: No, you should eat them on a plate.

* * *

Doctor, doctor, I've had stomach ache since I ate three crabs yesterday.
Did they smell bad when you took them out of their shells?
What do you mean "took them out of their shells?"

Stones

How do stones stop moths eating your clothes?
Because a rolling stone gathers no moths.

Stork

Why does a stork stand on one leg?
Because it would fall over if it lifted the other one.

Do you like my new baby sister?
The stork brought her.
Hmm, it looks as if the stork dropped her on her head.

Who brings monsters' babies?
Frankenstork.

Story

What do you call A Tale of Two Mosquitoes?
A bite-time story.

Teacher: I was going to read you a story called The Invasion of the Body Snatchers, but I've changed my mind.
Class: Oh why, ma'am?
Teacher: Because we might get carried away.

Who wrote Count Dracula's life story?
The ghost writer.

Igor: How was that science fiction movie you saw last night?
Dr Frankenstein: Oh, the same old story – boy meets girl, boy loses girl, boy builds new girl. . .

Did you hear the story of the three holes?
Well, well, well.

What's a giant's favorite tale?
A tall story.

String

What do you call a witch who is made of cotton and has lots of holes in her?
A string hag.

Skeleton: Doctor, doctor, I keep thinking I'm a yo-yo.
Doctor: Are you stringing me along?

How did the teacher forecast the weather with a piece of string?
She hung it up, and if it moved, she knew it was windy, and if it got wet, she knew it was raining.

Stupid

What did the stupid ghost do?
He used to climb over walls.

What do you call a stupid skeleton?
Bonehead.

Did you hear about the stupid wizard?
He couldn't remember if he used to be forgetful.

Did you hear about the stupid woodworm?
He was found in a brick.

What do stupid kids do at Halloween?
They carve a face on an apple and go bobbing for pumpkins.

A stupid glazier was examining a broken window. He looked at it for a while and then said, "It's worse than I thought. It's broken on both sides."

My friend is so stupid that he thinks twice before saying nothing.

Did you hear about the stupid photographer?
He saved burned-out lightbulbs for use in his darkroom.

Did you hear about the stupid monster who hurt himself while he was raking up leaves?
He fell out of a tree.

I don't know what it is that makes you stupid but whatever it is, it works.

The criminal mastermind found one of his gang sawing the legs off his bed. "What are you doing that for?" demanded the crook boss. "Only doing what you ordered," said the stupid thug. "You told me to lie low for a bit!"

Sty

What do you call a multistory pig-pen?
A styscraper.

What's pink, lives in a sty and drinks blood?
A hampire.

Submarines

Did you hear about the sailor that was discharged from the submarine service?
He was caught sleeping with the windows open.

Suicide

Did you hear about the cannibal who commited suicide?
He got himself into a real stew.

Witch: I'd like a new frog, please.
Pet Shop Assistant: But you bought one only yesterday. What happened?
Witch: It Kermit-ted suicide.

Sun

What do you do with a green monster?
Put it in the sun until it ripens!

What happened to the tailor who made his pants from sun-blind material?
Every time the sun came out, the pants rolled down.

Sunglasses

Why is a man wearing sunglasses like a rotten teacher?
Because he keeps his pupils in the dark.

Superstitions

Are you superstitious?
No. Then lend me $13.

Survival

How do you survive the electric chair?
Insulate your underpants.

Fatty: You look as if you've survived a famine – but only just.
Thinny: And you look as if you've caused one.

Swallow

What is the cannibals' favorite game?
Swallow my Leader.

What happened to the cannibal lion?
He had to swallow his pride.

What happened to the skeleton who was swallowed by a big fish?
He had a whale of a time.

What should you do if you swallow a lightbulb?
Spit it out and be delighted!

Doctor, doctor, my son's just swallowed some gunpowder!
Well, don't point him at me.

Swedes

Did you hear about the cannibal who went vegetarian?
He couldn't stop eating swedes.

Swim

Waiter, waiter! There's a dead fly swimming in my soup.
Nonsense sir, dead flies can't swim.

A man in a swimming pool was on the very top diving-board. He poised, lifted his arms, and was about to dive when the attendant came running up, shouting, "Don't dive – there's no water in that pool!"
"That's all right," said the man. "I can't swim!"

Boy: Mom, why can't I swim in Loch Ness?
Mother: Because there are monsters in it.
Boy: But Daddy's swimming there.
Mother: That's different. He's insured.

Why do you keep doing the backstroke?
I've just had lunch and don't want to swim on a full stomach.

⁂

Did you hear about the slow swimmer?
He could only do the crawl.

⁂

Jack: Dad, there's a man at the door collecting for a new swimming pool.
Father: Give him a bucket of water.

Sword
Why was the sword-swallowing monster put in prison?
He coughed and killed two people.

⁂

Did you hear about the sword swallower who swallowed an umbrella?
He wanted to put something away for a rainy day.

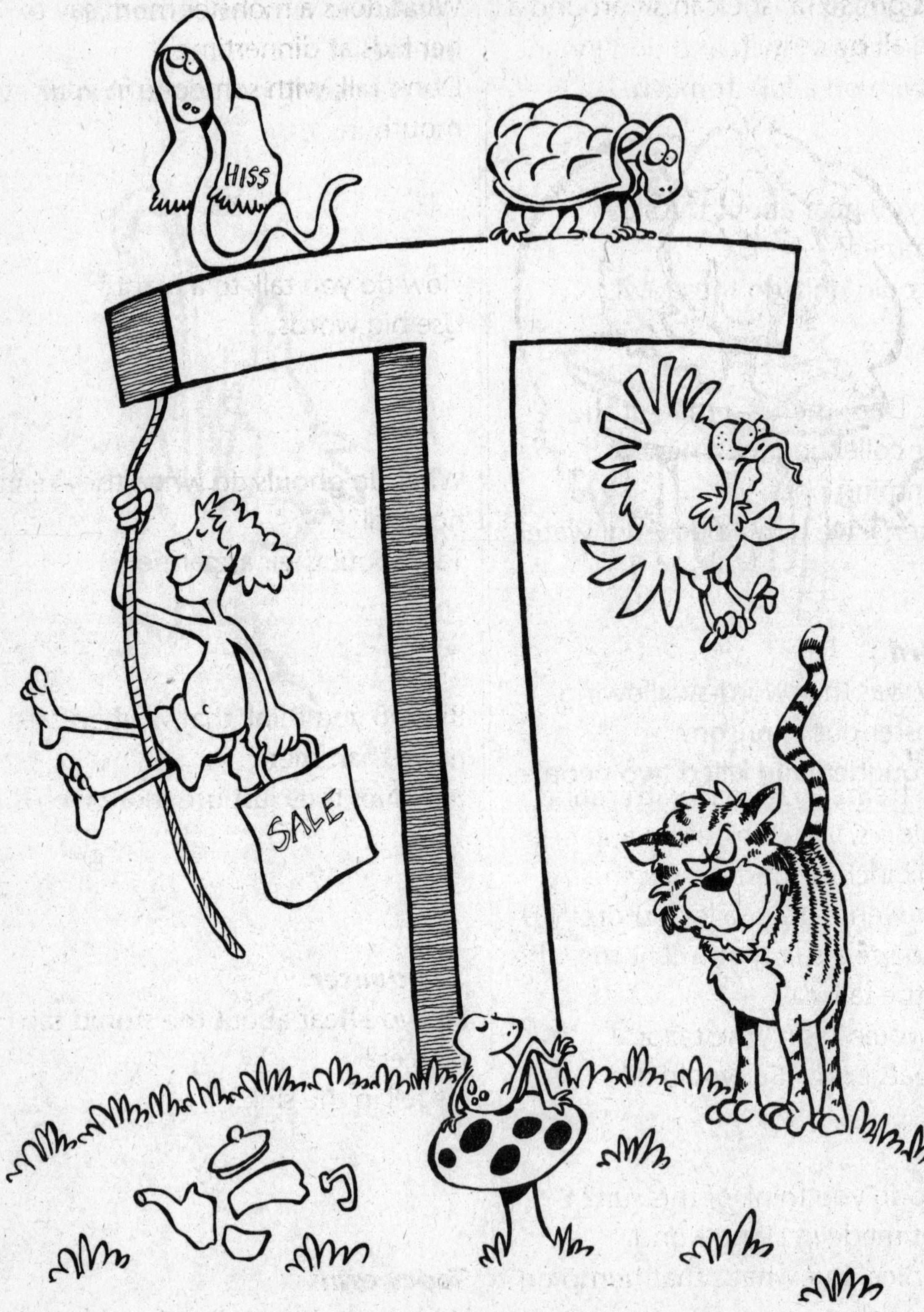
HISS
SALE

Table

She's got so fat she can sit around a table all by herself.

Tailor

An extremely tall man with round shoulders, very long arms and one leg six inches shorter than the other went into a tailor's shop. "I'd like to see a suit that will fit me," he told the tailor.

"So would I, sir," the tailor sympathized. "So would I."

What do you think of this suit? I had it made in Hong Kong.
Very nice, but what's that hump on the back?
Oh, that's the tailor. He's still working on it.

Talk

What does a monster mom say to her kids at dinnertime?
Don't talk with someone in your mouth.

How do you talk to a giant?
Use big words.

What do ghouls do when they're in hospital?
Talk about their apparitions.

Bill: Do you think that women talk more than men?
Ben: No, they just use more words.

Tap dancer

Did you hear about the stupid tap dancer?
He fell in the sink.

Tapeworms

What creepie crawlies do athletes break?
Tapeworms.

Tarzan

Where does Tarzan buy his clothes?
At a Jungle Sale.

Tax

Doctor, doctor, I keep thinking I'm an adder.
Oh good, could you help me with my tax return?

Tea

John: Do you feel like a cup of tea?
Don: Oh, yes.
John: You look like one, too – sloppy, hot and wet!

Knock knock.
Who's there?
Army Ant.
Army Ant who?
Army Ants coming for tea then?

✳

Doctor, doctor! Every time I drink a cup of tea I get a sharp pain in by nose.
Have you tried taking the spoon out of the cup?

Teacher

Knock, knock.
Who's there?
Teacher.
Teacher who?
Teacher-self French.

✳

Confucius he say: If teacher ask you question and you not know answer, mumble.

✳

Did you hear about the cross-eyed teacher who had no control over her pupils?

✳

Did you hear about the teacher who married the dairy maid?
It didn't last. They were like chalk and cheese.

✳

Why did the soccer teacher give his team lighters?
Because they kept losing all their matches.

It was sweltering hot outside. The teacher came into the classroom wiping his brow and said, "Ninety-two today. Ninety-two."
"Happy birthday to you. Happy birthday to you . . ." sang the class.

Carol: Our teacher gives me the pip.
Darryl: What's her name?
Carol: Miss Lemmon.

What do you call a teacher floating on a raft in the sea?
Bob.

What's your handicrafts teacher like?
She's a sew and sew.

What do you get if you cross your least favorite teacher with a telescope?
A horrorscope.

Ben's teacher regards Ben as a wonder child. He wonders whether he'll ever learn anything.

Mother: Why do you call your teacher "Treasure"?
Girl: Because we wonder where she was dug up.

"Do you know," said the teacher to one of her pupils who had BO, "that we call you the wonder child in the staffroom?"
"Why's that, ma'am?"
"Because we all wonder when you're going to wash!"

Teapot
Helen: Mom, do you know what I'm going to give you for your birthday?
Mom: No, dear, what?
Helen: A nice teapot.
Mom: But I've got a nice teapot.
Helen: No you haven't. I've just dropped it!

Teenager

"Very well, my boy," said the manager, "I'll hire you. I take it you're not afraid of early hours?"
"Oh, no, sir," said the teenage applicant, "you can't close too early for me!"

Teeth

Why didn't the monster use toothpaste?
Because he said his teeth weren't loose.

What did the Abominable Snowman do after he had had his teeth pulled out?
He ate the dentist.

Why was the man arrested for looking at sets of dentures in a dentist's window?
Because it was against the law to pick your teeth in public.

What did one tooth say to the other?
Get your cap on, the dentist is taking us out tonight.

Why does a vampire clean his teeth three times a day?
To prevent bat breath.

Why did the vampire give up acting?
He couldn't find a part he could get his teeth into.

Why do you forget a tooth, as soon as the dentist pulls it out?
Because it goes right out of your head.

What's the best thing to put into a pizza?
Your teeth.

Patient: Tell me honestly, how am I?
Dentist: Your teeth are fine, but your gums will have to come out.

What sort of an act do you do? I bend over backwards and pick up a handkerchief with my teeth.
Anything else?
Then I bend over backwards and pick up my teeth.

"Your teeth are like the stars," he said,
As he pressed her hand, so white.
He spoke the truth, for, like the stars,
Her teeth came out at night!

Television

What is the safest way to see a witch?
On television.

How did the ghost song-and-dance act make a living?
By appearing in television spooktaculars.

Doctor, I keep stealing things. What can I do?
Try to resist the temptation, but if you can't, get me a new television.

I can't understand the critics saying that only an idiot would like that television program. I really enjoyed it.

Daughter: What's on television tonight, Mom?
Mother: Same as always – a vase of flowers and a bowl of fruit.

Thank you

Werewolf: Doctor, doctor, thank you so much for curing me.
Doctor: So you don't think you're a werewolf anymore?
Werewolf: Absolutely not, I'm quite clear now – see my nose is nice and cold.

"Did you thank Mrs Pillbeam for teaching you today?" Alec's mom asked him when he came home from school.
"No, I didn't. Mary in front of me did and Mrs Pillbeam said 'Don't mention it' so I didn't."

What did Frankenstein's monster say when he was struck by lightning?
Thanks, I needed that.

Theater

What do ghosts see at the theater?
A phantomime.

※

Where does a werewolf sit in the theater?
Anywhere he wants to!

※

The box-office clerk at the theater went to the manager's office to tell him that there were two horses in the foyer. "Two horses?" exclaimed the manager in surprise. "What on earth do they want?"
"Two stalls for Monday night."

※

What happens if a big hairy monster sits in front of you at the movie theater?
You miss most of the film.

Three

Statistics say that one in three people is mentally ill. So check your friends and if two of them seem okay, you're the one.

※

What always starts with a tie?
A three-legged race.

※

Doctor, doctor, I can't stand being three feet tall any longer.
Then you'll just have to learn to be a little patient.

Throw

How do you stop a werewolf chasing you?
Throw a stick and shout "Fetch!"

Thunder

What happens when a band plays in a thunderstorm?
The conductor gets hit by lightning.

Tickle

How can you tell which end of a worm is its head?
Tickle its middle and see which end smiles.

※

How do you make a skeleton laugh?
Tickle his funny bone.

※

Ticks

What kind of insects live on the moon?
Lunar ticks.

What happened when the werewolf swallowed a clock?
He got ticks.

Tiger

Who went into the tiger's den and came out alive?
The tiger.

What did the stupid ghost call his pet tiger?
Spot.

Have you ever seen a man-eating tiger?
No, but in the cafe next door I once saw a man eating chicken!

Tiles

What kind of tiles can't you stick on the wall?
Rep-tiles.

Time

Knock, knock.
Who's there?
Fanny.
Fanny who?
Fanny the way you keep saying "Who's there?" every time I knock!

What did the Loch Ness Monster say to his friend?
Long time no sea.

How can you tell when witches are carrying a time bomb?
You can hear their brooms tick!

What time is it when you sit on a pin?
Spring time.

What did the clean dog say to the insect?
Long time no flea!

That boy is so dirty, the only time he washes his ears is when he eats watermelon.

What time is it when a monster sits on your car?
Time to get a new car.

If twenty dogs run after one dog, what time is it?
Twenty after one.

Tin
Why is a child learning to sing like someone opening a tin of sardines? Because they both have trouble with the key.

Tires
How did the witch feel when she got run over by a car?
Tired.

Toad
A workman had just finished laying a carpet in a witch's house when he realized he had lost his sandwiches. Looking round he saw a lump under the carpet. Not wanting to pull the carpet up again he just got a big plank of wood and smashed the lump flat. Then the witch came into the room with a cup of tea for him. "Here's your tea," she said. "My, you've laid the carpet well. Just one thing, though, have you seen my pet toad anywhere?"

What did the witch say to the ugly toad?
I'd put a curse on you – but somebody beat me to it!

Toadstool
How do you know when your garbage can is full of toadstools. Because there isn't mushroom inside.

What do frogs sit on?
Toadstools.

Toaster
What did the toaster say to the bread?
Pop up and see me some time.

Toffee
What's the difference between a schoolteacher and a train driver?
A schoolteacher says, "Spit out that toffee" and a train says, "Choo, choo."

Tomato
What is a vampire's favorite soup?
Scream of tomato.

Mommy, Mommy what's a vampire?
Shut up and drink your tomato juice before it clots.

Tomorrow
How do you keep a wizard in suspense?
I'll tell you tomorrow. . .

Cannibal Boy: I've brought a friend home for dinner.
Cannibal Mom: Put him in the fridge and we'll have him tomorrow.

Waiter, waiter! I don't like the flies in here.
Well, come back tomorrow, we'll have new ones by then!

Tongue
My girlfriend talks so much that when she goes on holiday, she has to spread suntan lotion on her tongue.

First Monster: I'm so thirsty my tongue's hanging out.
Second Monster: Oh, I thought that was your necktie!

They say she has a sharp tongue.
Yes, she can slice bread with it.

Tonsils

A mother monster marched her naughty little monster into the doctor's surgery. "Is it possible that he could have taken his own tonsils out?" she asked.
"No," said the doctor.
"I told you so," said the mother monster. "Now, put them back."

Tooth

Why did the termite eat a sofa and two chairs?
It had a suite tooth.

What comes out at night and goes Munch, munch, ouch!
A vampire with a rotten tooth.

As the judge said to the dentist: Do you swear to pull the tooth, the whole tooth, and nothing but the tooth?

Toothache

What's the difference between a vampire with toothache and a rainstorm?
One roars with pain and the other pours with rain.

Toothbrush

What do you get it you cross a porcupine with a giraffe?
A long-necked toothbrush.

Tornado

What is a tornado?
Mother Nature doing the twist.

Tortoise

The psychiatrist was surprised to see a tortoise come into his office.
"What can I do for you, Mr Tortoise?" asked the psychiatrist.
"I'm terribly shy, doctor," said the tortoise. "I want you to cure me of that."
"No problem.
I'll soon have you out of your shell."

A family of tortoises went into a cafe for some ice-cream. They sat down and were about to start when Father Tortoise said, "I think it's going to rain. Junior, will you pop home and fetch my umbrella?" So off went Junior for Father's umbrella, but three days later he still hadn't returned. "I think, dear," said Mother Tortoise to Father Tortoise, "that we had better eat Junior's ice cream before it melts." And a voice from the door said, "If you do that I won't go."

Touch

Knock knock.
Who's there?
Roach.
Roach who?
Roach out and touch somebody.

Towel

What do snakes have on their bath towels?
Hiss and Hers.

Tower of London

If King Kong came to England why would he live in the Tower of London?
Because he's a beef-eater.

Town

Knock knock.
Who's there?
Ghost.
Ghost who?
Ghost town.

Knock knock.
Who's there?
Ghent.
Ghent who?
Ghent out of town.

What is a ghost's favorite Wild West town?
Tombstone.

Toy
Only a week after Christmas an irate mom stormed into the toy shop. "I'm bringing back this unbreakable toy fire-engine," she said to the man behind the counter. "It's useless!"
"Surely your son hasn't broken it already?" he asked.
"No, he's broken all his other toys with it."

Train
What did the monster say when he saw a rush-hour train full of passengers?
Oh good! A chew-chew train!

What is evil and ugly and goes at 125 mph?
A witch in a high-speed train.

Where do ghost trains stop?
At devil crossings.

Why do you have to wait so long for a ghost train to come along?
They only run a skeleton service.

Monster: I've got to walk 25 miles home.
Ghost: Why don't you take a train.
Monster: I did once, but my mother made me give it back.

Did you hear about the boy who had to do a project on trains?
He had to keep track of everything!

Trampoline
Mrs Jones: Well, Billy, how are you getting along with the trampolining in PE?
Billy: Oh, up and down, you know.

Travel
How do toads travel?
By hoppercraft.

What does a witch get if she's a poor traveler?
Broom sick.

What steps should you take if you see a dangerous yeti on your travels?
Very large ones.

※

Mrs Broadbeam: Now, remember, children, travel is very good for you. It broadens the mind.
Sarah, muttering: If you're anything to go by, that's not all it broadens!

※

What people travel the most?
Romans.

Tree
Teacher: Mason, what is the outer part of a tree called?
Mason: Don't know, sir.
Teacher: Bark, boy, bark!
Mason: Woof-woof!

Tricks
When do ghosts play tricks on each other?
On April Ghoul's Day

※

Why don't ghosts make good magicians.
You can see right through their tricks.

Trifle
A monster went shopping with sponge-fingers in one ear and jelly and custard in the other. "Why have you got jelly and custard sponge in your ears?" asked the sales girl.
"You'll have to speak up," said the monster. "I'm a trifle deaf."

Trumpet
Eddy's father called up to him, "Eddy, if you don't stop playing that trumpet I think I'll go crazy."
"I think you are already," replied Eddy. "I stopped playing half an hour ago."

※

With whom does an elastic trumpet player play?
With a rubber band.

Why did Ken keep his trumpet in the fridge?
Because he liked cool music.

Turkey

Why is a turkey like an evil little creature?
'Cos it's always a-gobblin'. . .

Twins

What happens if you see twin witches?
You won't be able to tell witch witch is witch.

Did you hear about the Tyrannosaurus monster twins?
They were both called Rex.

Teacher: What is the plural of mouse?
Infant: Mice.
Teacher: And what is the plural of baby?
Infant: Twins.

Typing

Typing teacher: Bob! Your work has certainly improved. There are only ten mistakes here.
Bob: Oh good!
Teacher: Now let's look at the second line, shall we?

What type of people do vampires like?
O positive people.

What kind of typewriters do vampires like?
Blood type-writers.

George is the type of boy that his mother doesn't want him to associate with!

The pupils in the 12th grade, who had learned to type, were being interviewed by prospective employers. Lisa was asked her typing speed. "I'm not sure," she replied. "But I can delete at 50 words a minute."

UNIVERSE
THIS
WAY

Udder

What happened when the ghostly cows got out of their field?
There was udder chaos.

What do you call a huge, ugly, slobbering, furry monster with cotton wool in his ears?
Anything you like – he can't hear you.

Ugly

First Witch: I'm not ugly. I could marry anyone I pleased!
Second Witch: But that's the problem – you don't please anyone.

Teddie: What's that terribly ugly thing on your shoulders?
Neddie: Help! What is it?
Teddie: Your head!

She's so ugly that when a wasp stings her it shuts its eyes.

Umbrella

What do you call a skeleton who goes out in the snow and rain without a coat or an umbrella?
A numbskull.

Umpire

If you have a referee in football, and an umpire in tennis, what do you have in bowls?
Goldfish.

Uncle

Did you hear about the cannibal spider that ate his uncle's wife?
He was an aunt-eater.

✳

My uncle spent a fortune on deodorants before he found out that people didn't like him anyway.

✳

My uncle's got a wooden leg.
That's nothing. My auntie has a wooden chest.

Under

Why are skeletons so calm?
Nothing gets under their skin.

✳

Did you hear about the boy who sat under a cow?
He got a pat on the head.

✳

I reckon Mom must be at least 30 years old – I counted the rings under her eyes.

How do you milk a mouse?
You can't – the bucket won't fit under it.

Undercover
A boy went to a Halloween party with a sheet over his head. "Are you here as a ghost?" asked his friends.
"No," he replied, "I'm an unmade bed."
Another boy wore a sheet over his head. "Are you an unmade bed?" asked his friends.
"No, I'm an undercover agent," he replied.

Understand
What bee can never be understood?
A momble-bee.

Anyone who isn't confused here doesn't really understand what's going on.

Underpants

How do you survive the electric chair?
Insulate your underpants.

Undertaker

Patient: Doctor, doctor, I feel terrible. I can hardly breathe, I can't walk, I keep having palpitations and my skin is covered in nasty blotches.
Doctor: Oh dear.
Patient: Are you writing me a prescription?
Doctor: No, a note for the undertaker.

How do undertakers speak?
Gravely

Do undertakers enjoy their job?
Of corpse they do.

Why did the undertaker chop all his corpses into little bits?
Because he liked them to rest in pieces.

What did the undertaker say to his girlfriend?
Em-balmy about you.

Underwater

Who was the first underwater spy?
James Pond.

What insect can fly underwater?
A bluebottle in a submarine

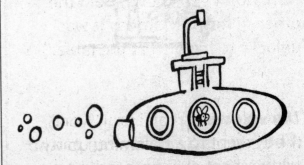

Universe

The monster from outer space decided to go on a trip around the universe, so he went to the rocket office to book a ticket to the moon. "Sorry, sir," said the attendant, "the moon is full at the moment."

Unlucky

Two schoolboys were talking about their math lessons. "Why do you suppose we stop the tables at 12?" asked one.
"Oh, don't you know?" said the other. "I heard Mom say it was unlucky to have 13 at the table."

The unluckiest man in the world: the deep sea diver coming up who met his ship going down.

Unpopular

Why was the moth so unpopular? He kept picking holes in everything.

Why is Dracula so unpopular? 'Cos he's a pain in the neck.

Up and Down

First Trampolinist: How's life?
Second Trampolinist: Oh, up and down, you know.

Useful
What kind of snake is useful on
your windscreen?
A viper.

Vacuum cleaner

Teacher: Barbara, name three collective nouns.

Barbara: The wastepaper basket, the garbage can and the vacuum cleaner.

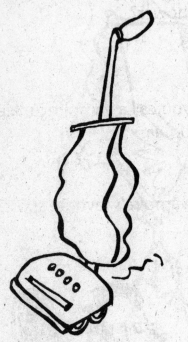

Vampire

What happened to the two mad vampires?
They both went a little batty.

✳

What do vampires cross the sea in?
Blood vessels.

✳

What do vampire footballers have at half-time?
Blood oranges.

✳

Why did the vampire take up acting?
It was in his blood.

✳

Who plays center forward for the vampire football team?
The ghoulscorer.

✳

Which vampire ate the three bears' porridge?
Ghouldilocks.

✳

Which vampire tried to eat James Bond?
Ghouldfinger.

✳

When do vampires bite you?
On Wincedays.

✳

Why did the vampire enjoy ballroom dancing?
He could really get into the vaultz.

✳

What is the first thing that vampires learn at school?
The alphabat.

✳

1st vampire: How things?
2nd vampire: Terrible! Today I received a letter saying I'm overdrawn by 50 pints at the blood bank.

Why is Hollywood full of vampires?
They need someone to play the bit parts.

Why wouldn't the vampire eat his soup?
It clotted.

What's a vampire's favorite animal?
A giraffe.

Why was the young vampire a failure?
Because he fainted at the sight of blood.

What is the vampire's favorite slogan?
Please Give Blood Generously.

How does a vampire clean his house?
With a victim cleaner.

What does a vampire stand on after taking a shower?
A bat mat.

What do you call a vampire junkie?
Count Drugula.

What is a vampire's favorite sport?
Batminton.

Why do vampires hate arguments?
Because they make themselves cross.

✳

The Vampire's Victim – by E. Drew Blood

✳

I Saw a Vampire – by Ron Fast

✳

Escape from the Vampire – by Jess N. Time

✳

Did you hear about the vampire who died of a broken heart?
He had loved in vein.

✳

Knock knock.
Who's there?
Jamie.
Jamie who?
Jamie'n you're a vampire?

✳

Knock knock.
Who's there?
Twyla.
Twyla who?
Twylight is when the vampires and ghoulies come out to play.

✳

Did you hear about the vampire who got married?
He proposed to his girl-fiend.

✳

Knock knock.
Who's there?
Neil.
Neil who?
Neil down before the vampire king!

✳

Two men were having a drink together. One said, "I'd rather live with a vampire than with my wife." "Why's that?" asked the other. "Because she's always trying to bite my head off," he replied.

✳

Why did the vampire have pedestrian eyes?
They looked both ways before they crossed.

✳

What do you call a vampire after it is one-year-old?
A two-year-old vampire.

✳

Why was the vampire thought of as simple-minded?
Because he was a complete sucker.

✳

What's a vampire's favorite hobby?
In-grave-ing.

What do vampires gamble with?
Stake money.

Varnish

Jill: How awful that your Aunt drowned in a tub of varnish.
Jack: Yes, but what a finish.

Vase

Mom, you know that vase that's been handed down from generation to generation?
Yes.
Well, this generation's dropped it.

Vast

What do sailors say when they see a fat person on a ship?
A vast behind!

Vegetable

What vegetable needs a plumber?
A leek.

What's a fresh vegetable?
One that insults a farmer.

What is a skeleton's favorite vegetable?
Marrow.

Vegetarian

What does a vegetarian earn?
Celery.

Why did the cannibal go on a vegetarian diet?
He went off people.

Venetian

How do you make a Venetian blind?
Poke him in the eye.

Ventriloquist

Suresh: Whatever will Clive do when he leaves school? I can't see him being bright enough to get a job.
Sandra: He could always be a ventriloquist's dummy.

Vet

Doctor, doctor, I keep thinking I'm a canary.
I can't tweet you, go and see a vet.

Vicar

Did you hear about the vicar who turned up at the wrong funeral?
He made a grave mistake.

Victim

A cannibal chief was just about to stew his latest victim for dinner when the man protested, "You can't eat me – I'm the manager!"
"Well," said the cannibal, "soon you'll be a manager in chief."

Knock knock.
Who's there?
Vic.
Vic who?
Victim of a vampire.

※

Knock knock.
Who's there?
Jerome.
Jerome who?
Jerome alone through the woods looking for victims?

※

What does Dracula say to his victims?
It's been nice gnawing you.

※

Knock knock.
Who's there?
Rome.
Rome who?
Roming around looking for victims.

※

What eats its victims two by two?
Noah's Shark.

Video

John kept pestering his parents to buy a video, but they said they couldn't afford one. So one day John came home clutching a package containing a brand-new video. "Wherever did you get the money to pay for that?" asked his father suspiciously.
"It's all right, Dad," replied John, "I traded the TV in for it."

Vikings

How did the Vikings communicate with one another?
By Norse code.

DOT-DOT-DASH

Village

Knock knock.
Who's there?
Aida.
Aida who?
Aida whole village 'cos I'm a monster.

Villain

How did the villain try to get out of being hanged?
He said he never wore a necktie.

Why was the villain on the gallows smiling?
He was knot-happy.

Vinegar

What do you call a witch's cat that drinks vinegar?
A sour puss.

Violin

Music Student: Did you really learn to play the violin in six easy lessons?
Music Teacher: Yes, but the 500 that followed were pretty difficult.

A little monster was learning to play the violin. "I'm good, aren't I?" he asked his big brother.
"You should be on the radio," said the brother.
"You think I'm that good?"
"No, I think you're terrible, but at least if you were on the radio, I could switch you off."

What sort of violin does a ghost play?
A dreadivarius.

✳

What were the Chicago gangster's last words?
Who put that violin in my violin case?

My brother's been practicing the violin for ten years.
Is he any good?
No. It was nine years before he found out he wasn't supposed to blow out.

✳

Stephen, it's time for your violin lesson.
Oh, fiddle!

Viper
Why did the viper want to become a python?
He got the coiling.

✳

Which snakes are found on cars?
Windscreen vipers.

✳

Knock knock.
Who's there?
Viper.
Viper who?
Viper your nose!

Virus
What did one virus say to another?
Stay away, I think I've got penicillin.

Vitamin
Which bee is good for your health?
Vitamin bee.

Vulture
Why don't vultures fly south in the winter?
Because they can't afford the air fare.

✳

Why did the vulture cross the road?
For a fowl reason.

Where do the toughest vultures come from?
Hard-boiled eggs.

What do you call a vulture with no beak?
A head-banger.

Why couldn't the vulture talk to the dove?
Because he didn't speak pigeon English.

How do we know vultures are religious?
Because they're birds of prey.

What do a vulture, a pelican and a taxman have in common?
Big bills!

How can she be so fat? She eats like a bird!
Yes, a vulture!

Wait

What do you do if you find a black mamba in your toilet?
Wait until he's finished.

※

What do bees do if they want to use public transport?
Wait at a buzz stop.

※

What should you do if a zombie borrows your comic?
Wait for him to give it back.

Waiter

Waiter, waiter! There's a dead spider in my soup.
Yes, ma'am, they can't stand the boiling water.

※

Waiter, waiter! There's a spider in my soup. Send for the manager!
It's no good, sir, he's frightened of them, too.

※

Waiter, waiter! What's this creepy crawly thing doing in my dinner?
Oh, that one – he comes here every night.

※

Why do waiters prefer monsters to flies?
Have you ever heard anyone complaining of a monster in their soup?

※

What will a monster eat in a restaurant?
The waiter.

※

Waiter, waiter! What's this fly doing in my soup?
The butterfly stroke by the look of it sir.

Waiter, waiter, there's a bird in my soup.
That's all right, sir. It's bird-nest soup.

Waitress
What's the best way to see flying saucers?
Pinch the waitress.

Walk
Knock, knock.
Who's there?
Gopher.
Gopher who?
Gopher a walk over the cliff.

How did the octopus lovers walk down the road?
Arm in arm in arm in arm in arm in arm in arm in arm.

Why did the monster walk over the hill?
It was too much trouble to walk under it.

Wall
"The walls in my apartment are very thin," a young girl complained to her friend.
"You mean you can hear everything that's going on next door?"
"Not just that: when they peel onions I start to cry!"

Wallet
Gordon: My wallet's full of big bills.
Graham: All unpaid, I expect.

War

Why did the python go to war?
He was coiled up.

Wart

What do you say if you meet a toad?
Wart's new?

How do man-eating monsters count to a thousand?
On their warts.

❋

What do you get if you cross a galaxy with a toad?
Star Warts.

Wash

What does a black mamba do in the bathroom?
Tries to wash his hands.

❋

Teacher: What's the difference between a buffalo and a bison?
Student: You can't wash your hands in a buffalo, sir.

Wasps

Where do you take a sick wasp?
To waspital.

❋

What is the wasps' favorite song?
Just a Spoonful of Sugar.

❋

What did the bee say to the wasp who he tried to make honey?
Don't wasp your time!

❋

Waiter, waiter! There's a wasp in my dessert.
So that's where they go to in the winter.

❋

Wasps – while everyone runs a mile when they see one, why does it take hours for them to work out how to get out of a room, even after you've opened the window that they're standing on?

Watch

I got a gold watch for my girlfriend.
I wish I could make a trade like that!

Watchdog

What do you get if you cross King Kong with a watchdog?
A terrified mailman.

☀

Why does the Hound of the Baskervilles turn round and round before he lies down for the night?
Because he's the watchdog and he has to wind himself up.

Water

Sign in a cafe: All drinking water in this establishment has been personally passed by the management.

☀

Son: Dad kept asking for glasses of water when he was in hospital.
Daughter: I expect that's how they knew he was going out of his mind.

Water-polo

Did you hear about the stupid water-polo player?
His horse drowned . . .

Weatherman

Why don't cannibals eat weathermen?
Because they give them wind.

Wedding

At a very classy wedding, one of the guests broke wind. The bridegroom was furious and rounded on the guilty party. "How dare you break wind in front of my wife?" he roared.
"Sorry," said the guest. "Was it her turn?"

☀

What happened at the cannibal's wedding party?
They toasted the bride and groom.

✹

Two men were remembering their wedding days. "It was dreadful," said Albert. "I got the most terrible fright."
"What happened?" asked Algie.
"I married her," replied Albert.

Week
Which day of the week do ghosts like best?
Moandays.

✹

How many days of the week start with the letter T?
Four: Tuesday, Thursday, today and tomorrow.

Weight
How do witches lose weight?
They join weight witches.

✹

He's watching his weight.
Yes, watching it go up!

✹

I wouldn't say our English teacher is fat, but when she got on a Speak Your Weight machine it surrendered.

Well
Witch: Doctor, doctor, I don't feel well.
Doctor: Don't worry, you'll just have to go to bed for a spell.

✹

Why do demons get on so well with ghouls?
Because demons are a ghoul's best friend.

Werewolf
Who are some of the werewolves cousins?
The whatwolves and the whenwolves

✹

What do you get if you cross a werewolf with a hyena?
I don't know, but if it laughs I'll join in.

✹

What happened to the werewolf who ate garlic?
His bark was worse than his bite.

※

Where does a werewolf sit in the theater?
Anywhere he wants to!.

※

What do you call a werewolf who drinks too much?
A whino.

※

The Bad-Tempered Werewolf – by Claudia Armoff

※

How I Became a Werewolf – by Olive Alone

※

Why did the boy take an aspirin after hearing a werewolf howl?
Because it gave him an eerie ache.

※

Why shouldn't you grab a werewolf by its tail?
It might be the werewolf's tail but it could be the end of you.

※

I used to be a werewolf but I'm all right nooooooooooooooooooow!

※

Why are werewolves thought of as quick-witted?
Because they always give snappy answers.

※

First Werewolf: Nerg.
Second Werewolf: Nerg, nerg, yug.
First Werewolf: Don't start changing the subject.

Wet
Who was wet and slippery and invaded England?
William the Conger.

※

What is wet and slippery and likes Latin American music?
A conga eel.

※

Why were the ghosts wet and tired?
They had just dread-ged the lake.

Whale
How do you weigh a whale?
On Whale Weigh Scales.

※

Which ghost sailed the seven seas looking for rubbish and blubber?
The ghost of BinBag the Whaler.

Whistle
Why do bees buzz?
They can't whistle.

What is green and sooty and whistles when it rubs its back legs together?
Chimney Cricket.

White
That girl looks like Helen Black.
She looks even worse in white.

Whole
Teacher, in pet shop: I'd like to buy a hamster, please. How much do they cost?
Pet shop owner: $10 apiece.
Teacher, horrified: How much does a whole one cost?

Mother: I told you not to eat cake before supper.
Daughter: But Mom, it's part of my homework. "If you take an eighth of a cake from a whole cake, how much is left?"

Wife
What did the executioner say to his wife?
Only thirty chopping days to Christmas.

First cannibal: My wife's a tough old bird.
Second cannibal: You should have left her in the oven for another half an hour.

First man: My wife eats like a bird.
Second man: You mean she hardly
eats a thing?
First man: No, she eats slugs and
worms.

❋

Me and the Wife – by Ian Shee

❋

My wife has a slight impediment in
her speech. Every so often, she has
to stop to breathe.

❋

A monster walked into a shop
selling dress fabrics and said, "I'd
like 6 meters of pink satan for my
wife."
"It's satin, sir, not satan," said
assistant. "Satan is something that
looks like the devil."
"Oh," said the monster, "you know
my wife?"

❋

A man who forgets his wife's
birthday is certain to get
something to remember her by.

❋

I'm suffering from bad breath
You should do something about it!
I did. I just sent my wife to the
dentist.

❋

Mr Brown: I hate to tell you, but
your wife just fell in the wishing
well.
Mr Smith: So it works!

Wig
What kind of wig can hear?
An earwig.

❋

Witch: Officer you must help. I've
just lost my wig.
Police officer: Certainly, ma'am,
we'll comb the area.

Wiggly
What's yellow, wiggly and
dangerous?
A maggot with a
bad attitude.

Wind
Knock knock.
Who's there?
Augusta.
Augusta who?
Augusta wind will blow the witch
away.

❋

Trees are planted to stop the wind. A hickory can break wind at 40 meters.

Window

Doctor, doctor, I keep thinking I'm a moth.
So why did you come to see me?
Well, I saw the light in the window . . .

✳

Bill: Did you hear about the stupid window cleaner who put a sign at the top of his ladder?
Ben: What did the sign say?
Bill: Stop.

WHO MOVED MY SIGN?

Who broke the window?
It was Andrew, Dad. He ducked when I threw a stone at him.

✳

How do you cure a headache?
Put your head through a window, and the pane will disappear.

✳

Don't look out of the window, Lavinia, people will think it's Halloween.

Winter

Why do skeletons hate winter?
Because the cold goes right through them.

Wish

First zombie: Do you still hold your girlfriend's hand?
Second zombie: Yes, but I wish the rest of her would visit more often.

✳

Barbara: I wish I'd been alive a few hundred years ago.
History teacher: Why?
Barbara: There'd have been a lot less history to learn.

✳

Mom, can I have 10 cents for being good?
All right, but I wish you could be good-for-nothing!

※

Annie: Mom, can I have the wishbone?
Mother: Not until you've finished your greens.
Annie: But I want to wish I won't have to finish them!

Witch

What has handles and flies?
A witch in a garbage can.

※

What did the doctor say to the witch in hospital?
With any luck you'll be able to get up for a spell.

※

Why did the witch wear a green felt pointed hat?
So she could walk across snooker tables without being seen.

※

How do witches tell the time?
By looking at their witch watches.

※

What do you call a witch who climbs up walls?
Ivy.

※

What happened when the witch went for a job as a TV presenter?
The producer said she had the perfect face for radio.

※

What do you call a witch with one leg?
Eileen.

※

What goes cackle, cackle, squelch, squelch?
A witch in soggy trainers.

※

What goes cackle, cackle, boom?
A witch in a minefield.

※

Why did the witch go to the psychiatrist?
Because she thought everybody loved her.

※

Why won't a witch wear a flat cap?
Because there's no point in it.

※

What do you call a witch that stays out all night?
A fresh air freak.

※

Why did the witch consult an astrologer?
She wanted to know her horror-scope.

🎇

How can you make a witch itch?
Take away her "W."

🎇

What does a witch enjoy cooking most?
Gnomelettes.

🎇

Never Make a Witch Angry – by Sheila Tack

🎇

Going On A Witch Hunt – by Count Miout

🎇

My Best Friend, The Witch – by Ann Otherwitch

🎇

I saw a Witch – by Denise R. Knockin

🎇

How to be a Witch – by Ruth Less

🎇

How to Escape from a Witch – by Shelby Lucky

🎇

Knock knock.
Who's there?
Witch.
Witch who?
Witch witch would you like it to be?

🎇

Knock knock.
Who's there?
Gus.
Gus who?
Gus what!
There's a witch in the ditch!

🎇

Knock knock.
Who's there?
Eunice.
Eunice who?
Eunice is a witch – I thought you should know.

🎇

What did the young witch say to her mother?
Can I have the keys to the broom tonight?

Witch Doctor
Waiter, waiter! There's a fly in my soup.
Yes, that's the manager, sir. The last customer was a witch doctor.

Wizard

Why did the wizard wear red, white and blue suspenders?
To keep his pants up.

What do you call a wizard from outer space?
A flying sorcerer.

※

What is evil and bearded and lives under the sea?
A wizard with an aqualung.

※

What did the wizard say to his witch girlfriend?
Hello gore-juice!

※

Why did the wizard jump off the top of the Empire State Building?
He wanted to make a hit on Broadway.

※

What do you call a wizard who only casts good spells?
A charming fellow.

※

What do you call a wizard who lies on the floor?
Matt.

※

What do you call a wizard lying in the gutter?
Dwayne.

※

Who did the wizard marry?
His ghoul-friend.

※

What do you call a wizard who has fallen into the sea in a barrel?
Bob.

※

What did the wizard say at the end of a long, hard day?
I'm going gnome.

※

When a Wizard Knocks on Your Door – by Wade Aminit

※

Did you hear about the wizard who can sculpt lots of things out of skull bones?
Apparently he has a high degree of witchcraftsmanship.

Woman

Teacher: Who was the first woman on earth?
Angela: I don't know, Sir.
Teacher: Come on, Angela, it has something to do with an apple.
Angela: Granny Smith?

Why did the woman take a load of hay to bed?
To feed her nightmare.

Wood

He's got a chip on his shoulder.
It's probably from the block of wood above.

Barry: You're like uncultivated woodland.
Gary: Really?
Barry: Yes, totally dense.

Wooden

Who was that at the door?
A man with a wooden leg.
Tell him to hop it.

What goes ninety-nine clonk, ninety-nine clonk?
A centipede with a wooden leg.

Dracula: Have you seen the new monster from Poland?
Frankenstein: A Pole?
Dracula: Yes – you can tell from his wooden expression.

Did you hear about the girl who got engaged to a chap and then found out he had a wooden leg?
She broke it off, of course . . .

Woodworm

What did the woodworm say to the chair?
It's been nice gnawing you!

One woodworm met another.
"How's life?" she asked.
"Oh, same as usual," he replied, "boring."

Surveyor: This house is a ruin. I wonder what stops it from falling down.
Owner: I think the woodworm are holding hands.

※

Knock knock.
Who's there?
Woodworm.
Woodworm who?
Woodworm cake be enough or would you like two?

Word

What's another word for a python?
A mega-bite.

※

Why do bees hum?
Because they've forgotten the words.

※

When Ben hit his thumb with a hammer he let out a few choice words. Shocked by her son's outburst, his mother said, "Don't you dare use that kind of language in here."
"William Shakespeare did," replied Ben.
"Well, you'd better stop going around with him," said Mom.

※

What word allows you to take away two letters and get one?
Stone.

※

School Principal: I've called you into my office, Peter, because I want to talk to you about two words I wish you wouldn't use so often. One is "great" and the other is "lousy."
Peter: Certainly, sir. What are they?

※

Three men were in the dock, and the judge, who had a terrible squint, said to the first, "How do you plead?"
"Not guilty," said the second.
"I'm not talking to you," snapped the judge.
"I didn't say a word," said the third.

※

Crossword Fan: I've been trying to think of a word for two weeks!
Friend: How about a fortnight?

World

Geography teacher: How can you prove that the world is round?
Ben: But I never said it was, sir. I'm speechless.
Geography teacher: Good, just stay that way.

※

Who conquered half the world, laying eggs along the way?
Attila the Hen.

※

One Irishman was showing off his knowledge to another, so he asked him if he knew what shape the world was. "I don't," said the second.
"It's the same shape as the buttons on my jacket," said the first.
"Square," said the second.
"That's my Sunday jacket," said the first. "I meant my weekday jacket. Now what shape is the world?"
"Square on Sundays, round on weekdays," said the second Irishman.

※

Roy: They say ignorance is bliss.
Rita: Then you should be the happiest boy in the world.

Worm
What is the worms' favorite band?
Mud.

※

Who is the worms' Prime Minister?
Maggot Thatcher.

※

What do you get if you cross a worm with an elephant?
Big holes in your garden.

What is the best advice to give a worm?
Sleep late.

※

Collecting Wriggly Creatures – by Tina Worms

※

Fisherman: What are you fishing for sonny?
Boy: I'm not fishing, I'm drowning worms.

※

Knock knock.
Who's there?
Worm.
Worm who?
Worm in here isn't it?

※

Doctor, doctor, I feel like an insignificant worm.
Next!

Writing

"Melanie," said the teacher sharply, "you've been doing Rebecca's homework for her again! I recognized your writing in her notebook."
"I haven't, sir," declared Melanie. "It's just that we use the same pencil!"

Written

What was written on the hypochondriac's tombstone?
I told you I was ill.

Wrong

Why did the witch lose her way?
Because her hat was pointing in the wrong direction.

Centipede to pal: I just hate it when I start the day off on the wrong foot.

❋

Teacher: If you add 20,567 to 23,678 and then divide by 97 what do you get?
Jim: The wrong answer.

❋

What is a dimple?
A pimple going the wrong way.

❋

Maisie: Where were you born?
Daisy: In the local hospital.
Maisie: I always thought there was something wrong with you!

❋

She always has an answer to every problem.
Yes, but they're always wrong.

Wrote

Who wrote books for little bees?
Bee-trix Potter.

❋

Who wrote Count Dracula's life story?
The ghost writer.

Letter X has so few jokes of his own that some of the other letters of the alphabet have kindly lent him some of theirs so he doesn't feel too left out!

What do you get if you cross a witch's cat and a canary?
A cat with a full tummy.

What do you get if you cross a snake with a pig?
A boar constrictor.

What do you get if you cross a man-eating monster with a skunk?
A very ugly smell.

What do you get if you cross the Loch Ness Monster with a shark?
Loch Jaws.

What do you get if you cross a caretaker with an elephant?
A 20-ton school cleaner.

What do you get if you cross an elephant with the abominable snowman?
A jumbo yeti.

What do you get if you cross a vampire with Al Capone?
A fangster!

What do you get if you cross a zombie with a boy scout?
A creature that scares old ladies across the road.

What do you get if you cross a yeti with a kangaroo?
A fur coat with big pockets.

What do you get if you cross a vampire with a car?
A monster that attacks vehicles and sucks out all their gas.

❄

What do you get if you cross a sheep-dog and a bunch of daisies?
Collie-flowers!

❄

What do you get if you cross a zebra and a donkey?
A zeedonk.

❄

What do you get if you cross a sheep and a rainstorm?
A wet blanket.

❄

What do you get if you cross a centipede and a parrot?
A walkie-talkie.

❄

What do you get if you cross a vampire with a flea?
Lots of worried dogs.

Xmas
Here's your Christmas present. A box of your favorite candies.
Wow, thanks! But they're half empty!
Well, they're my favorite candies too!

❄

What do Scully and Mulder look into in December?
The X-mas files.

✳

What do angry rodents send each other at Christmas?
Cross mouse cards.

✳

What did the fireman's wife get for Christmas?
A ladder in her stocking.

Father: Would you like a pocket calculator for Christmas, son?
Danny: No thanks, Dad. I know how many pockets I've got.

Teacher: Who can tell me where Turkey is?
Dumb Donald: We ate ours last Christmas, ma'am.

What does the bee Santa Claus say at Christmas?
Ho-hum-hum.

X-Ray

Monster: Doctor, doctor, what did the X-ray of my head show?
Doctor: Absolutely nothing.

What happened to Ray when a ten-ton truck ran over him?
He became X-Ray.

Xmas Eve

She's so dumb she thinks Xmas Eve is a tug of war.

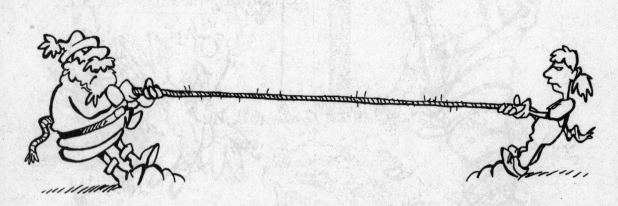

Yak

Which is the most dangerous animal in the Northern Hemisphere?
Yak the Ripper

Yankee Doodle

What do you call an American drawing?
A Yankee Doodle.

Yard

Why did the ghost work at Scotland Yard?
He was the Chief In-Spectre.

Yarn

What did Mrs Spider say to Mr Spider when he explained why he was home late?
You're spinning me a yarn.

Yawn

Did you hear about the schoolboy who was so lazy he went around with his mouth open to save him the trouble yawning?

Year

"What's the matter?" one man asked another.

"My wife left me when I was in the bath last night," sobbed the second man.

"She must have been waiting for years for the chance," replied the first.

Why did the mummy leave his tomb after 3000 years?
Because he thought he was old enough to leave home.

✳

Did you hear about the witch who did a four-year course in ugliness?
She finished it in two.

✳

Will you remember me in one day's time?
Of course I will.
Will you remember me in a week's time?
Of course I will.
Will you remember me in a year's time?
Of course I will.
Will you remember me in ten years' time?
Of course I will.
Knock, knock.
Who's there?
See, you've forgotten me already!

Yellow

What has brown and yellow stripes and buzzes along at the bottom of the sea?
A bee in a submarine.

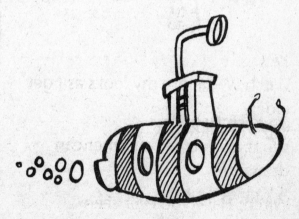

What is large, yellow, lives in Scotland and has never been seen?
The Loch Ness Canary

✳

Why did the witch wear yellow stockings?
Because her grey ones were at the cleaners.

❋

What's yellow and very poisonous?
Witch-infested custard.

❋

What's yellow and flashes?
A banana with a loose connection.

❋

What is yellow and goes click-click?
A ball-point banana.

❋

He reminds me of a bowl of custard.
Yes, yellow and thick.

Yes
Witch: Will I lose my looks as I get older?
Wizard: With luck, yes.

❋

Witch: Have you ever seen someone who looked like me before?
Girl: Yes, but I had to pay admission.

❋

Waiter, waiter! There's a fly in the butter.
Yes sir, it's a butterfly.

Yesterday
It's gone forever – gone forever I tell you.
What has?
Yesterday.

❋

Teacher: Billy. Didn't you hear me call you?
Billy: Yes, ma'am, but you told us yesterday not to answer back.

❋

I was doing my homework yesterday and I asked my dad what a circle is.
He said it was a round straight line with a hole in the middle.

Yeti

What's the difference between a very old, shaggy Yeti and a dead bee?
One's a seedy beast and the other's a deceased bee.

✳

How can you tell if a Yeti's been in the fridge?
There are paw-prints in the dessert.

What happened to the big shaggy yeti when she crashed through the screen door?
She strained herself.

✳

What do you give a seasick yeti?
Plenty of room.

✳

Where are yetis found?
They're so big they're hardly ever lost.

✳

Why shouldn't you dance with a Yeti?
Because if it trod on you you might get flat feet.

✳

How does a Yeti get to work?
By icicle.

✳

The Hungry Yeti – by Aida Lot

✳

Did you hear the joke about the fierce yeti?
It'll make you roar.

✳

Where do you find wild yetis?
It depends where you left them.

Yoghurt

My mother-in-law is so ugly she can make her own yoghurt by staring at a pint of milk for an hour.

Yokel

"Tell me," said the hiker to the local yokel, "will this pathway take me to the main road?"

"No, sir," replied the rustic, "you'll have to go by yourself!"

Why was the little bird expelled from school?
She was always playing practical yolks.

Yo-Yo

What goes BUZZZZZ, ZZZZZUB, BUZZZZZ, ZZZZZUB?
A bee stuck to a yo-yo.

Yolk

There was once a man who always went to work on an egg. One morning it wouldn't start, so he phoned the AAA. They told him to pull out the yolk. He did, and the egg started. When he got to work he phoned the AAA to thank them for their help, and told them his egg was all white now.

Teacher: What did Robert the Bruce do after watching the spider climbing up and down?
Girl: He went and invented the yo-yo.

※

Skeleton: Doctor, doctor, I keep thinking I'm a yo-yo.
Doctor: Are you stringing me along?

Young

What do you get if you cross a worm with a young goat?
A dirty kid.

※

What's the difference between a nice young lady and a fresh loaf?
One's a well-bred maid and the other's a well-made bread.

※

Why was Dracula always willing to help young vampires?
Because he liked to see new blood in the business.

※

I need a smart boy, said the boss to the young applicant. Someone quick to take notice.
Oh, I can do that, sir. I had it twice last week.

Yum Yum
What did the monster say when he saw Santa Claus?
Yum Yum.

Zebra

There were ten zebras in the zoo.
All but nine escaped. How many
were left?
Nine!

What's black and white and makes
a lot of noise?
A zebra with a set
of drums.

What do you get if you cross a
zebra with an ape man?
Tarzan stripes forever.

Now you see it . . . now
you don't.
What are you looking
at?
A black cat walking over
a zebra crossing.

Zombie

What do you call zombies in a
belfry?
Dead ringers.

Who do zombie cowboys fight?
Deadskins.

⁂

What did the zombie's friend say when he introduced him to his girlfriend?
Good grief! Where did you dig her up from?

⁂

Where do zombies go for cruises?
The Deaditerranean.

⁂

What did the zombie get his medal for?
Deadication.

⁂

Why was the zombie's nightclub a disaster?
It was a dead and alive hole.

⁂

How do you know a zombie is tired?
He's dead on his feet.

⁂

Doctor: Are you still having trouble with your breathing?
Zombie: Yes, I am.
Doctor: We'll see if we can put a stop to that.

⁂

What do little zombies play?
Corpses and robbers.

Zoo

Why did the witch buy two tickets to the zoo?
One to get in and one to get out.

⁂

First monster: I was in the zoo last week.
Second monster: Really? Which cage were you in?

⁂

First Witch: I took my son to the zoo yesterday.
Second Witch: Really, did they accept him?

⁂

Some vampires went to see Dracula. They said, "Drac, we want to open a zoo. Have you got any advice?"

"Yes," replied Dracula, "have lots of giraffes."

❋

Come on, Charles, I'll take you to the zoo.
If the zoo wants me, let them come and get me!

❋

Mary's class was taken to the Natural History Museum in New York. "Did you enjoy yourself?" asked her mother when she got home.
"Oh, yes," replied Mary. "But it was funny going to a dead zoo."

Young Chris was definitely more than a bit dumb; when his pal asked him how he had enjoyed his day at the zoo, he replied, "It was a total con! I saw a sign that said To The Monkeys, so I followed it and saw the monkeys. Then I saw another sign that said To The Bears, so I followed that and saw the bears. But when I followed a sign that said To the Exit, I found myself out on the street."

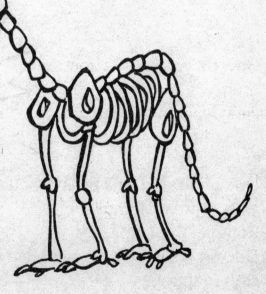

Zoom

There were two mosquitoes watching blood donors giving their blood. "It's not fair," said one to the other. "They're happy to lie down and let someone drain a pint of blood, but if we zoomed down for a quick nip, they'd do their best to kill us."

Your favorites

Here's a space for keeping a note of your favorite joke for each letter of the alphabet. Or why not use the space for writing down some jokes that you've made up yourself?

A

B

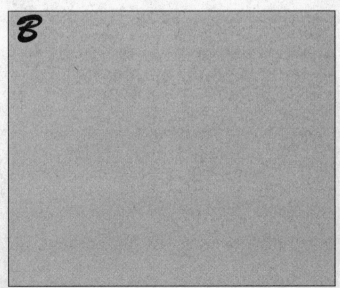

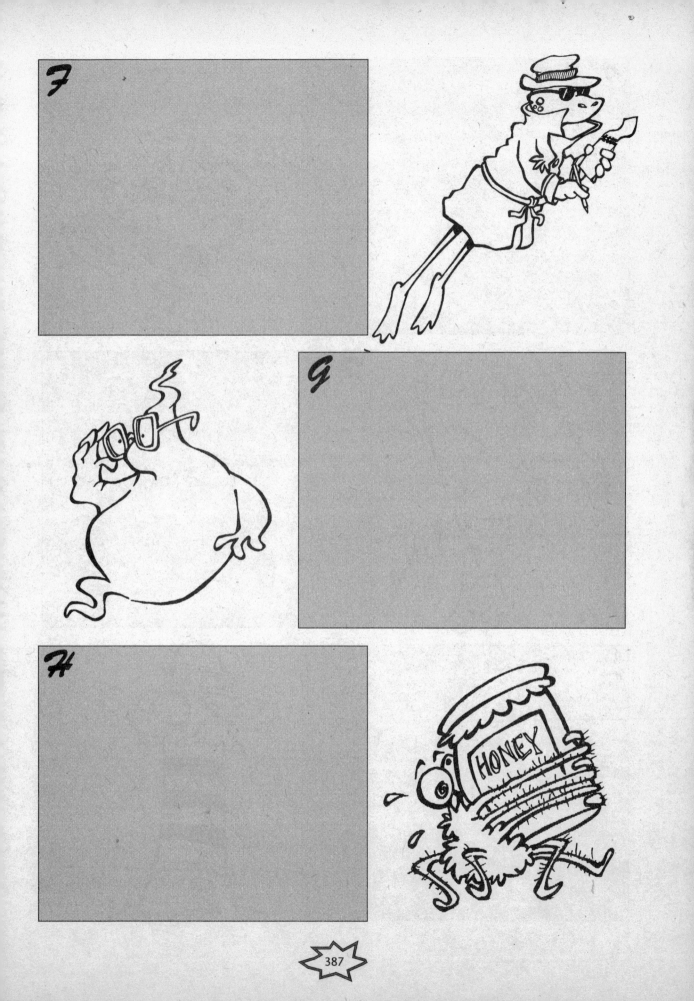

I & J

K

L

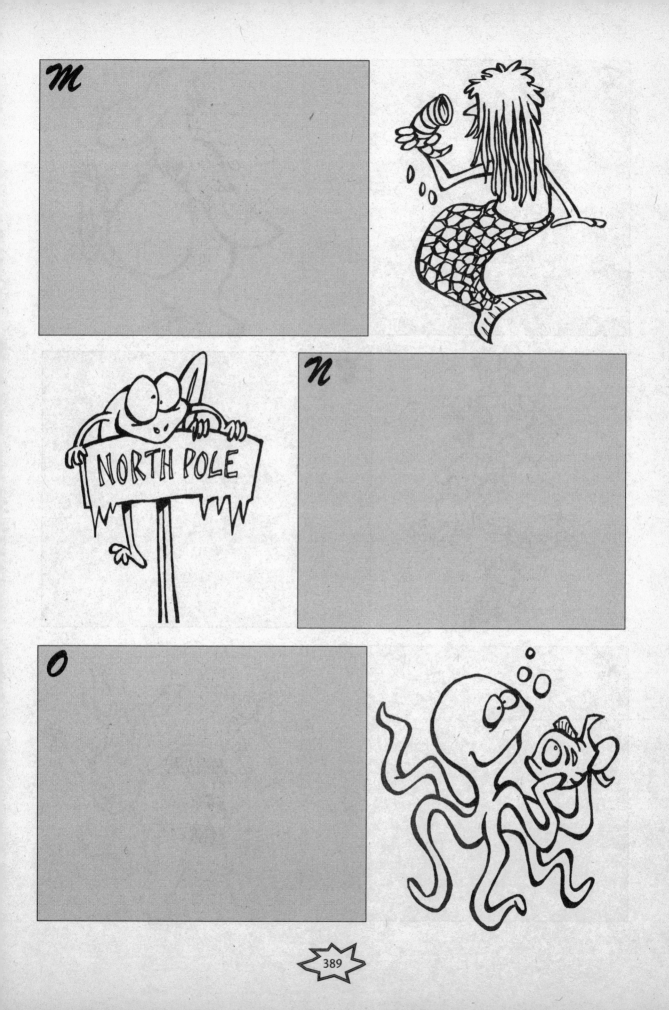

v

w

x, y & z

392

The Biggest Book of Mazes in the World   £5.99
The ultimate puzzle challenge, which will keep even the brightest minds occupied for hours.

The Puzzle Factory   *Sue Preston*   £3.99
The ultimate puzzle challenge, to keep even the brightest minds occupied for hours.

The Biggest Book of Puzzles in the World   £5.99
Nutty word games, mad mazes, codes to crack and hundreds more puzzle challenges.

Dance Stories   *Felicity Trotman*   £4.99
Wonderful collection of exciting, glamorous and romantic stories about the world of dance.

Fantasy Stories   *Mike Ashley*   £4.99
Some of the best fantasy stories of the century. Many have been written especially for this book, others are classics.

Robinson books are available from all good bookshops or can be ordered direct from the publisher. Just tick the title you want and fill in the form below.

Robinson Publishing Ltd, PO Box 11, Falmouth, Cornwall TR10 9EN
Tel: +44(0) 1326 374900 Fax: +44(0) 1326 374888 Email: books@Barni.avel.co.uk

UK/BFPO customers please allow £1.00 for p&p for the first book, plus 50p for the second, plus 30p for each additional book up to a maximum charge of £3.

Overseas customers (inc Ireland) please allow £2.00 for the first book, plus £1.00 for the second, plus 50p for each additional book.

Please send me the titles ticked above.

NAME (Block letters) ....

ADDRESS ....

....POSTCODE ....

I enclose a cheque/PO (payable to Robinson Publishing Ltd) for ....
I wish to pay by Switch/Credit Card

....Card Expiry Date ....